Individualism
and Moral
Character

Individualism and Moral Character

Karen Horney's Depth Psychology

JEFF MITCHELL

Routledge
Taylor & Francis Group

LONDON AND NEW YORK

First published 2014 by Transaction Publishers

Published 2017 by Routledge
2 Park Square, Milton Park, Abingdon, Oxon OX14 4RN
711 Third Avenue, New York, NY 10017, USA

First issued in paperback 2017

Routledge is an imprint of the Taylor & Francis Group, an informa business

ISBN 13: 978-1-138-51091-3 (pbk)
ISBN 13: 978-1-4128-5381-1 (hbk)

To my wife, Patricia, and my son, Leo

γνῶθι σαυτόν
"Know thyself"—Inscription on the Temple of Apollo at Delphi

"*Quelque découverte que l'on ait faite dans le pays de l'amour-propre, il y reste encore bien des terres inconnues.*" —François de La Rochefoucauld, Maxime N° 3

"Whatever discoveries one has made in the realm of self-esteem, there always remains ample unexplored territory."

Contents

Preface

The subject of the present work—namely, the psychological and moral ramifications of individualism—certainly qualifies as a sizeable matter. Indeed, one could argue that the concept of individualism is itself so broad as to disqualify it as the leitmotif of an extended inquiry into moral psychology. After all, many aspects of modern life have been impacted or even transformed by individualism, and the phenomenon has been studied by a wide variety of disciplines from a number of different angles. To make matters even worse, in neither the humanities nor the social sciences has a generally agreed upon definition of individualism prevailed, so that in some instances students of the subject have wound up talking past one another.

Despite these difficulties, I believe it would be wrongheaded to abandon individualism as a subject matter for inquiry on the grounds that it is too wide-ranging. To do so would be to run the risk of making the same mistake as the six blind men exploring the elephant in the well-known Jainist allegory. Based on the examination of only one part of the animal, each man draws a false conclusion about the nature of what he's touching: "It's a fan," "It's a wall," "It's a snake," and so forth. In fact, to a great extent both contemporary moral philosophers and personality theorists have committed a similar error by failing to adequately consider the relationship of their respective subject matters to the growth of individualism, which, as a fundamentally social process, has often seemed to them to fall outside their purview. With only scant attention paid to its cultural origins and genesis, the modern, individualized self has frequently constituted the starting point of investigation for ethicists and psychologists. Of course, every study must delimit its field of inquiry, but in order to be effective, such delimitation cannot omit essential elements of the intended subject matter. Unfortunately, the ahistorical treatment of modern selfhood has often tended to do just this, by suggesting that ethics and personal psychology should build their respective foundations on an understanding of the individual and his or her native tendencies and capacities. Such an approach is, of course, not only ahistorical but also ethnocentric, since it assumes that what is truly essential in human nature is pre-social and universal, and this assumption has been contradicted by over a century's worth of work in the social sciences.

Admittedly, the contributions of historiography, sociology, anthropology, and social psychology have served as an important corrective to the essentially atomistic conception of human nature we inherited from the Enlightenment. To some degree, psychology and philosophy have assimilated the new learning, but old intellectual habits die hard, and it is still the case that the psychoanalytic tradition in psychology, as well as the two most popular ethical theories, deontology and utilitarianism, have continued to cling to some key aspects of the Enlightenment conception.

As concerns moral psychology, perhaps the most important upshot of the Enlightenment heritage has been a general neglect of moral character. For their part, philosophers have tended to treat the study of morals as a normative science, the ultimate warrant of which rests upon an underlying principle or law. The identification and demonstration of this rule has constituted the Holy Grail of modern moral theory. The general assumption has been that any rational actor with knowledge of such a rule would be more or less adequately equipped to act in accord with the dictates of morality. Although it is typically allowed that application of the moral rule also implies a certain general knowledge of the human condition and some minimal familiarity with the particulars of the relevant situation, acquaintance with these facts is not viewed as being especially problematic, and so is often taken for granted. Another guiding assumption has been that only such self-awareness is required for right conduct as would be needed to reflectively render ethical judgments. Hence, from the standpoint of many moral philosophers, the sort of rich self-knowledge that can be gained through psychotherapy is largely irrelevant to acting morally.

Of course, Aristotelian ethics represents an important philosophical tradition according to which character *does* play an important role in moral reasoning. For Aristotle, right conduct is not primarily due to grasping the correct rule or rules, but to the acquisition and exercise of virtue. While his moral psychology has the merit of clearly identifying habit as a crucial component of morals, from a modern standpoint his theory suffers from two considerable drawbacks. Despite the fact that he acknowledges a subconscious dimension to mental life, Aristotle's introspectionist psychology is essentially one of conscious states, in which unconscious or subconscious processes receive little systematic attention. In addition, he generally trusts that the natural order includes a specific function for human beings, and that the best sort of people in the best sort of societies will be those who come closest to realizing their full potential. As it fortuitously turns out, Aristotle discovers that the men of the Greek upper classes nicely fit the bill, or at least well enough to permit him to identify and describe the virtues peculiar to human nature in general.

In Aristotle's defense, we should be quick to point out the nearly total absence of social science in his day, as well as the relatively nascent state of individualism in ancient Greece. Due to the former circumstance, Aristotle is poorly equipped to deal with the influence of social and cultural biases on his own thinking. As his modern reader knows, he is prone to legitimating the institutions and practices of his time, such as slavery or the inferior social position of women, by arguing that they derive more or less directly from the natural order of things. Greece provided him with neither the historical nor the ethnographic knowledge we take for granted today, knowledge that could have led him to adopt a more critical attitude toward the claims of his culture.

By contemporary standards, the Greek city-states of the classical period were culturally homogeneous, and tradition and custom were still the dominant elements of Greek social life. Although male citizens enjoyed more opportunity for advancement and a greater range of occupational options than their Homeric predecessors, social class remained an important factor in determining the individual's destiny. Likewise, while classical society was more differentiated than its Homeric ancestor, it was far from achieving a modern degree of autonomy between social systems. In Aristotle's Athens, for instance, there was no clear separation of church and state, nor between the political and judicial functions of government.

In this world, custom and birthright, and not individual preference and choice, still enjoyed pride of place. Against such a backdrop, it was natural for Aristotle to assume that there existed *a* fixed catalogue of the virtues for the citizen. Indeed, this state of affairs could help to explain why his moral psychology failed to adequately address the subconscious aspects of selfhood, since in a society that was still largely bound by tradition, such personality factors generally made but a modest contribution to human affairs. As a rule of thumb, the greater the freedom accorded to the individual to shape his or her own path through life, the more significant personality becomes as a factor in decision making. Unfortunately, by the time personality and its underlying processes became inescapable topics for psychologists—by the late nineteenth century—a metaphysical divide between facts and values had been erected in the intellectual culture, so that moral character was often considered to fall outside the compass of psychology.

The following essay is an attempt at theoretical reconstruction and synthesis. It is my contention that both the capacity of the modern individual for reflective morality, as well as his or her propensity for harboring submerged conflicts, have largely resulted from the growth of individualism. The fact that modern identity is mainly achieved, rather than ascribed, creates a gap between the self and its roles, which can permit the development of a critical frame of mind toward existing social arrangements and norms. Under less favorable circumstances, however, the same gap can become a haven for indistinct and conflicting desires.

I open the essay with a futuristic vision of extreme individualism borrowed from Philip José Farmer's novella, "Riders of the Purple Wage." I then proceed to offer a working definition of "individualism," and examine the growth of individualism from the perspective provided by C. R. Hallpike's three-tiered model of social evolution. In addition, I give a brief defense of Hallpike's notion of social evolution.

The second chapter extends the argument made in the first by examining how the growth of individualism has involved the individuation of identity. To this end, I discuss Hallpike's use of Lawrence Kohlberg's scheme of moral development and explore the relationship between growing social complexity and the emergence of self-aware individualism. I argue that the construction of personal identity is largely a response to the loss of a unifying cultural pattern in societies of the advanced type. The chapter concludes with a consideration of Karen Horney's view of the genesis of character disorders and the relations between personality, identity, and the unconscious as they appear in the light of her theory.

The third chapter constitutes the second phase of my argument, in which I propose an alternative to the Freudian view of depth psychology. The chapter begins with a discussion of the shortcomings of orthodox psychoanalysis, followed by a consideration of John Dewey's metapsychological alternative to instinct-based models of human nature (of which psychoanalysis is the most important representative). I also defend Dewey's view against several objections to it raised by psychoanalytic social theorist Philip Rieff.

In the fourth chapter I turn my attention to modern moral philosophy and offer a genetic critique of the "legislative" tradition in ethics. I then lay the basis for an alternative understanding of ethics by nesting the general theory of value within George Herbert Mead's objective relativism. In the final section of the chapter, I argue that the notion of good taste captures not only aesthetic judgments but also judgments of conscience. I try to establish that the conception of moral judgment as a form of taste constitutes a cogent alternative to deontology, utilitarianism, and virtue ethics.

Chapter five is dedicated to showing that Karen Horney's reconstruction of psychoanalysis succeeded in removing the objectionable elements from Freud's brainchild while at the same time building upon his genuine insights. I further argue that the assumptions informing her personality theory are consistent with Dewey's metapsychology.

In the final chapter I make the case that Horney's version of psychoanalysis constitutes a moral psychology. I argue that our civilization suffers from poor morals—in that we poorly understand the moral problems of the individual—and that Horney's approach has a significant contribution to make in improving our grasp of these problems. I show that, despite her focus on individual psychology, Horney was aware of the social and political dimensions of her subject matter, as is evidenced by her identification of the cultural influences at work in self-deception, and in the connection she drew between personal growth and democracy. Finally, I defend her moral psychology against several possible criticisms.

Acknowledgments

I would like to thank Arkansas Tech University for awarding me a yearlong sabbatical, during which I was able to complete a major portion of this book. In addition, I would like to express my gratitude to my family and friends for putting up with me during my prolonged labors. I'm particularly indebted to my mother-in-law and father-in-law, Annie and Pierre Rivière, for their unstinting hospitality and generosity over the course of multiple summers spent at their home in France. They always saw to it that I had an office workspace, and they did their best to accommodate my writing schedule, even when it meant violating all manner of French custom.

Finally, I owe a special debt of gratitude to Bernard J. Paris, who was generous enough to read a preliminary draft of the book and provide me with more than a few insightful criticisms and comments. While I absolve him of responsibility for the views expressed in the present work, as well as for any and all remaining errors and imperfections, I believe that the final product benefitted considerably from his suggestions.

1

Individualism and Social Evolution

A Future Reminiscent of the Present

In 1967 a compilation of speculative fiction, edited by Harlan Ellison, appeared under the title *Dangerous Visions*. The anthology comprised thirty-three original short stories by some of the best science fiction authors of the day, including the likes of Larry Niven and Philip K. Dick. Seven of the stories went on to win sci-fi's prestigious Hugo and Nebula awards, and *Dangerous Visions* went down in the annals of speculative fiction as one of the finest collections ever produced. Editor Ellison's recipe for success was the creation of a platform for daring departures from the standard sci-fi fare. He allowed his contributors to venture stylistically where no imaginative writer had gone before, and accepted the sort of controversial subject matter usually rejected by other editors at the time.

Ellison wrote a brief foreword to each story in the volume, and in his preface to the contribution by Philip José Farmer, entitled "Riders of the Purple Wage," he remarks that it is quite simply the finest tale in the book. Farmer's novella (it also happens to be the longest piece in the anthology, coming in at something over thirty thousand words) does manage to stand out in what is a memorable collection. "Riders" dazzles with a torrent of historical and literary allusions, sexual innuendos, and double entendres. On a first reading, Farmer's scintillating vocabulary and present-tense narrative, which disconcertingly moves from dream state to waking life to recollection, can be somewhat overwhelming. "Riders" is a tale that blossoms best on a second or even third perusal. The prose style is too experimental, and the text too densely layered with meaning, for a first reading to be very enjoyable. One's initial trip into this world of the future is so fraught with a sense of alienation and uncanniness that the considerable humor of Farmer's tale is hard to fully appreciate. Although "Riders" may constitute a dangerous vision, it is doubtlessly a comic one. The story's comic range extends from the bawdy to the more tongue-in-cheek, and humor constitutes a key element in the novella from beginning to end.

Without the comic relief, Farmer's world of tomorrow would be considerably bleaker. His tale follows roughly a day in the life of Chib, a young painter living in Los Angeles in the year 2166. Like other large cities of the twenty-second century, LA is a multilevel, fully enclosed metropolis whose inhabitants no longer need to work for a living, since they receive the "purple wage," a public dole provided to all citizens. This is a world of plenty, and its denizens seem singularly bent on finding self-fulfillment. Education, even at the postsecondary level, is free, and the government encourages everyone to engage in lifelong learning. Art in its various forms is pursued with great seriousness and intensity, and disputes over aesthetic matters periodically result in brawls and riots. For those who grow jaded to the comforts and amusements of twenty-second-century civilization, an outlet has been provided in the form of reserves, where the disenchanted can "return to nature" as hermits or members of reconstituted tribes. With a guaranteed income, and access to a wide variety of creature comforts (including highly advanced medical technology), the main problem confronting the individual is one of meaning: What exactly is one supposed to do with one's long life?

"Riders" is essentially a coming-of-age tale set in a social world that has entered an advanced state of anomie. The story's plot involves Chib's relation to his grandfather, who has been hiding out from the authorities ever since he stole $20 billion from a federal deposit bank a quarter of a century earlier. The reader is given to understand that Grandpa Winnegan's heist was more an act of rebellion against governmental encroachment into civil society than a crime committed for the sake of self-aggrandizement. Even though a currency recall that took place shortly after the robbery rendered the loot worthless, the government continued its pursuit of Winnegan, due, perhaps in part, to his public popularity. A final showdown between Winnegan and the federal agents assigned to his case brings the story to its close.

In his final communication to his grandson, Winnegan refers to himself as the "Wise Old Man in the Cave," and this epithet in fact neatly summarizes his role in the novella. Farmer employs the 120-year-old nonconformist to introduce an informed and critical perspective into the world of 2166. His great age, irreverent temper, and underground lifestyle all serve to render Winnegan an outsider to the century in which he lives, and it is his descriptions of the existing social order that best bring out its anomie.

One contemporary dictionary of sociology defines "anomie" as "a condition of society or of personal relation to society in which there exists little consensus, a lack of certainty on values or goals, and a loss of effectiveness in the normative and moral framework which regulates collective and individual life."[1] The breakdown of norms in Farmer's speculative version of LA is perhaps most evident in the sexual mores of the twenty-second century. A relatively new religious group known as the Panamorites has been so successful in promoting the benefits of physical love between parents and their offspring that incest is no longer commonly viewed as taboo. The story's protagonist, Chib, is portrayed as having a strained relation to his mother that is mainly due to lingering resentment he feels over her decision to discontinue sexual relations with him when he was sixteen. Like many of his compatriots, Chib is bisexual. By the mid-twenty-second century, heterosexuality has largely lost its normative status, leaving sexuality itself more ambiguous than ever before. Freed from such time-honored cultural constraints as the prohibition on incest and the determination of sexual orientation based on gender, sexual conduct has become primarily an affair of personal inclination, choice, and whim.

Another Panamorite contribution to American culture has been the institution of "Naming Day," an occasion on which any citizen who has reached the age of majority may select a new name that reflects his or her identity and temperament. For instance, Chib's full name is Chibiabos Elgreco Winnegan. The inspiration for the first name is somewhat obscure, but it's implied that Chib's namesake is a character who appears in Longfellow's famous poem, *The Song of Hiawatha*. The more obvious inspiration for Chib's middle name is the great sixteenth century painter: an understandable conceit for an aspiring artist. The names of other characters in "Riders"—such as Rousseau Red Hawk, a neo-AmerIndian *né* Julius Applebaum, and Huga Wells-Erb Heinsturbury, a female science fiction writer—are similar postmodern pastiches. Farmer has a journalist praise the support given by the government for this national custom, and the interviewer cites it as evidence for the state's ongoing commitment to individualism. Naming Day is a natural development of the cultural pattern of this society, since it renders unto the individual what supposedly by right belongs to the individual. After all, what is more closely tied to one's sense of self than one's name?

Yet tradition normally dictates that this most personal of terms is bestowed upon us by others. The underlying rule of Farmer's imaginary social order runs along the lines of "Where there was social ascription, there shall be individual choice and achievement."

The hyper-individualism of the brave new Los Angeles produces exaggerated forms of the vices associated with earlier versions of individualism. Egotism, narcissism, and hedonism reign supreme. Chib's mother, for instance, is almost the personification of gluttony: hugely overweight, she spends all her waking hours drinking and gambling with a cohort of equally debauched friends. Although generally less hedonistic and more self-disciplined, virtually all of the other characters in "Riders" come across as being strikingly self-centered. The one human relationship in the story that seems to involve real warmth and altruistic concern is that between Chib and his grandfather. In his final letter to Chib, the old man counsels his grandson to have confidence that he will find others who will love him as much or even more than his grandfather has. Grandpa Winnegan adds that, even more importantly, Chib must develop the capacity to love them back, and the story ends with his challenge to Chib: "Can you do this?"

In his afterword to the tale, Farmer explains that the immediate inspiration for "Riders" came from a lecture he attended about the growing need for social planning, and he cautions that the story is set in just one of many possible futures. He also remarks that, for a technical writer and science fiction author, he had become oddly indifferent by the late 1960s about the then-looming prospect of putting man on the moon. The crucial problems facing humanity are, at best, only indirectly related to the exploration and colonization of space, and if the resources required to adequately address the former detract from humanity's adventure on the final frontier, then so be it. People, he asserts, are more important than space rockets.

What lends "Riders" its peculiar poignancy is Farmer's projection of current social trends into a near future that acts like a fun-house mirror, distorting and exaggerating certain familiar features. The image thereby produced is, unfortunately, more alienated than alien. This fictional universe, where so many adults remain emotional adolescents forever in quest of identity, is suspiciously easy to imagine; indeed, with his story of the future Farmer has succeeded in giving us some insight into the present. By extrapolating the potential course of certain developments in the contemporary world, he provides a telling literary illustration of the interplay between personality, morals, and social environment.

Such interplay is widely recognized in day-to-day life and regularly furnishes plot material for writers, topics for columnists, and campaign issues for politicians. In the realm of theory, however, the complex interactions between feelings, personal value judgments, and mores have only rarely received the attention they merit. Many philosophers and social scientists still labor under the metaphysical preconception that facts and values share little or no common ground. Acceptance of the notion that "is" and "ought" stand for incommensurable categories of judgment has led to the creation of moral philosophies in which psychological considerations are seen as irrelevant to ethical reasoning and psychotherapies in which value judgments are held to play no legitimate role.

Farmer's cautionary tale of the future provides us with an insightful description of the plight of the modern individual, and it could serve as a corrective to the ideological blind spots of professional theorists. However, since "Riders" is a work of fiction, it can only furnish us with a basic intuition of the connection between personality, morals, and social structure. In order to turn this inkling into an argument, we will have to sharpen our focus and clearly identify our conclusions as well as the evidence that supports them. It is to this task that we now turn.

Individualism

There is a direct relationship between the extent to which a culture is lacking in individualism and the degree to which it strikes visitors from modern societies as alien. In fact, if there is any one sociological feature that is definitive of modernity, it's individualism. Since antiquity it has set the agenda for ethics and politics in those societies where it has taken root. Its march through virtually all major aspects of modern social life has had a profound impact upon our mentality and our morals. To date, it has flourished best in the West, and it is in Western societies that it continues to develop and intensify, though it is also making important inroads into non-Western cultures. Despite the fact that it has been with us since at least the Greco-Roman period, we are still reeling from its consequences, and every indication is that there is more to come.

Because the term "individualism" is used in a variety of contexts with a corresponding array of different meanings, a definition is in order. That the task of adequately defining this word is more complicated than might first appear is due to the central role that it and its cognates have played in social inquiry since the rise of social contract theory in the seventeenth century. "Individualism" and "individual" have typically been incorporated into theoretical frameworks as dualistic counterparts to words such as "collectivism" or "society," and so have become unusually fraught with metaphysical and moral meanings. Obviously, few questions are more basic to social theory than those concerning the respective natures of the individual and the collective, and the relations pertaining between them. Despite the fundamental importance of these issues for the study of society, they still represent open questions for many students of the field.

In his well-known *General Sociology* of 1905, Albion Small opens his chapter on the individual with the following observation:

> Today's sociology is still struggling with the preposterous initial fact of the individual. He is the only possible social unit, and he is no longer a thinkable possibility. He is the only real presence, and he is never present. Whether we are near to resolution of the paradox or not, there is hardly more visible consensus about the relation of the individual to the whole than at any earlier period. Indeed, the minds of more people than ever before are puzzled by the seeming antinomy between the individual and the whole.[2]

Small is writing at a time when the atomistic individualism of the Enlightenment—that is, the view that society was essentially the result of a voluntary association of individuals—had become untenable for many investigators. The conception of the individual as a rational being whose chief mental traits and faculties were primarily due to nature rather than to nurture was largely contradicted by the findings of the relatively new historical and cultural sciences. The application of the modern historical method to the study of social practices and institutions, such as religion and law, revealed that many "self-evident" or commonsensical ideas were, in fact, the outcomes of specific historical developments. For instance, in his much admired *Ancient Law*, which was first published in 1861, Sir Henry Sumner Maine argued that in Roman law the contract as a voluntary and binding agreement between individuals was preceded by a long and desultory phase in which the family, rather than the individual, figured prominently. In this early period of Roman law, obligations and prerogatives attached to persons in virtue of their status in the family, and were not based upon a freely chosen commitment.[3] In addition to the contributions made by the historical disciplines, the work of field

6

ethnographers in the late nineteenth century did much to cast doubt upon the belief in a universal and fixed human nature.

Small's working answer in *General Sociology* to the apparent antimony of the individual and society is to reject the assumption of any sort of dualism between the two and to shift the investigative focus instead to the social process. The benefit to be had by this change of methodology is that when the social process is taken as the fundamental unit of analysis, neither the individual nor the group is excluded from scrutiny. However, in *The Process of Government*, Arthur F. Bentley was able to show that Small did not go far enough in overcoming the old dualism.[4] The latter proposes an interpretation of society in terms of "social forces" which are rooted in the desires or wants of the persons who make up society. Small classifies these desires by six main types of end or interest—health, wealth, sociability, knowledge, beauty, and righteousness—and allows that there may be a considerable degree of variation within each category among individuals. Bentley's objection to Small's theory is that by grounding the social forces in the psyche of individuals he actually does little to shed additional light on the social processes that he is attempting to explain and, indeed, much to obfuscate matters. Small's theoretical framework suggests that desires or wants constitute the primary causes of social phenomena, and yet Bentley points out that he provides no evidence which would establish the existence of said desires independently of the social phenomena that they are purported to cause. As it stands, Small's taxonomy of desire constitutes an ad hoc rationalization and oversimplification of social processes.

Although Small explicitly rejects a dualistic understanding of the relationship between the individual and society, Bentley maintains that his causal mechanism nevertheless relies upon just such a dualism. In the *Process of Government* he likens the explanatory model that posits feelings or mental faculties as causes of social phenomena to the movement of billiard balls on a billiard table. The feeling or faculty constitutes the first ball that is set in motion, and it strikes another ball—say, an individual or institution—causing it to be displaced and perhaps striking yet other balls in its turn. On this model, the actual causal mechanism behind social change is left implicit and unexplored.

Slightly more than four decades later, in *Knowing and the Known*, Bentley and his coauthor John Dewey christen the term interactionism for the billiard ball approach, which they contrast with transactionism, an epistemological methodology of more recent date, which they argue

7

should supplant interactionism. Bentley and Dewey provisionally characterize interactionism as a style of knowing wherein "thing is balanced against thing in causal interconnection."[5] They argue that interactionism was common to the natural sciences under the paradigm provided by Newtonian physics. Due to its success in elucidating physical phenomena, it served as the model for social scientific inquiry as well. Although the coauthors do not deny that the interactionist approach proved to be fruitful in the physical sciences, they argue that even in this domain it ultimately revealed its limitations and was abandoned when Newtonian physics was superseded by the physics of relativity. As a framework for inquiry into human affairs, they accord it less success. Interactionism was poorly suited to the study of human affairs due to its tendency to reduce phenomena into elemental causes and effects. While such a method could produce respectable results when applied to the relatively simple subject matters of physics or chemistry, when extended to the relatively more complex and multi-causal phenomena of the social world it was liable to produce the fallacy of oversimplified cause.

In *Knowing and the Known* Bentley and Dewey propound transactionism as the major alternative to the interactionist approach, and they describe it as follows:

> where systems of description and naming are employed to deal with aspects and phases of action, without final attribution to "elements" or other presumptively detachable or independent "entities," "essences," or "realities," and without isolation of presumptively detachable "relations" from such detachable "elements."[6]

The interactionist standpoint tended to suggest a universe of dualisms. For instance, Bentley shows in *The Process of Government* that many of the most prominent nineteenth-century social theorists tacitly assumed a dualism between thought and emotion, with one school looking to feelings or mental faculties as social causes, and the other to ideas or ideals. Under the sway of this dualistic presupposition, both schools fell into giving one-sided accounts of their common subject matter. The transactionist alternative proposed by Bentley is surprisingly simple, and consists in the seemingly mundane observation that emotions and interests do not occur without some sort of ideational content. Likewise, while feeling may not occupy the foreground in a given mental state, neither is it ever entirely absent. Bentley emphasizes that any effort to explain social phenomena purely in terms of affect is bound to fail, since by itself emotion can never provide the intentional feature of acts, and that intention as a structuring idea brings "the whole outside world into the reckoning."[7] From the transactionist standpoint, "feelings" and "ideas" are to a certain extent linguistic fictions, since they call to mind discrete entities when in fact they denote aspects or features of a mental state that is simultaneously affective and ideational. While for the purposes of analysis it may be useful to discriminate or highlight—say, the specifically cognitive aspect of a given mental state—it is highly speculative to then treat the singled-out aspects as distinct causal agents. From such speculation metaphysical dualisms are born.

Discriminations or namings in transactional analysis are made provisionally, and take their warrant as postulations that arise out of observation but also serve to guide further observation. As postulations, names are open to revision in the light of new observational and experimental data. It is in this methodological spirit that we shall treat the term "individualism."

Before proceeding to a working definition of individualism, however, we should note that in *Knowing and the Known* Bentley and Dewey express serious reservations concerning the continued employment of the terms "individual" and "society" in inquiry. In the eleventh chapter, entitled "A Trial Group of Names," the following comments are made under the entry for "individual":

> Abandonment of this word and of all substitutes for it seems essential wherever a positive general theory is undertaken or planned. Minor specialized studies in individualized phrasing should expressly name the limits of the application of the word, and beyond that should hold themselves firmly within such limits. The word "behavior" (q.v.) as presented in this vocabulary covers both individual and social (q.v.) on a transactional basis in which the distinction between them is aspectual.[8]

The companion piece, as it were, to these comments are found under the entry for "social," to wit:

> The word in its current uses is defective for all general inquiry and theory. See *Individual*.[9]

Bentley and Dewey's express intention in *Knowing and the Known* is to provide a set of firm names for use in the theory of knowledge and in logic. Because neither epistemological nor logical concerns are central to our project, we are perhaps justified in viewing their qualms about the words in question as less of a prohibition against their use than as a caution to treat them transactionally.

As a term, "individualism" has been employed in different domains, and perhaps the best-known instances of it are its economic and ethical varieties. However, given the purposes of the present study, we are primarily interested in individualism in a sociological sense. For this particular meaning of the word, one of the earliest and most influential references is Alexis de Tocqueville, who introduces the term in his monumental *Democracy in America* (1840) as follows:

> Individualism is a considered and peaceful sentiment that disposes each citizen to isolate himself from the mass of his fellows and to withdraw to the side with his family and his friends; so that, after thus creating a small society for his own use, he willingly abandons the large society to itself.[10]

In his sketch of individualism, Tocqueville traces its psychological and sociological features. From the standpoint of moral psychology, he contrasts it with egoism, treating both egoism and individualism as character defects. On his analysis, the former is an innate passion or instinct that is primarily emotive, whereas the latter stems, at least in part, from an error in judgment. He locates the main influences that predispose persons to find individualism attractive in the social and political environment of democracy. While selfishness in one form or another has always been with humankind, individualism is the vice of democratic eras.

Tocqueville argues that conditions inherent to aristocratic societies lead their members to closely identify their personal interests with those of their families. Because families in such societies often persist for centuries in the same class and locality, the average family member feels a bond with deceased ancestors as well as with potential future descendants.

As Tocqueville points out, in addition to furnishing its members with strong family ties, the aristocratic social order promotes social intercourse outside of the family through its relatively rigid class hierarchy. In such a social world, patriotic feeling typically takes the form of class allegiance. The fixed hierarchy also relates the individual to members outside of his or her class by rendering them either his or her superiors or inferiors, the former representing potential patrons, and the latter potential servants.

Tocqueville sees democracy as exerting a leveling effect on the old class structure. Aristocratic society, he observes, incorporated everyone in a long chain stretching from peasant to king, and democracy tears the chain asunder into so many disconnected links. Under democratic social arrangements, class mobility increases, both upward and downward. New families rise to prominence, and well-established ones sink into obscurity.

Perhaps the most important feature of the democratic era that he includes in his description of individualism is the growth of the middle class:

> As conditions become equal, a greater number of individuals will be found who, no longer rich enough or powerful enough to exercise a great influence over the fate of their fellows, have nonetheless acquired or preserved enough enlightenment and wealth to be able to be sufficient for themselves. The latter owe nothing to anyone, they expect nothing so to speak from anyone; they are always accustomed to consider themselves in isolation, and they readily imagine that their entire destiny is in their hands.[11]

In fact, his very definition of individualism seems designed to capture the essentially apolitical attitude of a prospering middle class.

Although Tocqueville's sketch of individualism is insightful, it would not well serve our purposes to simply adopt it as our working definition of the term. In the first place, his overall characterization of individualism as a vice seems too narrow given contemporary linguistic usage. In addition to its negative aspects, individualism is often associated by modern English speakers with beneficial character traits, such as self-reliance and the spirit of free enterprise (e.g., President Herbert Hoover's praise of "rugged individualism" as a distinctive and valuable feature of American culture). While we are certainly interested in the psychological dimension of individualism, to classify it among the defects of character at the beginning of our inquiry would seem to prejudge the matter.

A second shortcoming of Tocqueville's theoretical definition is that his dichotomy between aristocratic and democratic eras is too categorical for our purposes. For instance, there is a good case to be made for the assertion that aristocratic France on the eve of the revolution had a greater degree of individualism than, say, France of the High Middle Ages, and we should want a definition that will bear out this difference.

Although it is perhaps somewhat counterintuitive, individualism does not, of course, primarily describe individuals per se, but rather

11

social orders. As a social phenomenon, the clearest evidence for it is to be found in collective behavior, and so it would be prudent for us to gear our definition to our most reliable observations. By proceeding in this manner, we are not precluding discussion of specifically psychological aspects of individualism, but rather trying to establish the firmest basis we can for introducing such considerations.

In what follows, "individualism" will denote forms of social organization in which persons are vested with the authority in certain matters to make their own choices or to act in a manner of their own choosing without being overruled by others, even when the decision or course of action in question is unpopular. In these matters, the individual is acknowledged to have the final say-so. The legitimacy of the individual's prerogative in a given area may be founded upon custom or law, or a mix of both. For instance, according to our definition, ancient Rome underwent a growth of individualism when Roman law made the transition from status to contract described by Maine. Common forms of this structural individualism in modern society include an adult's right to wed or to vote in an election.

We should add as a word of caution that an augmentation in individualism should not be automatically construed as either an amelioration or deterioration of the human condition, nor should it be viewed as necessarily resulting in an increase of freedom. Given our working definition of the term, concrete forms of individualism are social arrangements that confer upon the individual the power to choose among a certain range of options, and thus prevent other people from forcing him or her to choose otherwise or to renounce choosing altogether. Obviously, such socially protected opportunities for personal choice allow all manner of motivations and considerations into the decision-making process, and these interests run the full gamut, from the silly to the serious, the self-serving to the altruistic, the ignoble to the noble. Individualism is home to both calculating narcissism and creative humanitarianism.

We should also be wary of simply equating a gain in individualism with a gain in freedom. While it is true that actual instances of individualism furnish persons with added "elbow room," it would be misleading to always identify the removal of constraint with an increase in liberty, unless we were to assume a strict dualism between social constraint and personal freedom. That no such dualism exists is evident from the fact that persons only come to have some degree of control over themselves and their environment by assimilating social disciplines and practices, such as speaking and reading.

Our argument assumes that individualism constitutes a hallmark of modernity. However, this supposition does not necessarily imply that pre-modern societies are wholly lacking in individualistic elements, or that social development has followed a steadily increasing curve from prehistoric communalism to contemporary individualism. A word of caution is in order here because the reader of Durkheim's classic and highly influential study of social development, *On the Social Division of Labor*, could come away with the impression that pre-modern societies are almost completely unacquainted with individualism. Durkheim draws a well-known distinction between two forms of social solidarity that he believes to be characteristic, respectively, of pre-modern and modern social orders. "Mechanical solidarity" is typical of the former and refers to a type of social coordination based upon shared attitudes and values. Since there is relatively little craft specialization in traditional societies, their individual members share essentially the same stock of knowledge and beliefs. Durkheim likens pre-modern social orders to some of the simplest forms of animal life, such as sponges, which are actually little more than multicellular colonies lacking muscles, nervous system, and internal organs. Sponge cells are only partially differentiated and function with a relatively low degree of coordination among one another.

At the opposite pole of the animal kingdom we find complex organisms such as mammals, whose structure is characterized by a high degree a cellular specialization and coordination. In mammals, cells have differentiated to such an extent that they make up organs that have taken over specific physiological functions. In fact, a complex life-form comprises an interdependent system of organs, and in this regard is an apt metaphor for a complex society. Like their zoological counterparts, complex societies depend upon a harmonization of their differentiated parts. Industrialized economies, for example, require an intricate interface of producers, transporters, wholesalers, retailers, and consumers. Durkheim refers to the organizational principle of modern society as constituting an "organic" form of solidarity. In social orders of the organic type, individuals often differ considerably in knowledge and know-how, and there may even be considerable variance in attitudes and values from person to person.

Although quite broad, Durkheim's description of the two patterns of solidarity well captures the key structural differences between primitive societies and those of the modern type, as long as we bear in mind that by qualifying a society as "primitive" we merely mean what is typical of an original or early stage of societal development. "Primitive" in this sense is understood to be a descriptive term and is by no means intended to convey a value judgment as to the overall worth and superiority or inferiority of any given society to any other. Unfortunately, Durkheim's pair of concepts, while in many respects useful, is somewhat misleading when applied to the study of individualism. This shortcoming is due to the connotations of "mechanical" as routine, lacking spontaneity, and unaware (connotations which, incidentally, are also present in the original French). As a guiding idea the concept of mechanical solidarity has the unhappy tendency of leading to a subtle transfer of its reference from the group to the individual. The impression thereby created is that of individuals whose behavior rigidly follows the dictates of custom, and of a social world that offers little leeway for personal expression to its members. In fact, Durkheim sometimes conveys just this image of primitive social life in *On the Social Division of Labor*:

> In lower societies, the very external form of conduct is predetermined even to the details. The way in which man must eat, dress in every situation, the gestures he must make, the formulae he must pronounce, are precisely fixed.[12]

As we shall see, this characterization is inconsistent with what ethnographers have actually reported about life in the least developed societies. Durkheim's view also suggests an oversimplified conception of human history as a long march from servitude to self-determination, an idea that finds a distinct echo in some modern political ideologies.

The main problem, however, with the thesis that individualism has grown in a continuous and incremental fashion is that it does not square with what ethnographers have observed in hunter-gatherer societies. Based on his own fieldwork and on a broad study of the relevant literature, anthropologist C. R. Hallpike has proposed the term "atomistic society" to refer to foraging cultures and to some of the less developed agricultural societies.[13] The atomistic social order is primarily founded on kinship relations between individuals. In fact, there are no roles in such cultures that could take precedence over kinship: social atomism knows neither chief, nor priest, nor judge. Atomistic societies also lack corporate groups, such as clans or secret societies. In the absence of any significant political or social hierarchies, atomistic arrangements are generally egalitarian. Members enjoy roughly equal access to power, prestige, and wealth, and the occasional attempt by an individual to claim more than his or her allotted share is usually frowned upon. In fact, atomistic cultures are noted for their anti-authoritarianism and emphasis upon freedom from social constraint. Respect for the individual is correspondingly high, and in general there is a focus upon the pursuit of self-interest.

The immediate implications of atomistic individualism for our argument are twofold. In the first place, there is obviously enough individualism present in these cultures to render misleading Durkheim's use of "mechanical" to describe their pattern of social solidarity. In the second place, the presence of individualism in primitive societies contradicts the view that human history has been the scene of a more or less constant progression from bondage to freedom. More importantly, however, the ascertainment of atomistic individualism raises the question as to its relationship with individualism in modern industrial societies. Noting that various ethnographers of atomistic cultures have called attention to their surprisingly "modern" features, Hallpike argues that there are some crucial differences between atomistic and modern individualists that make the egoism of the former distinct from that of the latter.

He identifies four characteristics that are typically present in modern individualism, but that are lacking in the atomistic variety.[14] In the context of modern industrial society, one way in which individuals conceive of their relation to the group is by means of ethical principles or rules, such as the idea that it is incumbent upon all who are capable of contributing to the common weal to do so. Moral principles are typically universal or at least very general in scope, and potentially revolutionary in impact, since the abstract ethical standpoint they call into being suggests the existence of an authority independent of and superior to those of custom and tradition. Social atomism is wholly unacquainted with such abstract rules for conduct, and employs a very different strategy for regulating intercourse between individual and group. Major forms of behavior are determined by socially ascribed roles (e.g., gender-specific tasks in food procurement), and what is not required or forbidden by custom is left open to a balancing act between individual self-assertion and public pressure. For instance, although

15

atomistic societies have no judicial institutions or mediators, they have developed a number of other techniques for resolving conflicts. Some of the most common strategies in the atomistic repertoire include teasing, ridicule, and gossip. Hallpike remarks that atomistic societies are clearly "shame cultures," meaning that their members learn to fear socially unacceptable behavior due to the public humiliation it would bring. He argues that in more advanced societies, the fear of external sanctions sometimes develops into a sense of guilt that no longer has need of any audience—real or imagined—since the individual is judged at the bar of his or her own conscience.

The second feature Hallpike identifies as absent in atomistic individualism is any notion of principled opposition to time-honored practice and popular opinion. All ethical objections of this sort presuppose the fulfillment of at least two cognitive requirements—namely, knowledge of a moral standard that is missing or only partially in evidence in the status quo, and awareness of the faulty nature of current social arrangements. As we have already seen, hunter-gatherers and primitive agriculturalists inhabit a world that is structured by a set of concrete rules, but in which there is no recognized public forum for the creation of new rules or the evaluation of old ones. Atomistic societies have none of the institutions or governing bodies whose function it is in more complex societies to deal with rules. Sustained discourse and debate about rules naturally leads to the hunt for rules about rules (in order to properly identify the ones worth following), of which ethical principles constitute one variety. The codes of conduct that exist in social atomism are implicit in the body of custom that is the perennial gift of one generation to the next, but these dictates do not constitute the explicit object of any ongoing discourse. Hallpike notes that ethnographers of atomistic societies have repeatedly testified to the difficulty atomists experience when asked to provide rules or schemas for their own social arrangements. Despite their implicit, "working" knowledge of these codes, atomistic informants seem to lack the ability to conceive of social systems as wholes (a capacity, it's worth noting, that inevitably involves a significant degree of abstraction). Since most ethical objections to the status quo presuppose an awareness of the social system in which the practice being held up for evaluation is embedded, members of atomistic societies are obviously at a serious disadvantage when it comes to articulating social and ethical critique.

Despite its emphasis upon personal independence and self-assertion, atomistic individualism also lacks a conception of the individual as an entity who exists independently of his or her statuses and roles. Although members of atomistic societies obviously don't have the rich assortment of corporate and political identities that serve to bond modern individuals to their complex social orders, what roles and statuses do exist are ascribed. From the atomistic standpoint, there is no distinction between one's social ascriptions and one's identity. Unlike his or her modern counterpart, the atomistic individual does not experience the need to "find" him- or herself, since the individual's identity has always been a matter of common knowledge. Identity in these societies is not a matter of choice, but of fate.

The fourth element missing from atomistic individualism is the capacity for the sustained examination of one's own consciousness or of that of another. Hallpike points out that in the languages of primitive peoples words used to describe states of mind often reveal an implicit "physiological psychology," in which mental processes are partially assimilated with physiological functions. The early Greeks, for instance, conceived of thought in terms of breath and speech, and located the seat of cognition in the lungs. Hallpike argues that atomistic psychological vocabulary bespeaks of an awareness of inner states of mind that is narrow and highly selective. The focus of this terminology would appear to be directly observable phenomena that can provide important indications for how to act in the near future. In other words, what merits description are those aspects of interpersonal situations that could conceivably have consequences of an immediate and practical nature for the observer. Because the linguistic priority is on actions and their effects, intentions, motives, and other inner states tend to be neglected. A more discerning psychological vocabulary would presuppose an interest in mental description for its own sake that does not exist in the atomist context. Hallpike notes that in his fieldwork in Africa and Papua New Guinea, which involved the collection of hundreds of interviews, his informants never spontaneously introduced considerations of thought or intention when discussing the conduct of others that went beyond very cursory descriptions of anger, fear, sorrow, and the like. During his four years in the field the sole exception to this rule he encountered was a male informant who, in addition to being very intelligent, had worked for many years with Catholic missionaries.[15]

In Hallpike's three-tiered evolutionary scheme, the developmental stage that follows social atomism is known as corporate order. As their title suggests, societies of corporate order are those in which

17

membership is based on ascriptive criteria derived from categories other than that of kinship. Although kinship may still—and usually does—constitute a criterion for membership, it is supplemented by new forms of association, such as clans, age-grade groupings, secret societies, and special purpose sodalities (for ceremonies, warfare, etc.).[16] The creation of such corporate groups allows for the inclusion of greater numbers of individuals within the society than could be achieved through atomistic arrangements. In addition to enabling wider membership, corporate structures invest certain social roles with authority, such as a membership in a village council or a clan headship. The creation of formal offices whose powers exist independently of any given officeholder allows for both the emergence of genuine political authority and improved legal procedures. These new powers require legitimation, and the typical solution involves an identification of the social order with the underlying order of the universe. Religious belief and ritual come to articulate and enact the cosmological significance of the social world.

The primitive individualism of atomistic cultures is sharply curtailed in corporate order societies, since members of the latter often relate to one another as representatives of different groups. A person's overall prestige is a function of his or her roles and statuses, and Hallpike notes that corporate order inevitably establishes hierarchies among different classes (e.g., nobles over commoners, old over young, men over women, etc.). Morality is conventional, in the sense that good behavior is that which conforms to role stereotypes and custom. Although identity is also ascribed in atomistic cultures, the atomistic ascriptions are less comprehensive than corporate ones because the roles assigned to the individual are primarily derived from kinship and face-to-face cooperative activities. With the appearance of corporate structures, roles arise in which the individual undergoes a higher degree of social integration.

Consider, for example, the changes wrought by the emergence of hereditary nobility, a not uncommon feature of corporate order. All aristocracies exist as a matter of convention, and their perpetuation typically requires the observance of a more or less elaborate code of conduct. For the noble, class considerations are, of course, central in matters of marriage and reproduction, where bloodlines must be maintained, but may permeate other aspects of life as well. The marks of good breeding can be extended to encompass the aristocrat's education, choice of occupation, pastimes, manner of speech, mode of dress, and so forth. In those corporate order societies with an established aristocracy, being noble is, in short, usually a way of life, but a way of life that is only possible to the extent to which the individual adopts the perspective of his or her class. In other words, within corporate order the individual learns to privilege the perception of himself or herself that is obtained from the group perspective. There exists, as yet, little awareness of society as itself constituting a whole or system that can, in turn, be considered from the standpoint of the individual. Actually, it is the distinct consciousness of one's social order as constituting one among many possible arrangements that heralds the appearance of individualism of the modern type.

Hallpike terms the third and final stage of development in moral understanding "transcendence." He locates the first appearance of this phase in a number of early state societies around 500 BCE, roughly in the middle of the period designated the "Axial Age" (from approximately 800–200 BCE) by the German philosopher Karl Jaspers. During this era, a new social awareness arose in Greece, Israel, China, Iran, and India. Its key feature was the ability to take society itself as an object of thought. The capacity to conceptualize the social order as a whole ushered in the post-conventional stage of moral understanding; customs, rules, and laws could now be grasped as elements of a specific social arrangement, an arrangement that could be organized differently and perhaps even improved. In other words, the status quo lost its sacred inviolability and became subject to the social imagination. The factors responsible for this expansion of social awareness are numerous and complex, but among the most important Hallpike cites are the emergence of the state, the social consequences of warfare and conquest, and the development of trade and industry.[17]

The rise of the state and its associated bureaucracies tended to undermine the older group structures founded on kinship and heredity, at least among the upper social strata. Hallpike argues that, as the state grew in size and complexity, rulers naturally became interested in awarding administrative positions based on merit, since the job of governing increasingly required competency and specialization. By weakening the prerogatives of family ties and hereditary claims, rulers had a freer hand to select persons of talent. Warfare, and particularly campaigns of conquest, tended to mix populations and disrupt established patterns of land ownership by descent groups. In addition, the growth of trade and commerce usually weakens social relations based on ascribed rank and status by introducing economic self-interest as

19

a motive that vies with the group-oriented motives of corporate order. The development of economic life also usually encourages increased contacts with other societies, and through these contacts the particularity of the individual's own culture and language are impressed upon consciousness. We have seen how, according to Hallpike's developmental scheme, the simplest forms of society accommodate a significant degree of individualism, only for this individualism to largely disappear in the intermediate stage of development, and then reappear in a new form in societies of the modern type. Overall, the elements present in modern individualism but lacking in its atomistic counterpart render the latter less self-aware than the former. This key difference will provide us with a significant clue for understanding the specific nature of modern selfhood.

Social Evolution

Some readers may object that our presentation of individualism is seriously flawed because it depends upon an account of societal evolution, and that social phenomena cannot be legitimately described in evolutionary terms. In order for this criticism to be applicable to Hallpike's theory, however, it would have to be the case that social processes manifest no common patterns of development, since such patterns are essentially what he means by "evolution" as regards the study of human cultures. From a purely conceptual standpoint, it seems unlikely that all social change would be so idiosyncratic as to prevent the appearance of any common motifs. Take, for example, the creation of certain types of technology. In every culture that ever independently discovered writing, it's highly probable that the spoken word preceded the written one. Of course, it would not have been logically impossible for some society to use writing as its original form of communication, but given human physiology and the conditions of prehistoric life, the likelihood that writing arose first must be estimated as exceedingly low. Similar considerations hold as well for the domestication of fire and the discovery of heating food, and the reader can probably readily draw further illustrations from the history of technology. These examples underscore the fact that the world's various cultures do, after all, inhabit the same world and are made up of the same primate species. Notwithstanding differences between local environments and racial types, there does exist the backdrop of a shared physical universe and biological structure. Given the common parameters of the human condition, it would, in fact, be surprising if no general patterns emerged in the formation of societies.

Hallpike's claim is that large and structurally complex societies were preceded by relatively smaller and simpler ones, and that this process of growth can be ordered into a series of general phases, in which earlier stages serve as prerequisites for the emergence of later ones. The actual development of any given society is contingent upon a wide variety of factors, so that social evolution is by no means an inevitable process. Assuming, however, that Hallpike's description of the pattern of social transformation is accurate, we should expect that if a culture does develop, then it will pass through one or more of the various stages outlined by him in the order in which he lists them. Absent direct intervention or influence from a more advanced society, we shouldn't, for example, find any instances of hunter-gatherers bypassing the stage of corporate order and nevertheless achieving the creation of a literate, highly differentiated civilization.

Although societal evolution generally proceeds from relative simplicity to relative complexity, Hallpike cautions that we should beware of confusing the complex with the complicated.[18] Regarding social structures, he construes "complex" as referring to what is necessarily composed of multiple parts, whereas "complicated" suggests that at least some of the intricacy in question is due to poor design, lack of planning, and the like. In fact, he argues that the appearance of social complexity has often involved the *simplification* of previous cultural patterns. Despite their overall structural simplicity, primitive cultures often relate individuals to one another through highly involved forms of association and classification. Their social patterns are complicated because they are undifferentiated and particularistic, and they contrast strongly with modern social systems, which have undergone a process of rationalization through the division of labor.

Due to their lack of differentiation, small-scale societies typically have practices and institutions that serve multiple purposes. Hallpike cites the Konso of Ethiopia as an example.[19] A corporate-order society, this Cushitic people distributes political power across a variety of different social roles—including regional priests, council elders, warriors, and lineage heads—in an elaborate, uncentralized system. Customs and activities in primitive societies are also frequently invested with religious meanings so that tasks such as gardening or the construction of a dwelling are not undertaken solely for the mundane motives of meeting human needs for nourishment and shelter, but also participate in a cosmological system. The division of labor gradually dismantles such complicated cultural patterns by creating social subsystems that exist for certain express purposes. The distinct goal or goals of the subsystem promote the development of means-ends rationality and its associated values, such as efficiency and expertise. Oddly enough, therefore, the appearance of a specialized subsystem can represent an increase in structural complexity, but at the same time constitute a simplification of the former cultural pattern.

The theory of social evolution that informs Hallpike's study of moral understanding is primarily descriptive. Although he discusses various factors involved in social development, he does not attempt to provide a general explanation for why such development occurs or fails to occur in particular instances. As concerns societal evolution, the central thrust of his argument is aimed at establishing that it has taken place, and that its general features are accurately characterized by his tripartite scheme. To this end, he presents a wealth of evidence gleaned from across the social sciences and humanities. He asserts neither that social evolution is inevitable, nor that relatively more developed societies are inherently superior to relatively less developed ones, nor that human history is the story of Progress, wherein we moderns are morally superior to our predecessors.[20]

There are at least two different ways in which one could argue against Hallpike's account. Perhaps the most obvious approach would be to find empirical counterexamples to his evolutionary scheme. Although this avenue of criticism has the merit of being direct, it's not necessarily the most promising, given the author's expertise and his extensive review of the anthropological literature. The other tack would be to show that his theory of social evolution fails in principle. Since Hallpike's theory asserts that modern complex societies have developed from simpler, primitive forms of social life, an effective criticism would be to demonstrate that while any given society may undergo change, no society can actually develop. On this view, although a social order may alter in structure, such changes merely represent a reorganization or reshuffling of old elements into a new arrangement.

The problem with this description of the history of social life is that it refuses to acknowledge a number of commonplace facts. It is bound to simply disregard the emergence of social differentiation and structural complexity, increases in population size, as well as the appearance of novel group characteristics and qualities. Since "evolution" and "development" are commonly held to describe trends toward increased complexity and the appearance of new qualities and characteristics in the history of organic life-forms, it's unclear why their application should be denied to the social world.

Notes

1. *Collins Dictionary of Sociology* (London: Collins, 2006), s.v. "anomie or anomy."
2. Albion Small, *General Sociology: An Exposition of the Main Development in Sociological Theory from Spencer to Ratzenhofer* (Chicago: The University of Chicago Press, 1905), 443.
3. Sir Henry Sumner Maine, *Ancient Law, Its Connection with the Early History of Society and Its Relation to Modern Ideas* (New York: Henry Holt and Company, 1906), 81–82.
4. Arthur Fisher Bentley, *The Process of Government: A Study of Social Pressures* (Chicago: The University of Chicago Press, 1908), 26–37.
5. Arthur Bentley and John Dewey, *Knowing and the Known* (Boston: Beacon Press, 1949), 132.
6. Ibid., 133.
7. Bentley, *The Process of Government*, 37.
8. Bentley and Dewey, *Knowing and the Known*, 193.
9. Ibid., 195.
10. Alexis de Tocqueville, "Of Individualism in Democratic Countries," in *Democracy in America: Historical–Critical Edition of De la démocratie en Amérique*, ed. Eduardo Nolla, trans. James T. Schleifer, vol. 3 (Indianapolis, IN: Liberty Fund, 2010).
11. Ibid.
12. Emile Durkheim, *The Division of Labor in Society*, trans. George Simpson (New York: The Free Press, 1933), 289.
13. C. R. Hallpike, "Atomistic Societies," chap. V in *The Evolution of Moral Understanding* (Alton, PA: The Prometheus Research Group, 2004), 187–217.
14. Ibid., 216–217.
15. Ibid., 180–181.
16. Ibid., 219.
17. Ibid., 284–289.
18. Ibid., 153–156.
19. Ibid., 155.
20. Hallpike is careful to stress that the evolution of moral understanding involves an increasing degree of sophistication in thought about issues with moral import. In other words, his claim is that there has been a development in how moral problems are comprehended, and this, of course; is quite distinct from the assertion that morals and moral character have generally improved over the course of human history. He understandably distances himself from any pronouncements to the latter effect.

2

The Individuation of Identity

Although we usually count identity among an individual's most personal possessions, it has, of course, an inherently social aspect as well. A human being living completely apart from any social order or group—supposing that such an existence were possible—would have no need of identity. One can easily imagine such a loner performing all the activities compelled by human biology without the benefit of name, title, rank, or status. Animals provide us with ample evidence that the symbolic accouterments of identity are not indispensable for physical survival. Identity, then, is not required for navigating the world of nature: Its native sphere is that of society. The need for a proper name, for example, automatically arises in a setting where the individual is one among others of the same kind.

A person's sense of identity potentially includes many different elements: physical appearance, gender, memories, and even possessions and location. By the term "identity" we will understand the individual's beliefs and attitudes concerning those personal attributes that he or she habitually relies upon to relate to others. In other words, for our purposes "identity" means one's sense of self in relation to society, and it points to the individual's inner dispositions toward his or her social roles and statuses. For instance, in modern societies persons can adopt a wide range of attitudes toward their line of work, from viewing their occupation as a necessary evil to treating it as the single most important activity in their lives. Individuals can also differ significantly in their degree of self-awareness, and the concept of identity does not imply that one is necessarily conscious of all the attitudes that one holds toward oneself: Identities can, and often do, incorporate conflicting attitudes and erroneous beliefs. Consequently, they can be more or less integrated, as well as more or less stable.

Each individual self actually represents a unique coordination of "selves" that arise through the enactment of social roles. George Herbert Mead coined the term "generalized other" to refer to the intersubjective stance or organized set of attitudes that makes coordinated activity within a group possible. In a team sport, such as basketball, the individual team member must acquire the "generalized other" of the group in order to interact in an appropriate manner with his or her teammates. That is, the individual player must be able to take himself or herself as an object of thought within the conceptual framework that unifies and structures the group. The individual has to grasp the end toward which the group strives and understand the means employed to achieve it. Mead points out that in early childhood it is possible to distinguish a stage of behavior that is preliminary to participation in organized games. Playacting with objects or other people involves mentally adopting someone else's standpoint. Consider, for example, the little girl who takes on the role of mother and assigns her doll the role of child. Such play is less complex than that of games and sports, since it is open ended and not subject to explicit rules. Nevertheless, it is inherently social. In the next section, we will trace how social roles and rules come to constitute fundamental elements of personal identity.

Kohlberg and Hallpike on the Stages of Moral Understanding

A key part of Hallpike's theory of moral understanding is his view that the well-known stages of moral development described by the psychologist Lawrence Kohlberg roughly correspond to stages in social evolution. We need to consider this aspect of Hallpike's theory in some detail, since the nature of the individual's identity is closely related to his or her capacity for moral reflection. As concerns the first stage in societal evolution, social atomism, Hallpike argues that the moral comprehension of most of its members is well described by the second stage in Kohlberg's famous schema. Overall, Kohlberg recognizes three major divisions in moral development—namely, the pre-conventional, conventional, and post-conventional levels. Originally each level was subdivided into two stages, but eventually the last stage, the sixth, was dropped from the schema. This stage was labeled "Universal Ethical Principles," and was abandoned due to the fact that it was insufficiently supported by empirical data. The first stage in the pre-conventional level is often entitled the "Punishment and Obedience" orientation, since within this perspective right and wrong are merely a function of conforming or failing to conform to the decrees of external authorities. An action is bad due to the fact that it is sanctioned, and the primary moral interest lies in avoiding punishment. The social perspective of this orientation is highly egocentric, and there is little insight into the mental lives of others. In fact, the rightness or wrongness of any given act is essentially identified with the type of behavior—approbative or punitive—that it elicits from authority figures, and the moral agent's intentions or motives are not taken into account.

The second stage in the pre-conventional level is sometimes known as "Instrumental Hedonism," and it reflects an increased ability to project oneself into the shoes of the other. Reciprocity makes its appearance at this stage, as the individual becomes aware that others have their own interests, and that these can sometimes conflict with those of one's own. The new sensitivity to the reciprocal nature of interpersonal relations finds a specifically moral expression in the notion of fairness. What is fair receives a literal or concrete interpretation in terms of equal exchange and keeping up one's end of a deal. Although the overall orientation is still quite egocentric, there is the new recognition that in life with others it is sometimes necessary to give in order to receive. Instrumental hedonism's motto could be, "If you scratch my back, I'll scratch yours."

Hallpike argues that this orientation bears a close similarity to the moral outlook of social atomism in several important respects. Relationships in atomistic societies, particularly among hunter-gatherers, are primarily based upon family bonds and individual allegiances. With the exception of kinship roles and statuses, band members' relations to one another are not mediated through groups. Given their mode of existence, foraging societies can generally meet the needs of their members with a minimum of cooperation. Corporate groupings based on class, occupation, ethnicity, etc., are not present. Individuals are reared to be autonomous, and to respect the autonomy of others. The individualism of social atomism is usually rugged, in the sense that the emphasis upon self-sufficiency is not balanced by an ethic of altruism. Hallpike notes that the ethnographic literature on hunter-gatherers often reveals an interpersonal climate of mutual indifference. For instance, anthropologists studying these societies have repeatedly reported the abandonment of the sick, and a general lack of empathy when misfortune befalls a fellow member of the band. While foragers usually observe egalitarian codes of sharing, Hallpike points out that the stress they place on balanced reciprocity should not be mistaken for a genuine spirit of generosity. In fact, the egalitarian ethic of hunter-gatherers actually bespeaks of a lack of trust in others, an absence that Hallpike attributes to the weakness of their social structures.[1]

Ethnographers have often observed that social relations among foragers are marked by their brittleness, and Hallpike contends that the central tension in these societies is that between "self-assertion and conformity to group norms."[2]

The parallels between Kohlberg's instrumental hedonist orientation and the ethos of social atomism are patent. Assuming that Hallpike's thesis is correct, and that psychological ontogeny recapitulates socio-logical phylogeny, as it were, what does this tell us about the nature of identity in these societies? As we have already seen, identity in social atomism is mainly a function of kinship and, to a lesser extent, affinities between individuals. Gender and age certainly make their contributions as well, insofar as they help determine social roles and statuses, such as mother or hunter, child or elder. Most of the individual's identity, then, is ascribed, though the emphasis upon personal autonomy and self-sufficiency does accord some measure of freedom to the individual. These cultures generally value non-interference and shy away from employing formal social constraints, as is often witnessed by their permissive child-rearing practices. In consequence, we should expect that a certain degree of liberty is allotted to temperament. Hence, underlying individual tendencies (e.g., to be reserved or submissive) enjoy some space for free development. In addition, the relative loose-ness and fluidity of band membership that has often been noted in the literature endows members with some degree of choice in their associations. We have already remarked that avoidance is the main mechanism for resolving group conflict in social atomism, and that it is often facilitated by the relative ease with which an individual can change living groups.

Despite these concessions to individuality, the overall picture of identity that emerges under social atomism is one of ascription. How-ever, we should take care not to confuse this cultural assignment of identity with cultural regimentation à la Durkheim. It's not so much that the social atomist is directly squeezed into a specific mold as that atomistic societies provide their members with very few opportunities to develop unconventional interests and abilities. Although it may seem slight when considered from the standpoint of external behavior, there's a significant psychological difference between performing an act due to direct social pressure and performing the same act for want of other options. In the latter case, the individual's behavior is only indirectly constrained by social circumstances, so that he or she may not expe-rience the cultural channeling of his or her conduct as an absence of freedom. In a discussion of traditional religious education among Jews as it existed prior to the Second World War in the villages of Eastern Europe, anthropologist Dorothy Lee provides a nice illustration of such channeling, which she terms "cultural compression."[3]

As Lee observes, by the standards of contemporary pedagogy nearly everything about the religious instruction of young boys in the close-knit *shtetl* communities was ill conceived. Typically the youngsters began their schooling before the age of five and sometimes were only three years old when they first entered the *kheyder*, or religious primary school. The instructional day was ten hours long, and the *kheyder* was normally in session five and a half days a week. Learning often took place in poorly lit, crowded rooms where the boys were seated on long, backless benches flanking a table. Pupils began their educational career with rote memorization of prayer texts in Hebrew, a language they could not understand, with little effort made to impart to novices the meaning of what they memorized. After the prayer book came reading of the Torah, which was eventually followed by study of the Talmud. The materials were wholly age inappropriate, and apparently little concession was made to the limited attention spans of young children or to their need for sensory stimulation and physical activity. *Kheyder* teachers were notorious for being ill suited to their profession and for their willingness to employ corporal punishment in order to elicit the correct answers and desired behavior from their charges. The *kheyder*, in short, had all the makings of a dysfunctional learning establishment of the first order.

And yet, instead of instilling a lifelong loathing for formal education, the *kheyder* often seems to have had the opposite effect upon its pupils. According to Lee, many of its graduates developed a genuine love for learning and scholarship, and as adults even looked back upon their early schooling with a certain degree of fondness. Lee finds one of the keys to this apparent enigma in the cultural role that was accorded to religious education among *shtetl* Jews. In these communities a man's status as a good Jew and as a community member with full standing directly depended upon exercise of the skills acquired in religious instruction. Only through reading prayers and studying scripture could a man correctly worship God and arrive at a sound understanding of the Law, which would provide him with necessary guidance in fulfilling his social responsibilities. So, from the perspective of the boy, the arduous trek through formal religious instruction was a necessary stage of the journey into manhood. Having witnessed their own fathers reciting prayers and poring over sacred text and scholarly commentary, they often regarded the rigors of their early education as more privilege than burden. In this regard Lee cites a conversation she had with one of her own students, a Bessarabian Jew who entered the *kheyder* at the age of three. Remarking that she found the conditions of his early schooling appalling, he replied, "Miserable? I was learning the language of the ritual; I was learning to say the chants like my father and my older brother. I was proud."[4] Lee notes that her student's attitude was echoed in many of the reports she examined of other *kheyder* graduates. The sole culturally acceptable path available to *shtetl* boys was indeed narrow, but because they usually found it to be meaningful, the hardships of the *kheyder* were generally viewed as worth enduring and did not spoil the entire experience.

Lady Murasaki's *The Tale of Genji*, the great eleventh-century Japanese romance, provides Lee with another illustration of cultural compression. The first part of the novel focuses on the amorous adventures its hero, Genji, undertakes at the imperial court. Lee remarks that on her first reading of the work she was shocked by the degree to which the conduct of Genji and his mistresses is dictated by custom: Genji's lovers must write him morning-after letters, in which everything from epistolary form and content down to the type of ink, paper, and calligraphy to be employed is prescribed. When the hero participates in ceremonial events, what he wears is strictly determined by conventions that extend even the type of undergarments to be worn.[5]

The aristocratic world depicted by Lady Murasaki impressed Lee above all as being highly regimented and impersonal. However, the anthropologist realized that she had failed to grasp this universe from the perspective of its inhabitants, and on a second reading she discovered a dimension of subtle nuance in the performance of custom that she had at first missed. Lady Murasaki portrays the hero and some of his mistresses as free spirits, who, although they employ conventions, are able to express their will and creativity through them. These strong personalities stand out in contrast to more mundane characters, whose actions are almost wholly conventional in the sense that they represent a docile and unreflective performance of the required forms. To those who grew up with them and knew nothing else, the considerable constraints of court life in feudal Japan were probably not primarily experienced as checks on individual initiative, but rather as the grammatical rules necessary for effective and stable social interaction.

The second level in Kohlberg's scheme of moral development is that of conventional morality. Like the first, pre-conventional level, it contains two stages, often referred to as the "good boy, nice girl" and "law and order" orientations. In the former, the self has become closely identified with some of its social roles. In light of this expanded notion of selfhood, new interests and loyalties emerge. The individual is now concerned to conform his or her behavior to the expectations of others, and to the conventional expectations attached to certain roles (e.g., being a good daughter or sister). The new sense of responsibility toward others springs from a heightened awareness of the immediate social environment, and from a new appreciation of the family and other local groups as being inherently valuable. Kohlberg emphasizes that the wish to toe the line of stereotypical expectations is an expression of a general desire to actively support the groups with which the individual has identified. Whereas the pre-conventional attitude toward cooperation was based on a logic of *quid pro quo*, the conventional one assumes that at least some social arrangements make a legitimate claim upon the individual—a claim that should be respected regardless of the consequences. The general cognitive perspective of the good boy, nice girl orientation is, in fact, that of the interpersonal. For the first time, intention becomes an important consideration in the evaluation of conduct. In addition, emotional states with a specifically social component, such as respect, trust, and gratitude, are judged to be important aspects of the individual's interpersonal relationships. The self comes to evaluate its own behavior through the eyes of others, and seeks their approval.

The transition to the law and order orientation essentially represents an expansion of the interpersonal perspective to include social organization extending beyond the face-to-face level. The novel cognitive element in this orientation is the comprehension of social groupings as systems that condition the human relations within them. The insight that the rules and roles defined by the group determine how individuals should treat one another engenders a newfound respect for law as essential to the maintenance of social order. Despite their reverence for legal authority, persons with this perspective do often recognize that in rare instances conflicts may arise from the competing claims of law and moral duty.

If Hallpike's theory of moral evolution is correct, then the conventional standpoint first emerged in societies of corporate order.

By integrating the individual more fully into group life, corporate order eliminated the rugged individualism of social atomism. Within the world of corporate order, few moral questions arise because, insofar as the individual knows his or her place in society, he or she knows what is to be done. In other words, morality is almost purely customary. The norms governing various offices are a matter of public knowledge and enjoy nearly universal acceptance.[6] As in social atomism, there is relatively little attention paid to the inner life of the self, and mores center on acts and not intentions.

In several respects, modern team sports constitute a good analogy for the moral viewpoint of corporate order. When, for example, it's asserted that a professional baseball player is a good batter or out-fielder, we assume that the truth-value of the claim can be objectively assessed according to the prevailing standards of the sport. Batters and outfielders perform specific functions that are defined by the rules governing baseball, and they can be adjudged as good or bad according to their job performance relative to the records of other players, past and present. Whether or not a given player is a great batter is not a matter of personal opinion. If we but extend the evaluation of role performance to also include the role actor's overall moral worth, we should get a sense for the moral viewpoint constituted by corporate order. As Hallpike and other writers, such as Alasdaire MacIntyre, have observed, in these societies the individual is not conceived of as existing prior to social relationships, but rather is actually thought of as being constituted by them. There is no notion of an inner or real self that stands behind or beyond all the roles occupied by the individual, a self that is only incompletely expressed in any given role, and that even transcends the sum total of all its social engagements. From the standpoint of corporate order, such an entity would appear to be more wraithlike than mortal. According to the lights of corporate order, actual persons can be known and evaluated through their relations to other persons.

The third and final division in Kohlberg's scheme is the post-conventional level. Cognitively speaking, the transition to this level includes the realization that society is not an eternal and immutable part of nature, but rather a status quo that always involves some degree of artifice. The nearly absolute authority enjoyed by law and custom under the conventional standpoint is called into question by the new awareness that the social order is distinct from the natural one, and at least partially the result of human endeavor. Given these insights, doubts and questions commonly arise about the legitimacy of the rules governing group life. Whereas the individual with a conventional outlook will accept the authority of a tradition simply because it is a tradition, the post-conventional moral actor will want to know what makes it a worthwhile one. Strictly speaking, conscience in a modern sense only appears at the post-conventional level because it is only within this perspective that the attempt is made to provide a rational justification for moral judgments. Morality is no longer primarily a "given" but becomes, in at least some instances, a choice to be made or even a problem to be creatively solved.

As we have already noted, the mature version of Kohlberg's scheme lists only one stage or type of orientation for the post-conventional level, which is sometimes called the social contract orientation. For the first time, a clear distinction is drawn between public and private goods. As regards the latter, this orientation recognizes that values may be relative to groups and even to individuals. It also acknowledges that differences of personal opinion concerning some moral issues are widespread, and that individuals should enjoy the right to hold and express these opinions. In addition to the freedom of thought and expression, a number of other rights are usually seen as having universal application, although the list of rights may differ somewhat from person to person.

Individuals with this standpoint often employ different rationales to justify the ethical authority of human rights. They may have recourse to the idea that such rights are necessary for the form of social life agreed upon by the members of society, or that they stem from the natural law, or that they are grounded in utilitarian considerations. Regardless of the justification given, the distinction between ethics and law plays an important role in the social contract orientation. Rather than conceiving of the law in the absolute and fixed terms of the conventional perspective, it is the law as living process and formal procedure that now comes into view. The emphasis is upon law as a way for self-interested individuals to fairly and peacefully resolve conflicts. Insofar as the legal system serves to safeguard the integrity of democratic government, it is also valued as a means for building consensus. Furthermore, the social contract orientation is legalistic in its very conception of the individual moral actor, since the most important model for personal moral duties is that of contract. The individual is thought of as a free agent, who must respect certain ground rules and fulfill certain duties necessary to the continued existence of the social order, but who otherwise chooses his or her legal and moral commitments. While many of the individual's social roles actually come with certain legal obligations attached (e.g., being someone's employee, spouse, or parent), others may fall outside the law but still lend themselves to a contractual understanding, as in friendship, where there is generally some expectation of reciprocity, be it however vague and informal.

In his description of the social contract orientation, Hallpike notes that individuals with this outlook often find it difficult to integrate the ethical and legal perspectives.[7] On the one hand, the fact that the law is viewed in less literal or absolute terms at this stage stems from the understanding that ethical considerations have a legitimate role to play in legal reform and the legislative process. On the other hand, it is also generally acknowledged that in a free society it is a bad idea to legislate morality, meaning that at least some moral decisions are better left up to the individual. Hence, there is a tension between the notion that ethical principles can serve to create social consensus and the view that morals are relative to the individual.

Much of the confusion is due to a philosophical tradition that has assumed that the core subject matter of ethics is rules or principles. For the past several centuries, Western moral philosophy has been dominated by the hunt for an underlying law that would serve to ground all moral judgment. If such a law existed, one would expect that its application to similar situations would result in similar outcomes. Consequently, the personal contribution to moral judgment would be minor. However, concurrent with this philosophical search for objective moral truth, Western nations have gradually granted their members more and more personal liberties, and hence expanded the potential sphere of moral choice for the individual. Western philosophy has been an active participant in the growth of contemporary individualism by furnishing arguments on its behalf, of which social contract theory has been the most influential representative. Collectively speaking, philosophers have, therefore, been in the somewhat awkward position of arguing vigorously for freedom of choice, while simultaneously trying to produce an ethics in which that freedom is largely irrelevant beyond the black-and-white option of choosing to either respect or disregard the dictates of morality.

Hallpike criticizes the monism of the major ethical theories and argues for a pluralist approach that would recognize the important role played by individual judgment in moral reasoning.[8] In addition, he points out that Kohlberg's conception of the post-conventional moral orientation very much bears the bias of ethical monism.

34

Indeed, the sixth developmental stage, which Kohlberg later abandoned as appearing too infrequently to merit incorporation into the scheme, was entitled the universal ethical principle orientation. In it, ethics becomes purely a matter of conscience and rests upon abstract principles such as the Golden Rule or the categorical imperative. According to Kohlberg's original hypothesis, such principles exist independently of any social compact and draw their authority from logical traits that include universality, consistency, and comprehensiveness. Due to their highly formal and abstract character, the principles function as standards or criteria for the evaluation of concrete norms or laws. Since they define the nature of justice, rights, and personhood, the principles can be employed to determine whether or not any given concrete rule, whether moral or legal, passes ethical muster.

As Hallpike points out, Kohlberg's notion of the post-conventional moral orientation is almost wholly cognitive, and so fails to adequately address the roles habit and affect occupy in the good life. He notes that Kohlberg was generally dismissive of virtue as an important factor in moral development, since he identified it almost entirely with customary morality. On Kohlberg's view, genuine virtue is equated with conduct guided by a self-chosen ethical principle, and what usually passes for virtue or vice is merely outward behavior that conforms to the popular conventions of the day.

In subsequent chapters we shall see that Kohlberg's ethical cognitivism fails to take into account the unconscious and emotional aspects of personality, aspects that often exert an undue influence over reasoning and judgment in human affairs. We shall argue that this cognitivism is in large part the result of a legislative perspective that has predominated in modern moral philosophy. For the time being it is worth noting, with Hallpike, that Kohlberg expressly embraces John Rawls's theory of ethics.[9] The legislative standpoint that is explicit in Rawls's moral philosophy largely accounts for the relative absence of an ethic of altruism and care in Kohlberg's conception of post-conventional morality. As Hallpike observes, altruistic concern usually grows out of relations with particular persons, such as parents, siblings, friends, and neighbors.[10] Since the legislative perspective in moral philosophy naturally focuses on the ethical bare minimum required for group life in a modern social order, the specific character of actual interpersonal relations tends to receive short shrift.

Despite the flaws in Kohlberg's conception of the post-conventional moral standpoint, Hallpike argues that it does capture some crucial aspects of moral understanding in societies that have achieved the level of what he calls transcendence. We have already seen that Hallpike dates the origin of transcendent societies to the Axial Age. As regards morality, transcendence implies the implicit grasp of the ethical as a measure of conduct that is not necessarily embodied in any existing custom or social arrangement, and that does not draw its legitimacy from the mere fact of such embodiment. Indeed, the transition to transcendence involves the birth of the moral imagination: Actions are no longer right or wrong simply due to the dictates of tradition, but rather in the light of an ideal entertained by the self. This ideal may, of course, take many different forms, and can derive its validation from any one of a number of different sources, including speculative cosmology, divine command, or philosophical dialectic. Regardless of the manner of its justification, however, the moral dimension of conduct emerges as an object of reflection for the self, and this dimension is distinguished from the environing social and legal systems.

By the same token, the individual becomes aware of himself or herself as a person who is in some sense distinct from his or her social roles. This type of self-consciousness has often been recognized as the hallmark of modern individualism. Hallpike's study identifies increasing social complexity as the main factor in the development of individualism, a view shared by sociologist Rose Laub Coser, who argues that the crucial changes are those that directly impact the structure of social roles.[11] She pinpoints what she terms "role segmentation" and "complex role-sets" as key factors in promoting the self-aware and reflective state of mind that is emblematic of individualism.

A role-set consists of all the role partners related to someone in virtue of their status. For example, the role-set of a college professor would include the student body, faculty, staff, and administration of his or her institution. A simple role-set is one in which role partners differ little from one another in status, are rarely replaced by new occupants, and are more or less well acquainted with one another. The family, for instance, typically constitutes a simple role-set for its members. Complex role-sets, on the other hand, involve relations between individuals whose interaction is of a more transient nature and who sometimes occupy very different positions in the social system. For example, the coworkers and clients of the average corporate manager comprise a complex role-set.[12]

The ensemble of all the different status positions and social roles a particular individual fills is known as the status-set. The corporate executive's status-set includes not only his or her work relations but also those stemming from participation in other institutional and social contexts, such as family, church, school, and community. Generally speaking, the more complex the role-sets are that make up one's status-set, the more diverse are one's social relations. Coser refers to such pluralism and multiplicity in an individual's relationships as role segmentation, and she maintains that role segmentation is a vital source of cognitive enrichment. Frequent and omnifarious social contacts confront individuals with a variety of viewpoints and force them to hone their interpretational skills. By their very nature complex role-sets are usually harder to navigate than simple ones, since in the former we must often deal with people whose attitudes and motivations neither coincide with our own nor are known from previous experience. By contrast, simple role-sets, due to their habitual and relatively fixed nature, present the individual with fewer problematic situations that could serve to provoke reflection. Coser also suggests that a variety of role-sets are more likely to furnish the self with a diverse pool of interests and with an identity that does not depend upon any one role or relationship for its definition.[13] Although such an identity must often incorporate competing claims on the individual's allegiance that can be difficult to harmonize, the perspective that arises through grappling with these conflicts cannot be collapsed into that held by any particular group. She concludes that role-set complexity generally tends to promote the development of individual autonomy.

Individualism and Personal Autonomy

In societies in which a person's identity is mainly a matter of social ascription, the hold of custom over the individual's conduct seems to be much greater than it is in societies in which identity is primarily achieved. Although we have already touched on this point, it is worth further considering why this is the case, since the answers will provide us with some important clues for understanding the different nature of identity in traditional versus modern social orders. It seems fairly obvious that we cannot simply chalk up the greater sway of custom in atomistic or corporate-order societies to the force of habit, since habit remains an integral part of human behavior in modern societies. It is not, of course, the *capacity* for acquiring habit that has changed, but rather the *nature* of the habits acquired in the form of custom.

Perhaps the most obvious difference as concerns the situation of the individual in pre-modern versus modern societies is that the options for personal development in the former are relatively restricted. Social atomism, for example, is light on constraint, but also very limited in the cultural resources it makes available to the individual. A person of great native ability in music or math—or, for that matter, sport—would have little chance to develop to his or her full potential in a foraging society. Even a Mozart requires perfected musical instruments and notation, and a Gauss a useable system of numbers. As some philosophers since Hegel have been fond of pointing out, freedom in its fullest sense cannot be identified with mere lack of human interference in the activities of the individual. If we were to equate liberty with absence of social constraint, then we would have to judge the young child accorded the privileges of an adult by its parents to be as free as the average adult, at least within the realm of family life. But even in the absence of parental restrictions, the child would still be less autonomous than the grown up, since in many areas of life it would lack the capacity to make an informed decision. Instead of acting on the basis of desire that has ripened in the light of knowledge and experience, it would be especially vulnerable to the untoward influence of impulse and whim. A five-year-old might, for instance, decide to take up smoking merely because it looks interesting, without being able to fully appreciate the potential consequences of the decision. Genuine freedom involves the ability to make an informed choice between two or more live options. Depending upon the nature what is being decided, the availability of the options is itself often largely a function of technological and social development.

Not only are the material and social conditions for different courses of action often lacking in pre-modern societies, so is the mental perspective that helps to usher such options into being. Social life in these cultures is generally much more integrated than in modern civilization. Because they are pre-literate, the size and complexity of the cultural inheritance is limited to what can be transmitted from the living memory of one generation to the next. In fact, since these social orders have relatively few craft specialists, the preponderance of the cultural tradition is acquired by the average group member. In addition, members of the same society share the same living conditions and engage in the same activities, so that their perceptions and reactions tend to resemble each other as well. Such homogenous groups may constitute a sort of social filter that gradually and subconsciously removes disharmonious or jarring elements from preexisting arrangements. By the same token, these like-minded individuals would favor those innovations that make for greater vitality and coherence. Without the benefit of planners or a plan, distinctive cultural traditions of decorative design, dress, construction, and music could have arisen in this manner. Over time, general tendencies and preferences would have then crystalized within specific practices into fixed conventions.

Although it has an aesthetic aspect, the general tendency toward integration of the cultural pattern is rooted in a very practical circumstance. Only that which is capable of being communicated or shared can be incorporated into culture, and yet for any number of cultural pursuits the potential field of different elements is vast. To borrow a well-known example from Ruth Benedict,[14] the full range of sounds that can be generated by the human vocal apparatus far exceeds the phonetic needs of any language. Furthermore, any tongue incorporating them all would do so at the price of being too difficult for the average person to master. If they are to remain capable of being learned, most cultural practices must employ just some of the manifold elements potentially available to their practitioners. As concerns the overall culture itself, Benedict argues, the same holds true. The arc of possible human interests and values is enormous, and any given primitive culture employs just a fraction of those it could potentially utilize. The actual interests and values incorporated, of course, are at least partially due to the accidents of geography and history.

In societies in which tradition constitutes the predominant form of social authority, it is often possible to identify *a* pattern of culture, in which the "symbolic" culture of mores and metaphysical assumptions is of one piece with the "material" culture of food-gathering techniques, shelter-building technology, weapon making, and so forth. Furthermore, the cultural pattern is characterized by certain recurring motifs and ideals. Both atomistic and corporate-order societies are traditional in this sense, and both tend to display a relatively high degree of cultural integration compared to modern societies. As concerns the latter, their advanced division of labor has given birth to social systems that operate in relative autonomy from custom and cultural legacy. The authority of tradition has been replaced by that of secular rationalism, and institutions have been restructured in the light of certain explicit functions, functions for whose sake the institutions are expressly understood to exist. By contrast, one of the most striking features of societies in which a unifying cultural pattern prevails is the undifferentiated nature of their social practices. Many of these activities are multifunctional, and the various functions fulfilled by any given institution or practice often coexist without being organized into a formal hierarchy.

Dorothy Lee points out that a stumbling block to a better understanding of primitive societies has been the tendency of anthropologists to organize ethnographic material into categories culturally familiar to themselves and their readers. So, for instance, some textbooks on primitive societies compartmentalize their subject matter into different sections on economic activities, religious and magical beliefs, and artistic practices. Though such a presentation has an undeniable analytic appeal, Lee argues that it can be misleading because it is, in fact, often foreign to the cultures in question.[15] In the primitive social context, there is usually no clear dividing line between economics, religion, and art. Rather, according to Lee, what ethnographers actually observe are social situations that are structured by custom and that derive their meaning from an overall cultural framework. Hence, a given situation cannot be separated from its cultural context without robbing it of at least some of its meaning.

The integrated nature of primitive culture instills a mental backdrop in its members that is not conducive to analytical thinking. The ability to dissect a phenomenon or problem into its various parts often involves abstraction as well as the drawing of abstract distinctions, and where the weave of social life displays a dominant pattern, both mental operations are little called for in day-to-day activities. Abstraction is requisite for solving a great variety of problems since it permits the thinker to replace the complexity and richness of the actual situation with a simplified model that can be readily manipulated on the chalkboard of the imagination. Without such simplification, the mind would be swamped with all manner of irrelevant details, and essential connections between the basic aspects of the matter at hand would be easily lost. By making patent what is essential, and eliminating the superfluous, useful abstractions sharpen the mind's focus, and so are indispensable for analytical thinking.

Within the social orders under consideration, however, there is little need for abstraction because they primarily rely on custom rather than reason to accomplish their various tasks. In addition, the multifunctional nature of many customary activities probably constitutes a hindrance to abstract thinking, since the reduction that gives birth to an abstract concept is undertaken on behalf of a specific end. The fact that an agricultural activity is, say, intermeshed with religious observances would tend to discourage creative thinking about ways to improve how crops are raised because a change instituted for the sake of economics might interfere with proper relations with the world of spirits. It stands to reason that the more integrated a given cultural pattern is, the more natural resistance it will have to change, since the greater the degree of integration, the greater the likelihood that a modification in one sector will directly impact other areas.

The undifferentiated character of primitive practices and institutions disperses value across the ensemble of customs, making it difficult for the group member to isolate any one aspect of social life and assess its specific worth. As we have seen, practices in these societies are not organized in terms of a conscious adjustment of means to a specific end in the perpetual quest for increased effectiveness and efficiency. There are certainly human interests and preferences, but they are often implicit and generally taken for granted. The very distinction between fact and value, so fundamental to contemporary thought and such a source of consternation to moral philosophy since the eighteenth century, is alien to the primitive mind.

Contemporary thinkers often trace the origins of the is/ought gap identified by Hume to the birth of modern science and its rejection of teleological theories of natural phenomena. On this view, science progressively revealed an objective universe of facts in which the status of values became problematic. As concerns intellectual history, there is much to be said for this explanation, but we should not allow it to obscure the circumstance that the theoretical distinction between the "is" and the "ought" had a practical forerunner. In the realm of human activities and habits, it was not first and foremost science that paved the way for the divorce of facts from values, but social differentiation.

Each new social system institutionalized an abstract point of view that inevitably wrested some objects from their culturally assigned places and treated them as mere means to the achievement of distant ends. Within these differentiated systems even social roles were handled as instruments that could be perfected toward better fulfillment of their specific functions. The single most important historical example of this process is the emergence of the free-market economy, which eventually led to the dissolution of the feudal social order in which it was born.[16] Capitalism transformed labor by extracting it from the network of social relationships that had structured work in the medieval world. The customs that governed dealings between serfs and lords, as well as apprentices and guild masters, gave way to the mechanism of supply and demand, in which labor was reborn as a commodity. Work was no longer assigned as part of the individual's social status but instead involved a contractual relationship entered into by the laborer in order to receive a wage. For the employee, the job was primarily a means of livelihood, and for the employer the worker represented an economic resource. Within the context of this market economy, the distinction between means and ends is part of everyday life, as is the conception of value as relative to one's situation. The wage laborer recognizes that his or her work has a different value for others than it does for himself or herself. It is a relatively short step from such notions to the idea that values are fundamentally different than facts, and that the two exist independently of one another.

Actually, the contemporary demarcation between facts and values represents just one of a number of abstract discriminations that are essential for critical reasoning but usually absent from the vocabularies of pre-modern societies. Other important distinctions along the same lines include the divide between the subjective and the objective, between the human and natural orders, and between mind and body. Each of these differentiations has, of course, constituted a major topic in Western philosophy, and some of them have given rise to famous dualisms. Although philosophers have often differed in their metaphysical appraisals of these discriminations, they have generally acknowledged that there was at least an *apparent* difference between the subject matters being distinguished. Furthermore, they have also usually taken it to be part of the particular office of philosophy to explain the nature and meaning of these distinctions in human experience. In the context of primitive culture, many of the very words needed for such meta-analysis are absent. At least part of what is lacking in these societies is a certain "soft" technology of critical thinking, the most important element of which is doubtless writing.

As anthropologist Jack Goody and others have pointed out, literacy made a crucial contribution to abstract thinking. With the advent of writing thought became graphically "objectified" and hence available for scrutiny and manipulation in a way hardly possible as long as ideas could only be presented orally.[17] In fact, the sphere of human discourse was transformed by the invention of writing. Language's original habitat was the rough and tumble world of action, where the word was generally handmaiden to the act. Originally of one piece with behavior, language primarily represented a way of orchestrating group action. Its use as a medium of reflection was derivative and emerged only gradually in the process of civilization.[18] Goody notes that it is difficult for non-literate societies to develop critical or skeptical traditions of reasoning since they lack a convenient and reliable way of creating a permanent record of viewpoints at odds with the popular beliefs and common sense of the group. Writing immensely facilitates genuinely reflective thinking, or thought about thought. The written text can be dissected at leisure, compared to competing accounts, considered for its own sake, applied to a problem at hand, and so forth. Through writing individuals can create snapshots of their perspectives—perspectives that may well differ in significant ways from the attitudes generally handed down in the group. Writing makes possible a world of ideas in which the objects under consideration are themselves ideas, and because it permanently fixes in a visual form what would otherwise exist as a fleeting speech act, the relations between concepts can be more or less readily investigated and stored. Historically, the abstract vista provided by literacy has always preceded the meta-theoretical and self-conscious inquiries of logic, epistemology, and metaphysics.[19]

Hallpike argues that a major weakness of Goody's theory is that it tends to focus too narrowly on literacy as the active ingredient in a change of cognition, when, in fact, literacy is usually part of a broader social transformation that includes the appearance of urbanization, scholarship, formal schooling and the state.[20] In support of this contention Hallpike points out that the invention of writing in Mesopotamia preceded the birth of abstract speculation in Greece by thousands of years. Such a tremendous time lag obviously poses problems for the hypothesis that literacy is the key to higher cognition. In addition, Hallpike discusses empirical research that suggests formal schooling has a greater impact on the capacity for abstract reasoning than literacy.[21] In light of these criticisms, we should view literacy as a necessary, but not a sufficient, condition for the development of higher thought processes, and this is essentially the position that Hallpike himself adopts.

The higher cognition that Hallpike and the researchers he discusses have in mind basically corresponds to the highest stage of cognition in Piaget's famous developmental scheme. This stage is often referred to as the level of formal-operational thinking, the key characteristic of which is the capacity to reason hypothetically. In the stage that immediately precedes the formal-operational level, known as "concrete-operational" thinking, the individual is capable of recognizing basic logical relationships in order to solve practical problems. In addition to being able to deal with problems of a more abstract nature, formal-operational cognition involves the ability to perform "quality control" on one's own

43

thought processes. For example, instead of settling for the first solution that appears to work, as would the concrete-operational thinker, the formal-operational reasoner brainstorms a variety of possible solutions and seeks to identify those that are the most promising. In addition to the employment of this "hypothetico-deductive cognitive strategy," formal-operational cognition involves propositional thinking, or the arrangement and generalization of past discoveries and conclusions into abstract statements. Such propositions serve as the building blocks of reflective worldviews, or the conscious synthesis of experience into a critical understanding of reality. Piaget described formal-operational thinking as involving second-degree cognitive processes, or processes to the second power, because unlike concrete operations, which treat the subject matter of propositions, formal operations deal with the abstract relations between propositions.

In her book *In Defense of Modernity*, Coser makes an extended argument in support of the idea that social complexity promotes formal-operational thinking. She reasons that the structure of the *Gesellschaft*, or modern social order, does much to inculcate formal-operational cognition in its members because it involves them in "universalistic"—as opposed to "particularistic"—relations with each other.[22] She borrows these descriptive categories from Talcott Parsons, who designated as particularistic those relationships in which the individuals involved are unique and irreplaceable for one another, as in friendships or among family members. The interest and emotional investment in particularistic relationships is permeated by the individuality of the participants, such as personal traits or shared past experiences. Universalistic relations, on the other hand, are those in which role partners are replaceable, as is typical of many economic and bureaucratic transactions in modern societies. In universalistic relations it is the person qua role player who interests us, and not the individual per se. Coser contends that universalism allows for a more effective organization of goal-oriented behavior and so promotes intellectual flexibility. Of course, as she herself remarks,[23] some of our universalistic relationships eventually come to be invested with particularistic sentiment (e.g., the physician whom we eventually designate as our family doctor), but the existence of these mixed cases simply shows that the distinction between particularism and universalism is best interpreted not as a strict dichotomy, but rather as a continuum between two extremes.

Coser points to a number of studies that lend support to the idea that cognitive sophistication is related to societal complexity. For instance,

Lawrence Kohlberg and Carol Gilligan mention research that suggests that while a sizeable portion of the American population never achieves formal-operational cognition, in Turkey entire village populations fail to attain it.[24] A study undertaken by Michael Maccoby and Nancy Modiano found a significant cognitive difference between rural Mexican children and their counterparts in Mexico City and Boston: "The perceptual, concrete, difference-sensitive, organically oriented, village child is by age twelve in sharp contrast to the more abstract, functional, similarity-sensitive, cosmopolitan city child of the same age."[25] Other research has suggested that the presence or absence of formal schooling is a crucial factor—perhaps *the* crucial factor—behind these observed differences in cognitive skill (an assessment that we have already seen is shared by Hallpike). Sylvia Scribner and Michael Cole rely on their own fieldwork (among the Kpelle in Liberia), as well as that of Patricia Marks Greenfield and Jerome S. Bruner (among the Wolof in Senegal), and A. R. Luria (among central Asian peasants in the former Soviet Union), to support their inference that formal schooling promotes the ability to think abstractly.[26]

Hallpike discusses later work done by Scribner and Cole that provides additional evidence for their thesis concerning the cognitive effects of formal schooling.[27] In a study they conducted among the Vai of Liberia, the researchers found that of all the survey tasks they administered, those dealing with logic problems showed the strongest effects of formal education. Schooling not only augmented the number of correct answers but also impacted how answers were justified. The authors reported that an additional significant effect of classroom instruction was an increase in the skills necessary for debate and critical thinking. Even the highly traditional schooling undergone by Qu'ranic scholars appeared to promote critical reasoning skills, such as a heightened sensitivity to the relationship between language and thought. The opportunity to engage in abstract discussion and debate was demonstrated to be an important factor in equipping the individual to think critically.

Although the results of Scribner and Cole's work are not particularly surprising, they do clearly challenge the Enlightenment conception of rationality as being primarily a native capacity of individuals, a notion that still enjoys considerable currency. During the seventeenth and eighteenth centuries the rationalists argued that reason was an innate endowment of the self, an assertion that was denied by their opponents, the empiricists, who rejected the doctrine of innate ideas in favor of the view that reason was acquired. Even the empiricists, though, tended to construe rationality as an acquisition of individuals, since their underlying model for experience was the consciousness of an isolated, pre-social self. Locke and subsequent empiricists conceived of mind as independent of the world, although aware of it due to sense perception. The empiricism of the Enlightenment called upon the individual to be the guarantor of his or her own knowledge by evaluating ideas upon the basis of the sense data provided through personal experience. The epistemology of this era, both rationalist and empiricist, was mainly conducted from the standpoint of the knowing (and doubting) self, and so intellectual inquiry was conceived to be primarily individual, rather than communal, in nature. Dewey points out that the privileging of the individual standpoint in metaphysics and epistemology was a theoretical repercussion of what he terms "practical individualism."[28] The great social conflicts of the day, in politics, the economy, and in religion, involved the new claims of the individual over against the authority of tradition and custom. He argues that these concrete struggles for the right of the individual to greater self-determination found their philosophical expression in a metaphysical and epistemological subjectivism.

Individualism and Critical Thinking

Critical thinking is still often thought of first and foremost as an accomplishment of the self. After all, the very freedom of the individual largely rests on his or her ability to make informed judgments and decisions. Among modern democracies, most state-sponsored systems of education explicitly pursue the goal of cultivating critically minded citizens who can think for themselves. This objective dovetails with one of the most important working principles of democratic governance—namely, the belief that the state should generally refrain from restricting the individual's liberty of thought and action unless such interference is strictly necessary in order to prevent harm to others. Given the contemporary emphasis upon political individualism, and the underlying subjectivism in the view of rationality we have inherited from the Enlightenment, the social basis of critical thinking is often neglected or downplayed.

The work of Cole and Scribner highlights the fact that formal schooling institutes a new cognitive social environment. Following Y. A. Cohen, they list the following three characteristics of informal education: (1) it is particularistic, basing expectations for performance upon the learner's social status and relationships to others rather than upon his or her past achievements; (2) it promotes traditionalism; and (3) it fails to differentiate between the emotional and cognitive realms. In addition, they echo Mead's observation that informal education generally occurs through observation, and that verbal communication plays a relatively minor role in the informal learning process.[29] Formal schooling, on the other hand, tends to rely much more on the power of words. Greater recourse is had to language due to the abstract nature of the subject matter to be conveyed. Whereas informal education usually involves mastering concrete tasks in an environment that is already familiar to the learner, the classroom teacher must often call upon the student's imagination to supply key elements of the learning situation. A lesson in algebra or political science naturally requires more language about language than does a demonstration of how to fashion a spear or a dugout canoe. Hence, formal education tends to provide training in verbal skills and propositional thinking.

This thesis is confirmed by the fact that one of the best established effects of formal schooling on cognition is the tendency of classroom instruction to develop the pupil's capacity for taxonomic classification.[30] Such classification involves the establishment of sets based upon the presence or absence of shared characteristics. Studies of young children and members of non-literate societies have revealed that the "natural" or informal way of categorizing is based on everyday uses and settings. So, for instance, in a famous study by the Soviet psychologist A. R. Luria, unschooled Uzbek peasants were presented with pictures of a log, hatchet, saw, and hammer, and then prompted to create a taxonomic set that would exclude the inappropriate object. The peasants often failed to group the three tools together, opting instead to associate the log, the hatchet, and the saw, since these objects were all involved in wood gathering, or arguing that all four belonged together, since they were all required for construction work.

True taxonomic classification, by contrast, involves a theoretical standpoint that considers its subject matter for its own sake, separate from any concrete context involving practical interests. The guiding ideal of the theoretical attitude is to grasp things as they actually are, on their own terms, free from the subtle and not-so-subtle distortions of subjectivity. It is a point of view that is no one's in particular, and yet potentially available to all. The theoretical frame of mind roughly corresponds to Mead's notion of the "logical universe of discourse," which he characterizes as the most inclusive and extensive of all abstract social classes.[31] He equates this universe of discourse with a "system of universally significant symbols," a system whose universality stems from its grounding in the logical constants that inform all cognition.[32] Mead is careful to point out that the logical universe of discourse arises in communication, and that communication has as its necessary precondition a social process.

In modern society, what we have called the theoretical stance is not the exclusive property of any one class or group, and it can emerge in cooperative conduct wherever impartiality and fact-finding are essential. Although it is most closely identified with the figures of the scientist and the scholar, it has a vital role to play whenever it is important to accurately assess the strength or soundness of arguments and the truth-value of assertions. Nevertheless, it is more at home in some institutions than in others, and it can figure prominently in formal schooling. This brings us back to the point that critical thinking is misconstrued when it is mainly identified with the individual who adopts a critical stance in relative isolation from others. Although there is no doubt that many thinkers enjoy great autonomy in the exercise of their calling, the capacity for critical thinking represents an acquired skill that initially emerges through participation and communication with others.

In the classroom critical reasoning finds embodiment in the student-teacher relationship, with the latter requesting explanations, offering criticisms, introducing competing points of view, and so forth. Potentially, at least, the classroom represents a good opportunity for the cultivation of such thinking. In the upper grades the teacher's professional interest in the student is ostensibly intellectual. Ideally this focus on cognition orients the individual to consider his or her own thought processes in a more systematic fashion than he or she would outside of school, where all manner of other interests and considerations clamor for attention. Of course, the classroom setting does not magically confer immunity to distractions and competing interests, and the quality of any given student's attention depends on a number of different factors. Nevertheless, as concerns the promotion of formal-operational thinking, the school environment does have the advantage of being a social situation in which priority is clearly given to cognitive activity. The goal is for the pupil to internalize the generalized other of the logical universe of discourse—of which teacher-directed classroom discussion constitutes one instance—and so become capable of adopting a critical attitude toward his or her own thought processes. The goal, in other words, is to assist the student in becoming an independent thinker.

It would, however, be a mistake to assume that the social dimension of critical reasoning ends with the conclusion of formal education. Like any art, critical reasoning must be practiced in order to remain vital, and, like any artist, the individual guides and assesses his or her performance by reference to group standards, even if such references sometimes involve the modification or rejection of these standards. Because it is discursive, critical thinking can be communicated, and, at the very least, it involves a dialogue within the self. "Critical reasoning" is, of course, an abstraction, since all thinking involves a specific subject matter. Experience shows that effective thinking about specific issues and problems is usually promoted through participation in specialized communities for problem solving or inquiry. In addition to a given methodology and body of knowledge, such communities offer the individual a culture of critical thinking in which his or her solutions or hypotheses can be evaluated by qualified peers. Through the mechanism of peer evaluation, the innovations of the individual become the common property of the group. Even in highly formal disciplines such as mathematics, creativity requires the unique mix of experience, habit, and suggestion that is found only in the mental perspective of the individual. Individualism is, in fact, the wellspring of scientific and artistic creativity. The discoverer and inventor venture into unknown territory for which the group has no map. To some extent the innovator always steps beyond the borders of custom and conventional wisdom and must rely upon his or her intelligence and judgment as guides.

The intellectual and aesthetic contribution of individualism is not limited to the creative act, but also extends to criticism. Although a good thinker will try to anticipate possible objections to his or her proposal, the individual's ability to imagine every noteworthy critique is relatively restricted. We are, after all, largely creatures of habit, each with his or her own personal set of abilities, experiences, and value commitments that cannot be wholly revamped at will. For this reason, every intellectual discipline that wishes to remain vital cultivates its own culture of criticism. In any field where conclusions are drawn from inferences that are not purely deductive, but only probable, there is usually some room, however slight, for reasonable people to disagree. Furthermore, nearly all scientific theories involve some form of inductive reasoning. Given the considerable variation between individuals due to nature and nurture, when specialists are allowed to draw their own conclusions differences naturally arise, and such clashes over theory usually represent a native resource for systematic inquiry. Disagreement and debate among the experts often serves to clarify key concepts, identify underlying assumptions, and detect weaknesses in the prevailing view. Critical thinking is a widely practiced art in modern societies, and it is at once both an effect of individualism and one of its most important enduring causes. What we have termed critical thinking or reasoning essentially corresponds to Piaget's formal-operational stage of cognition. While we have discussed it primarily in reference to specific fields and disciplines, it also constitutes a significant force in human affairs in general, both public and private. Since the Enlightenment, the belief in the human potential for rationality has played a key role in legitimating democratic government and in promoting civil liberties. Modern social innovations such as public education and a free press were implemented with the need for an educated, well-informed citizenry in mind. Democratic governance is premised upon the proposition that members of such a citizenry will be adequately equipped for the public discussion and debate needed to build intelligent consensus.

Individualism and Self-Interest

In light of our discussion of critical thinking's institutionalization in modern societies, it is worth briefly reconsidering the dominance of custom in traditional ones. It should now be clear that if members of the latter seem, for the most part, to unquestioningly bow to the dictate of custom, it is because among them custom enjoys a near monopoly on authority. In non-literate societies, the impact of individual intelligence on day-to-day life is practically invisible, whereas the sway of tradition is apparent to all. The cultural heritage itself is not recognized as the product of human invention because it has arisen unconsciously and represents the largely unintentional contributions of many anonymous ancestors. Language, mythology, and even technical know-how have imperceptibly developed over the course of generations, with no historian present to record or reconstruct their respective tales. As we have seen, everyday life in these societies does little to inculcate the capacity for abstract thinking. Moreover, traditional social orders generally lack the basic "soft technology" requisite for critical thinking, such as abstract words and writing. Finally, the relatively integrated nature of the cultural pattern in structurally simple societies tends to prevent the emergence of the sort of value conflicts that are so characteristic of complex social orders. Members of the latter often find themselves occupying social roles that pull the self in opposite directions. Obviously, when the individual feels torn between conflicting customs, the customs in question suggest themselves as objects of thought. Is my ultimate loyalty to my family, or to the state? Can I simultaneously be someone's supervisor and friend, and, in my former role, give my friend a negative job evaluation? In formulating answers to such questions, the individual obviously cannot simply refer to custom because custom has in a sense broken down, or at least shown itself to be incomplete.

Inner conflicts pitting egoistic against altruistic motives are particularly common in advanced societies, due in large part to their living conditions. Structural competition is widespread, and its taproot is, of course, capitalism. The free market economy explicitly enlists individual self-interest as the main motivation for working, and the generic inducement offered to self-interest is money. By attaching a price tag to nearly every available service and material good, the market transformed money into a well-nigh universal incentive to action—universal in its allure because survival came to depend on having some, and because whatever money one possessed above the minimum amount needed for necessities could be used in so many different ways. As the saying goes, money speaks a universal language: Its appeal across so many of the old social divides, whether they be based on class, ethnicity, gender, or religion, derives from the fact that it can be employed to satisfy such a wide range of desires. Although popular opinion often attributes a pronounced penchant for hedonism to those who manage to acquire it in large amounts, money can in fact be put to the service of many non-materialistic ends. In sufficient quantities, for example, it can help to secure personal independence, create political influence, or achieve philanthropic goals. In short, money is the perfect medium of exchange for societies with a high degree of individualism because the individual can tailor its use to his or her heart's content—on the condition, of course, that the needed funds are available.

The social landscape created by a money-based economic system vastly increases the options for individualized behavior and has played an important role in setting the stage for the conflict between self-interest and the general welfare that has figured so prominently in modern moral philosophy. The structure of the modern economic order naturally orients its participants to think of themselves as autonomous actors. Social and political bonds that had formerly structured economic activities were ruptured by the growth of capitalism, a development that ultimately led to the emergence of the economy as a distinct social system. The medieval regime of status made way for

the modern one of contract, and the labor necessary for the continued material well-being of society was no longer secured through a
network of customary rights and duties, but instead obtained through
direct pecuniary reward. Within the market economy the individual
has the legal status of a free agent who is endowed with the power
to enter into contracts with other economic actors or entities, such
as companies. Since the publication of Adam Smith's *The Wealth of
Nations*, economists have assumed that participants in the economy
generally act toward the end of maximizing their personal utility. As
employer or employee, or buyer or seller, the economic actor seeks
to secure the best deal possible for himself or herself. Qua economic
player, the individual is indifferent to others unless they can somehow
benefit his or her bottom line. Although Economic Man/Woman is
obviously an abstraction that imperfectly describes the real human
beings who make up national economies, the abstraction has proven
to be accurate enough for the purpose of understanding and predicting
many economic phenomena.

In addition to the logic of self-interest, another component of any
economy that can be justifiably described as capitalist is competition.
In almost every major area of modern economic life, competition has
been introduced as the key mechanism for securing economic progress.
By mimicking the process of natural selection that takes place among
living beings, conventional wisdom holds that the market eliminates
inefficient and inept economic actors, and rewards the superior per-
formers, thus promoting their continued economic survival. Under
conditions of fair business guaranteed by the rule of law, "fit" economic
actors are supposed to succeed on the basis of attributes such as inno-
vativeness and heightened productivity, qualities that are assumed to
benefit the material well-being of society overall. While there is some
question as to what extent this theory accurately describes the real-
world complexities of modern economies, structural competition is a
fact of modern economic life. As such, it naturally creates conditions
in which the individual is led to identify his or her success as resulting
in someone else's loss, and vice versa. Although an efficient economy
may require some degree of the proverbial rat race, such programmed
competition tends to undermine the individual's sense of belonging to
the group.[33]

Egoism was not an invention of capitalism, and the reader will recall
the general lack of altruism ethnographers have noted in many atomistic cultures. However, in comparison to the modern social context,

the atomistic one offers relatively few occasions in which the ends of the individual directly conflict with those of the group. Egalitarianism among atomists sharply circumscribes the possibilities for the development of individuality. Where private property is limited to a few personal possessions, and where there is little social differentiation or stratification, the would-be expansive personality cannot unfold through amassing wealth, power, or social prestige. The cultural pattern of these societies generally provides few occasions in which the individual could choose to pursue a specific good to the exclusion of others. In modern society opportunities for self-seeking behavior are, of course, too numerous to list, and responsibilities and obligations to others must compete with a profusion of private interests and enjoyments.

The Integrative Function of Modern Identity

The title of the current chapter, "The Individuation of Identity," may strike some readers as rather redundant; after all, one meaning of "identity" is virtually synonymous with "individuality." In other words, any event or thing that can be individually distinguished has an identity. However, as we pointed out at the beginning of this chapter, we are employing "identity" in the sense of the individual's attitudes toward himself or herself in relation to others. As concerns this interpersonal identity, we have shown that there is a clearly recognizable pattern of increasing individuation that has been an integral part of the process of societal evolution. In practical terms, the growth of individualism in complex societies has meant that identity has progressively become more a matter of individual choice and achievement than of social ascription. Under an advanced division of labor, social systems become more autonomous, and often serve as motors of societal change, introducing innovations that disrupt the established patterns of custom and tradition. In Western societies since the Renaissance, relatively rapid developments in almost every major social sphere long ago surpassed the capacity of the moral or symbolic culture to provide the individual with an integrated identity for life with others.

Not only is there no generally accepted, unifying cultural pattern in these societies, but modern social systems sometimes conflict with one another. The most obvious examples of such tensions are generated by the free-market economy, whose profit motive often clashes with its politically and legally sanctioned mission of promoting the general welfare. All industrialized economies are, after all, political economies, in the sense that they are subject to governmental controls and guidance. Given the generally large populations of contemporary states and their corresponding responsibilities in domains such as defense, education, transportation, and health, most governments are important economic actors in their own right—that is, simply in terms of taxation and public expenditures, not to mention specific fiscal and trade policies. It is difficult to imagine how a contemporary state could avoid making decisions that significantly impact the economy. In addition, the well-nigh global triumph of capitalism by the end of the twentieth century has resulted in the widespread belief that the free market is superior to Communism in providing for the material well-being of society. Indeed, a number of countries, including the world's most populous, China, have adopted capitalism due to this conviction. Nevertheless, it has been evident since at least the Industrial Revolution that the market economy is not without its discontents.

Although the incentive of personal aggrandizement has served as a stimulus to individual initiative and enterprise, it has also often fueled a disinterest or even blatant disregard for the noxious side effects of certain economic activities. The historical record has shown that the goal of accumulating wealth in no way necessarily guarantees good stewardship of natural resources, care for consumer safety, concern for the well-being of employees, or respect for the democratic political process. Depending upon the nature of specific conditions, individuals and corporations have sometimes found it to be to their economic advantage to act in ways that actually detract from the public welfare. Time and again, excesses committed for the sake of the bottom line have led to calls for reform and, in some instances, to the creation of legislation specifically designed to regulate business and industry. It may well be that the pulsating heart of free enterprise is to be found in economic competition, but such competition has only proven to be generally beneficial to society when it takes place according to rules imposed by government and enforced by policing agencies and the courts. The historical record also reveals that, in order to be effective, governmental and judicial oversight must be continually adapted to the ever-changing nature of the economy.

At the level of the individual, the discord created by economic activities that augment profits but produce negative social repercussions can engender frustration or cynicism. It is by no means unusual, for instance, that in certain trades and industries the price of doing business is compliance with corrupt practices. If corruption is widespread in a particular market, economic survival may depend upon cutting the same corners that one's competitors do. The economic actor who would nobly play by the rules that everyone else flaunts will probably find himself or herself at serious competitive disadvantage. The basically honest person who winds up in a corrupt business culture is caught in a social situation that virtually guarantees at least the partial frustration of desire. In such instances, there may be no truly good recourse for the individual, who will inevitably experience himself or herself as a house divided.[34]

Perhaps the single most popular metaphor for the state of contemporary Western civilization has been that of fragmentation, which captures the loss of coherence and direction caused by the dissolution of a unifying cultural pattern. Although writers often differ over the extent and severity of this fragmentation, there is a general consensus that it constitutes a key feature of modernity (and, for that matter, post-modernity), and that fragmentation exists at the level of both the community and the individual. As concerns the latter, the progressive dissipation of a culturally assigned life narrative creates the need for the individual to articulate a personal identity. *With the growth of individualism, identity increasingly takes over some of the key functions of integrating the individual with his or her social world, functions previously performed by culture.* It provides the self with a template for interpersonal relations, sense of purpose, and self-esteem. The clearest statement of identity can be found in the narrative in terms of which the individual prioritizes the various ends and goods in his or her life. In a structurally complex social environment, the individual needs such a narrative and its pendant, identity, in order to integrate his or her various roles and activities into a coherent and meaningful whole.

The pressure to articulate an identity is, in fact, a direct consequence of institutionalized individualism. Members of contemporary Western societies—arguably the social orders in which individualism has developed to its greatest extent—are continually referred to their own self-interest and judgment as guides for behavior. One must choose one's line of work, spouse, friends, recreations, habitation, and so forth. Such "lifestyle" decisions often represent occasions for the individual to define himself or herself, since they generally involve selection among competing goods and so require one to discover what one actually prefers. The person who weighs and compares various goods naturally brings his or her own perceptions and previous judgments to bear on the issue at hand. Without the background of personal experience, the individual would have no points of reference by which to evaluate values. Needless to say, instances in which persons have the opportunity for genuine choice are also occasions on which inclination and personality often directly influence reasoning: indeed, not only judgment and thought fall under their unconscious influence but also perception, recollection, and imagination.

In their book, *The Homeless Mind*, authors Peter L. Berger, Brigitte Berger, and Hansfried Keller observe that modern identity is "peculiarly individuated."[35] They understand this individuation to be most clearly manifested in the prerogative the modern individual enjoys to arrange his or her own life free from the interference of outside authorities, provided that in so doing he or she does not harm others. The authors stress that, in addition to being legitimated by popular social and political ideologies, the individuated nature of modern selfhood is rooted in contemporary institutional structures and forms of consciousness.[36] As we have seen in our survey of societal evolution, the modern social order has resulted from the differentiation of various societal systems from a general cultural pattern. Within the pre-modern social context, the individual is treated as a known value, whose identity is primarily ascribed. From the standpoint of modern social systems, however, persons are typically viewed as variables whose precise identities are irrelevant to the functioning of the system in question. The difference, in short, is that between arithmetic and algebra. Archaic societies define persons concretely and holistically, whereas modern ones typically make no effort to treat individuals in their specificity, but approach them as rather narrow abstractions—for instance, as consumers, voters, litigants, and so forth.

Facts and Values

The highly differentiated social systems typical of advanced societies have indirectly provided support for the belief that a metaphysical divide separates facts from values. In many areas of social life the advanced division of labor has resulted in a fundamental divorce between doing and valuing, production and consumption, creation and appreciation. These social divisions have suggested that facts are objective and public, whereas values are subjective and personal, and that facts are open to observation and demonstration, whereas values are essentially non-rational and ultimately arbitrary or inscrutable.

The plight of the modern self is that his or her actions are often replete with social meaning, but that these social implications are only incorporated incidentally and sporadically as personal motives. On the one hand, contemporary goods are often highly mediated and abstract, and have required the development of communities based not upon shared kinship, ethnicity, or even territory, but rather upon shared ideals. Goods such as scientific knowledge or the freedom of expression have developed over generations and have involved the labor, dedication, and, in some cases, sacrifices of countless men and women. It is no exaggeration to say that the development of these goods required the parallel development of new forms of social solidarity and communal feeling, the extension of the individual's concern and loyalty from the tribe to the present generation to those as yet unborn.

On the other hand, modern social systems have generally relied upon enlightened (in the sense of adequately foresighted) self-interest as the carrot—or, alternatively, the stick—to secure the cooperation of the individual with the group. This is obvious in the case of capitalism, but is apparent in other areas as well. The rule of law, for instance, depends upon the threat of punishment, and punishment in the modern sense could be defined as whatever promises to intentionally injure the individual's self-interest. The theory of the social contract, which has long served as a way of legitimating democratic government, constitutes in its various forms an attempt to prove to the individual that enlightened self-interest dictates that he or she should submit to the rule of law and order. Even religion has not been exempt from the influence of individualism, and to one degree or another virtually all of the world's major religions today have incorporated the idea of personal salvation.

Modern reliance upon individual self-interest as the high road to social control is perhaps ultimately best interpreted as a strategy of the "lowest common denominator." Advanced societies differ from their predecessors in their sheer size and high degree of cultural pluralism. Given the fact that contemporary social systems function in populations that are typically large and culturally diverse, the appeal to self-interest is natural, since it cuts across nearly all demographic variables. After all, the mere fact of biological existence is enough to endow most persons with some needs and desires that are primarily self-regarding. Of course, in addition to the wants associated with the basic material requirements for human life, the vast majority of people have bonds to family members that are significant enough to be counted among the individual's genuine interests.

The noticeably secular orientation of the industrialized social order—as opposed to its ancestors—is at least partially due to the reorganization of social activities on a cross-cultural basis. Modernity has increasingly forsaken the metaphysical and speculative for the biological and social as a working foundation for group consensus. To a significant extent, the operative social philosophy of the modern world is "live and let live." While religious and moral beliefs may differ from person to person, material wants, the desire for creature comforts, and the interest in a certain minimum of social stability and safety are shared by most people. By virtue of focusing on the generic or cross-cultural elements of group life, contemporary social systems have become so highly differentiated and function-oriented that they operate more or less independently of any specific cultural pattern. As if by default, the soft or symbolic culture of value has been mainly relegated to the private sphere and to specific subcultures.

According to a popular modern view, morals are actually the rules required for group life. Durkheim, for instance, characterizes morality as "the indispensable minimum, that which is strictly necessary, the daily bread without which societies cannot live."[37] More recently, sociologist and communitarian Amitai Etzioni has argued that, "No society can function well unless most of its members 'behave' most of the time because they voluntarily heed their moral commitments and social responsibilities."[38] He asserts that the alternative to such shared moral commitments would either be chaos or a police state.[39] Although there is much to be said for Etzioni's call for moral renewal, the dichotomy he paints to support it is false because it overlooks the possibility of a social order constituted upon enlightened self-interest. Let us imagine a society exclusively composed of extremely self-centered and selfish individuals. Each and every person in this social world looks out primarily for "number one," and philanthropic actions are undertaken only when they promise to promote the happiness of the "philanthropist." Individuals regularly file for divorce when they decide that their current marriage is no longer personally satisfying, and grown children systematically commit their elderly parents to nursing homes as soon as it becomes convenient to do so. Needless to say, no one ever wittingly commits a heroic action for the sake of someone else. What might at first blush appear to be isolated acts of heroism will, upon analysis, turn out to be due to impulse, thrill seeking, the desire for attention, a death wish, and so forth. Friendships are based upon mutual pleasure and usefulness, and last only as long as they procure these goods.

Even parents' "love" for their children is grounded in the pleasure they take in their offspring. If a child becomes burdensome, it is foisted off on the state, the law permitting.

The vision presented by this society is neither morally uplifting nor particularly heartwarming. However, there's no reason to suppose that such a social order would degenerate into anarchy or require the heavy hand of a police state for its continued survival. In fact, the description of our hypothetical land of the self-seeking has a more than vaguely familiar ring to it. Etizioni's dichotomy would be valid if our society consisted of sociopaths (also known as psychopaths) since they tend to be impulsive and have poor behavior controls.[40] In other words, even though sociopaths certainly qualify as being both self-centered and selfish, they often fail to act in a manner that rationally promotes their own self-interest, which is one of the reasons why they are so over-represented in carceral populations. Since the threat of punishment is frequently insufficient to keep the sociopath in line, a society made up of sociopaths would conceivably slide into anarchy unless law and order were drastically enforced. We can assume, however, that individuals who are *merely* egocentric will generally be successful in curbing their antisocial impulses in order to avoid punishment. Furthermore, it stands to reason that they will grasp the wisdom of the social contract— that is, that they will recognize that it benefits them *as individuals* to live in a society in which the rule of law prevails. There is, of course, no reason why the rational egoist should not violate the rules when he or she can do so with a reasonable likelihood of getting away with it, and the authorities will have to be exercise permanent vigilance for weak spots or loopholes in the system. Nevertheless, policing such a society would not necessarily require a perpetual state of martial law, because the goal would merely be to make crime unattractive to most of the people most of the time. We should bear in mind that the self-centered do not necessarily have criminal tendencies. In a sufficiently affluent society of the selfish, most people would probably be content to pursue their lives within legal bounds. Even in those instances in which crime would actually pay, the anxiety aroused by the thought of being caught would be sufficient to deter the vast majority of the population from engaging in it.

According to the results of our thought experiment, a society entirely made up of selfish persons could survive without having recourse to draconian measures. Its Achilles' heel would be long-term planning, since the present generation would have little reason to make sacrifices for future ones. So, for instance, there would be slight interest in preserving natural resources or protecting the environment, provided that those currently alive could reasonably expect to escape any major negative ecological consequences during their lifetimes. As long as each ensuing generation manages to deal with the problems it inherits from its predecessors, society will survive, if not flourish. But maybe this scenario is too gloomy, since even very selfish people sometimes identify themselves with their children, seeing their offspring as part of their legacy. Therefore, perhaps even among exceedingly self-centered people there could arise a sense of concern for succeeding generations. In any event, it should be clear that an advanced society can tolerate a high degree of selfishness in its citizens, and some would even argue that contemporary Western civilization provides plentiful empirical evidence to this effect.

Notwithstanding the popularity of the view that mores constitute the backbone of society, it has belonged to the peculiar genius of modernity to make self-interest the basis of social legitimation. Self-interest is arguably the single most important natural resource for the free market, and the same self-interest fuels the liberal social order. In the political realm, representative government constituted through the balance of powers and the clash of political parties and special-interest groups has provided an ingenious mechanism for building consensus among self-interested individuals. In addition, modern law has furnished a way of resolving conflicts among citizens that does not directly depend upon a specific moral code. By removing mores as the keystone in the arch of society, modernity has transformed morality into a matter of individual conscience. The moral values that were once ensconced in tradition and custom have increasingly become the subject matter of individual reflection and judgment.

Whereas customary morality represented the standpoint of the group, reflective morality represents that of the individual.[41] However, we should not interpret this proposition as implying that in the modern world moral values are wholly subjective and entirely relative to the self. In its reflective form, moral judgment is essentially a comprehensive assessment of what should be done in a particular circumstance, an overall evaluation that may confirm established practice or reject the current way of doing things in the name of a better one. In the latter instance, the individual must often rely upon the moral imagination to project a creative reconstruction of the status quo, a reconstruction that may involve changes to existing customs or even laws. Insofar as the individual's assessment is intelligent and insightful, he or she will have grounds that can be used to persuade others to draw the same conclusion. Many grassroots social reforms are driven by groups of individuals who hold a common vision of a better future, and, to the extent that their claims are warranted, their proposals draw their meaning from a shared human context.

There is nothing particularly mysterious about the intersubjective nature of values, at least no more than there is about the intersubjective nature of language. Mead's theory of the significant symbol reveals the cognitive heart of human language to be the mental capacity to grasp that a symbol points to something beyond itself, and that it does so in roughly the same manner for oneself and others. The very fact of symbolic communication constitutes powerful evidence that we inhabit the same world and, to a considerable extent, undergo the same sensations. If matters were otherwise, and each person constituted his or her own solipsistic universe, communication would be rendered impossible, because there would be no basis for common meanings.

Confusion over the apparent arbitrariness of values arises when they are treated as original and primary, a view that is typically associated with a similar conception of facts. Many introductory logic textbooks still present facts and values in a manner that suggests that they function as the raw materials of arguments. Consider, for example, Charles L. Stevenson's influential distinction between disagreements in belief, which involve factual claims, and disagreements in attitude, which involve value claims (i.e., of approval or disapproval). The distinction implies that disagreements in belief can be resolved by an appeal to the facts, whereas disagreements in attitude frequently prove to be impasses for discussion, dead ends at which the interlocutors can at best agree to disagree. Stevenson's typology of disagreements overlooks the important circumstance that the claims that serve as the parameters or starting points for a given argument usually represent the outcomes of previous ones. Far from constituting first principles that can only be accepted or rejected, not justified, value judgments—insofar as they are reflective—are the results of inquiries that can be evaluated for their trustworthiness and accuracy.

For those readers who are acquainted with Dewey's logic, the conception of facts and values as the results of former inquiries will be familiar. In *Logic: The Theory of Inquiry* (1938), he argues that the distinction between theoretical judgments and practical ones is ultimately just one of emphasis, since scientific theories directly incorporate "operations of doing and making" in the form of experimentation.[42] Of course, we have done little more than indicate the general lines of an argument that Dewey works out in detail with admirable rigor in the *Logic*, and the interested reader is referred to that work, which to this day has not received the attention it deserves from professional logicians.

For our purposes, the most important point to bear in mind is that the considered value judgments of the individual can be meaningfully analyzed and assessed. On the one hand, analysis of particular judgments from the standpoint of a community of inquiry may reveal factors of which the individual is unaware but that nevertheless unduly influence his or her decision-making. For example, in subsequent chapters we shall show how Karen Horney's depth psychology can be fruitfully applied to understanding the unconscious impact of personality and character on moral reasoning. On the other hand, we must also recognize that sometimes an individual's judgment is pioneering, and can serve to enrich the experience of the group. In such instances, the valuation is in principle capable of being rationally reconstructed into an argument. However, because such arguments often involve a universe of discourse that presupposes firsthand experience of certain goods, the argument in question may be difficult or impossible to grasp for those who lack the requisite background. The psychopath, for instance, whose lack of empathy and shallow emotional life have led him or her to equate love with sexual desire and possession, will probably be incapable of comprehending the spontaneous generosity of genuine romantic love.

The Family as Moral Microculture

Due to the combined influence of a number of different factors, the moral landscape of modern society has grown increasingly variegated. One of the primary causes behind the diversification of modern morals has been the social and legal establishment of the spheres of public and private life. It is probably not a coincidence that the nineteenth-century discovery of early childhood as *the* critical period for the formation of personality came at a time when domestic life had already emerged as the largely private world we now know. Under the social conditions of modernity, the family has tended to become a sort of microculture of value. Most contemporary families have lost the vocational function they had in times past, when it was more common for a family line to have a traditional occupation and for the home and the workplace to share the same space. Consequently, the practical training that families could once offer their members has largely been replaced by formal schooling and vocational instruction that take place outside the home. In advanced societies the main educational task left to the family involves what is sometimes vaguely referred to as "values instruction," which is usually associated with conveying moral and social values, although of course it can include other types of value as well.

The economic demand for a mobile labor force and the process of urbanization have led to the decline of the homogenous type of traditional community in which a particular system of values based on shared labor, ethnicity, social class, or religious creed predominated. In general, provincialism has made way for cosmopolitanism, and cultural monism for cultural pluralism. In our advanced societies, with their complex networks of producers and consumers and their vast social systems that orchestrate the activities of millions of people, the family remains the single most important source of human immediacy. Rather than constituting a homogenous unit within an overarching cultural pattern, it has taken on a more individual character, and it is in this sense that it constitutes a microculture of value. Families within the same neighborhood, even in rural localities, often have different priorities. The Smiths may prize worldly success in business above all other goals, while their next-door neighbors, the Joneses, define themselves in religious terms. Consequently, the family unit has gradually acquired added importance when it comes to determining the sort of social goods the individual will first experience.

Most of the vocabulary designating moral goods consists of words whose meaning is vague, in the sense that terms such as "friendliness" or "generosity" are highly context-dependent, and tend to be construed by the individual according to his or her firsthand experience of human relationships. Different families may employ the same words but flesh them out with disparate meanings, or perform the same actions but with dissimilar attitudes. For example, many families observe holidays with relatives or take annual vacations, but differ considerably in the manner in which they perform these typical household projects. In one clan, family gatherings at Christmas are occasions for impressing the relatives with the beauty and elegance of one's home and decorations, and with one's good taste and graciousness as host. Subtle and not so subtle cues are given about the importance of observing good decorum and being polite. If certain familial tensions and disagreements exist—as they most always do—they will be kept beneath the surface, so as not to spoil the festive occasion. Conversation among the adults is cordial but not animated. Overall, the atmosphere will be quite restrained; indeed, an outside observer might even find it to be frosty.

In another family, the Christmas gathering is a rough and tumble affair, with relatively poor organization, even though the current hosts have held it at their home many times before. Preparations that could have been taken care of well in advance are always performed at the last minute, accompanied by a not insignificant degree of stress and bickering. One of the few certainties of the holiday season is that the main meal will not be served on time, but with a considerable delay. In general, members of the extended family take a no-holds-barred approach to each other, and rarely hesitate to openly disagree or vent criticism. There may even be some isolated incidents of harsh words and crying, but generally such outbursts are quickly forgotten. When compliments are paid to the host or hostess, they are heartfelt and accepted at their face value. Despite the chaotic organization and occasional flare-ups, the overall atmosphere is warm and natural.

We can easily imagine the surprise of someone reared in the self-conscious decorousness of the first household who happens to spend the holidays with the second family. At first, our visitor may be bothered by what strikes him or her as a decided lack of self-control among the family members. Are the emotional outbursts and shouting really necessary? Why can't those who have nothing nice to say simply say nothing? Indeed, it may take the newcomer quite a while to realize that the tumult of the get-together is an indication of the close ties most of the participants feel to one another. They are not overly concerned about offending each other because they sense that the bonds uniting them are resilient. Looking back at his or her own family experience, our visitor may for the first time grasp the stilted nature of the gatherings, and realize to what extent a show was being put on by common, albeit subconscious, consent. He or she intuits that beneath the surface there lurked genuine tensions, tensions that threatened to disrupt the relatively fragile relationships that were the norm throughout the extended family.

Another popular pastime of the modern household is the family vacation, an activity that can serve to provide us with an additional illustration of the individualized character of the contemporary family. In one small family, the parents pride themselves on taking extensive trips with their children during the summer; indeed, they often explain to their offspring how lucky the youngsters are to be visiting so many different places so early in life, particularly in comparison to the other families they know. The trips often entail many hours spent in the car, during which the children frequently become restless or bored. The quarters are cramped, and they are, after all, only children. When the youngsters become fidgety or complain about the long hours on the road, the parents chide them for their ingratitude and their indifference to new sights and sounds. Most of the destinations, chosen almost entirely by the mother and father, have pedagogic value: a seemingly endless assortment of parks, nature trails, monuments, and museums, with a decided emphasis on themes of interest to the parents. Sometimes the children actually enjoy the sightseeing, but just as often they must be dragged from one spot to the next.

Despite their protests to the contrary, the children often do wind up feeling guilty about the trouble they cause on the trips. Puzzled by their own misbehavior in the light of their good fortune, they attribute it to innate capriciousness and selfishness. It is not until they are adults and have gone on vacation with other families, or even have children of their own, that they begin to understand some of the underlying reasons for their earlier discontent. They may discover, for instance, that other families design their vacations with the limited attention spans of the young specifically in mind. It may even come as a revelation that some parents change their vacation plans to correspond to the spontaneous wishes of their children, or that many families approach vacations as occasions which should primarily be fun, and only secondarily educational, instead of vice versa. They may come across families who go to amusement parks, or go skiing, or who rent beach houses, order out pizza, and stay inside all day watching rented movies for the sheer decadent pleasure of it all! At a deeper level, it may begin to dawn on the grown children that their upbringing involved a high degree of subtle and pervasive thought control, which, although well intentioned, gradually alienated them from recognizing their own spontaneous desires and equipped them with a set of biases that prevented them from seeking new experiences.

An important factor in the diversification of familial microcultures has undoubtedly been the diversification of the family itself as a social group. Today this process is so advanced that in casual conversation the word "family" is often ambiguous and can refer to a traditional extended family, a nuclear family, a so-called "patchwork" family that includes children from prior marriages or relationships, a non-conjugal household, and so forth. Whereas some families still encompass strong extended family relationships, others have a much more restricted social base. The relative isolation of many nuclear families probably tends to exaggerate the influence of parents as role models and moral authorities, due to the absence of relatives who could develop close relationships to the children of the household. In close-knit extended families a grandparent, aunt, uncle, or even older cousin often becomes a confidant and advisor to the child and can provide him or her with an additional adult perspective on whatever problems the child is confronting. As a relative, the confidant is usually well acquainted with the parents and can, ideally, assist the child in taking a more realistic view of them, helping to put the parents and their ideas in perspective, or at least furnishing the child with some alternative viewpoints. Of course, in homes in which extended family members live together or are frequent visitors, the natural frictions produced by familiarity will often give the child some notion of how other adults view his mother and father. The fact that the institution of the godparent has enjoyed an essentially secular second life in many countries, after the relative atrophy of its original religious function, is perhaps at least partially due to the recognition that it can be helpful to have an advocate on the child's behalf in addition to the parents—an advocate whose role it is to look out for the child's best interests as a complete human being.

Personality and Identity

Personality does not develop independently of the social goods embodied in family life, but rather grows through internalizing them. Ideally, personal growth is a lifelong process that goes hand-in-hand with the construction of an identity, itself a work-in-progress throughout the individual's lifetime. Personality in the sense of temperament exists prior to the creation of an identity, but temperament simply represents certain attitudes and general lines of conduct to which the individual is naturally predisposed, such as being quick to anger, or shy, or easily distracted. Although such leanings are a part of personality, they do not, of themselves, a personality make. A mature personality is not merely an aggregate of different traits, but a pattern that involves a significant degree of organization. Personality is the individual's distinctive way of thinking and behaving, and as such it incorporates the individual's priorities and preferences, which implies a functional hierarchy of needs and desires. The individual's various characteristics and abilities generally do not exist in isolation from each other, but inform one another. It is not unusual, for instance, to find a good sense of humor paired with linguistic dexterity, or extroversion with an attraction to competition.

Personality develops through the individual's participation in society in a manner that is similar to the way in which we acquire language. On the one hand, the capacity to learn a language presupposes the existence of certain cognitive and anatomic capacities. On the other, without stimulation through participation in a linguistic community, the individual will never learn how to speak. In like fashion, mere temperament or disposition matures into personality and character through involvement in social roles. As a complex of custom involving specific goods and rules, social roles are at once the vocabulary and the grammar of personality. In everyday life they furnish us with the single most important guide of how to act in various situations, and so constitute the raw materials of moral character. In advanced societies, where custom has become an object of reflection, the lion's share of identity is constituted by the individual's particular interpretation of his or her social roles. Identity is, therefore, a crucial element of personality.

Our linguistic metaphor also provides an analogy for the individuation of identity. In a well-known essay entitled "The Problem of Meaning in Primitive Languages," anthropologist Bronislaw Malinowski argues that the ethnographer who would study a primitive language in the field would do best to approach it as a "mode of action."[43] Such a perspective is counterintuitive due to the ethnographer's experience of language in his or her own culture, where formal education privileges the written word over the spoken one. In writing, language functions primarily as a "countersign of thought," but this use of language is abstract and derivative. When the written word serves the ethnographer implicitly or explicitly as the model for linguistic analysis, it inevitably skews the comprehension of primitive speech, which is highly dependent on a context of common pursuits for its meaning. Within the primitive social situation, communication often takes place within group activities in order to coordinate the efforts of individuals. As an imminently practical tool that is employed in virtually all group undertakings, language is a pervasive part of the primitive scene that receives little attention for its own sake from group members.

It follows from Malinowski's analysis that primitive mind has no explicit awareness of grammar, or, for that matter, even a clear grasp of the difference between the emotive and cognitive meaning of words. Primitive mind exists within the medium of language but does not make this medium an object of interest, at least not in the sense of systematic investigation. Symbolic communication is simply taken for granted, and there is little or no conscious control of language per se. Much the same could be said of social roles within the same cultures—namely, they are accepted as a matter of course, and little attention it paid to their place in the overall social order. Like the linguistic act, the performance of a social role in the primitive setting is a package deal that involves an undifferentiated mix of thought, feeling, and action. The modern, well-educated speaker or writer can consciously wordsmith his or her language to achieve a specific effect, privileging, for example, rhetorical impact or technical accuracy, depending upon the end in view. In a similar fashion, modern role occupants can decide—albeit to varying extents—in what manner and to what degree to invest themselves in their given roles.

The pressure members of advanced societies feel to articulate a personal identity stems from the fact that these social orders do not rely on a common pattern of custom to meet their needs. The unifying force of tradition has been replaced by that of instrumental reasoning and enlightened self-interest. The shared cultural system of the *Gemeinschaft* has been undone by the discrete social systems of the *Gesellschaft*, thrusting the individual from a realm of social certainties into one replete with social possibilities. Given his or her circumstances, the modern individual needs the integration of personality that can be provided by a sufficiently strong sense of identity.

Modern society continually confronts the individual with lifestyle options. Granted, some people enjoy more alternatives than others, and there are even cases in which persons find their range of options severely—and sometimes permanently—limited. However, for most people life within the modern social order is a series of choices. Insofar as the individual chooses reflectively, he or she elaborates an identity. As Aristotle astutely observed long ago, key evaluative terms, such as "good" or "bad" and "better" or "worse," are teleological in nature—that is, they represent an assessment of how well or poorly whatever is being evaluated fulfills its specific function or purpose. As concerns most major social roles and activities, there usually exist commonly accepted standards of evaluation, so that once someone has assumed the office of elementary school teacher or taken up the sport of skydiving, that individual's performance can be assessed relative to what the general public or community of experienced practitioners have deemed to be praiseworthy. While it is extremely rare for either public or expert opinion to be unanimous about which standards should be used, there is often at least a working consensus of opinion, especially as regards misconduct or poor performance. For example, more people are likely to agree about what a good daughter should *not* do than about what she should do. Although the fact of such merely broad—as opposed to universal—agreement often appears quite imperfect and unsatisfying from the standpoint of ethical theory, it constitutes the single most important body of custom remaining in advanced societies. These widely held customs are the informal rules that serve to create the stability and trust that is a precondition for well-being in the family and for a flourishing civil society. While the rule of law alone could arguably suffice to ensure the continued survival of society, it would be a social world nearly bereft of positive group experiences. Customary expectations of behavior also furnish the individual with the basic set of habits and attitudes that serves as the foundation and touchstone for all moral reasoning and judgment.

There are, of course, instances in which community opinion is deeply divided—so divided, in fact, that custom loses much of its authority. Thus, for example, a tribal or clan ethic based on the principle of loyalty to one's in-group usually conflicts with the ideal of citizenship within the nation-state. As we have seen, such instances have played an important role in the development of individualism, since the conflict between two mutually exclusive customs virtually requires the individual to make a choice. Despite their significance for reflective morality, these clashes are the exception rather than the rule in everyday life; indeed, they fall into that proverbial class of exceptions that confirms the rule. A social world in which all customs were simultaneously problematic and up-for-grabs would be so chaotic as to constitute a general breakdown of morals. Implicit or explicit, informal or formal, rules of some type are required for the endurance of any group, insofar as the group is more than simply the aggregation of its members, because rules constitute a necessary precondition for the existence of social roles. Social roles are, in fact, essentially rules for interpersonal conduct that allow group members to anticipate one another's attitudes and behavior, and such anticipation is a prerequisite for complex and stable forms of cooperation.

Although convention is still a potent guide for the evaluation of social-role performances, there is markedly less agreement about what constitutes a good reason for entering into such roles in the first place. Should one become a parent primarily with regard to one's personal development and self-fulfillment, or out of concern for the happiness of one's spouse, or as part of one's duties as a devout Roman Catholic? It is in attempting to ground such decisions that the individual often articulates his or her identity. Since the terminology of evaluation is teleological in nature, potential role occupants frequently try to determine who they are, or at least who they should strive to become, when weighing whether or not to enter into a given role or status relationship. In other words, the individual assesses the office or activity in terms of how it will fit into or impact his or her overall life project, as conceived in a narrative self-understanding.

Personality and identity coexist in a symbiotic relationship. On the one hand, personality provides the immediate backdrop to the evaluation and selection of ends required for the creation of an identity. As children, our native and acquired proclivities furnish us with at least a cursory values orientation or ranking of goods and ends. On the other hand, it is only through the eventual construction of a stable identity that the personality can achieve integration and full-fledged expression. The hallmark of the mature and well-developed personality is its integration through an identity that harmonizes the individual's various roles and commitments into a coherent whole. The very desires and interests of such a personality have gained variety and depth through the performance of different social roles, since the self that occupies them has internalized the particular habits, attitudes, and ends associated with the roles in question. Depending in large part upon the nature of prevailing social and cultural conditions, the competitive impulse can manifest, for example, as a good-natured wish to see one's home team win, or as a vindictive desire to triumph academically over one's classmates. It is even conceivable that the same person could simultaneously harbor both sentiments.

The completely developed personality is, of course, an ideal that can at best be approximated. In much the same vein, we should bear in mind that identities are always constructed under imperfect social conditions. If a social order has embodied conflicting attitudes and values, it may be well-nigh impossible for even the most ingenious individual to author a personal narrative in which the conflicting elements are harmonized. Consider, for instance, the intellectual and spiritual plight of persons whose thinking about human affairs is dominated by prescriptions derived from religious dogma, but who employ the results and methods of the experimental sciences in their everyday lives. The need to overcome this and other cultural dualisms is a major theme in the thought of Dewey, who points out that the use of two incompatible standards inevitably weakens the mental grasp of the person who holds them.[44] It should also be noted that not all social roles are created equal. While role participation generally offers an opportunity to enrich the self with new perspectives and values, some roles are more enriching than others, and, of course, roles exist whose very nature makes them morally objectionable, such as being a member of a criminal organization.

Although we have argued that modern social conditions tend to promote the development of identity, we should also mention that individuals vary greatly in the degree to which their personality has been integrated through a consciously designed life narrative. While the modern individual must make lifestyle choices, it is almost always possible to do so unreflectively and in a superficial manner. No few members of advanced societies become expert at shallow living, adept at simply following the path of least resistance and siding with whatever happens to be the majority of the moment. Ethically dubious aspects of industrial, commercial, or professional activities may be uncritically accepted by the individual simply due to the fact that most of the people he or she deals with do not object to them. The highly differentiated nature of the modern social order facilitates a compartmentalization of the individual's behavior, insofar as different roles are often enacted in different settings and involve disparate groups of people. The sight of the person who adheres to the law of the jungle at the workplace, but who strives to be generous and loving at home, is not an uncommon modern spectacle.

We must take care to keep in mind that the formation of an identity, particularly in the initial stages, is primarily unconscious. As the child or adolescent begins to chart his or her unique course through the convoluted shoals of the modern social order, identity serves as a polestar for decision making. In a society that is so arranged as to require the individual to choose many of his or her social roles, it obviously helps to have some idea as to what sort of person one is, or at least what sort of person one should try to become. In a healthy course of development, the individual's early self-image incorporates interpersonal ends and goods that are valued for their own sake. Based upon positive experiences with others, the child or adolescent feels himself or herself to be an integral part of the group—normally, the family—and naturally adopts some of its interests as his or her own. The young person's identification with interpersonal goods such as mutual trust and respect grows out of firsthand contact with them and represents the dawning of a conscious appreciation of these values. What is attractive to the individual is so primarily due to its actual merits. Given his or her underlying sense of belonging and self-worth, the child or adolescent is in a position to actually pick and choose between competing ends. If a selected good turns out to be less attractive than it at first appeared, the individual will be able to acknowledge that fact and adjust accordingly. In other words, his or her identity is constructed on the basis of genuine desire rather than of need.

Personality, Identity, and the Unconscious

Unfortunately, what we have described as the healthy course of personality development is far from constituting a statistical average, since the process is subject to all manner of disturbances. Perhaps the major cause of personality dysfunction is a character disorder in one or more of the parents or caregivers. As Karen Horney observes in her magnum opus, *Neurosis and Human Growth*, the parent's own personality problems often interfere with his or her capacity to develop an empathetic and loving relationship with the child.[45] Unable to accurately gauge or perhaps even respect the child's needs and desires, the afflicted parent will consistently miss the mark, usually tending toward the sort of excess or deficiency Aristotle has taught us to associate with vice. The distorting lens of character disorder often clothes vice in the raiment of virtue. So, from the parent's perspective, his or her domination and intimidation of the child actually constitutes just the right measure of discipline, overprotectiveness is really prudence, a tendency toward emotional neglect becomes a wish to encourage the child to be independent, erratic parenting is actually an adult capacity for child-like spontaneity, and so forth. Even when no parental character disorder is present, there is no guarantee that the child's personality formation will be problem free. Parents, for example, who have had success with a certain approach in rearing their first child, may simply employ the same approach with their second, without making allowances for the differences in temperament between the two children. Or in a society undergoing rapid change, parents may persist in transmitting norms that are out of synch with the surrounding culture, and so leave their children feeling fundamentally divided in their loyalties.

Horney cautions that the genesis of a character disorder is always multi-causal.[46] Whatever the specific nature of the environmental and biological factors at work, the child is left feeling isolated and vulnerable in a social world that it vaguely perceives as menacing. Referring to this state as that of "basic anxiety," Horney argues that under its influence the child begins to lose touch with its spontaneous thoughts and feelings, what she describes as "the alive center" of the self. The child's natural reaction to the foreboding world in which it finds itself is to seek for safety, and this need for security adds an urgency to its human interactions that tends to make them inflexible and overly intense.

Horney identifies three basic mental postures the individual can adopt in his or her interpersonal relationships, stances she describes by using the spatial metaphor of moving toward, against, or away from others. The attitudes she has in mind are very broad, and merely represent, as it were, the three primary colors on the palette from which the infinitely varied shades of interpersonal attitudes are mixed. The posture of moving toward another person covers a wide range of sentiment and includes not only heartfelt affection and charitable impulses but also the attitude of submission. By moving against others Horney means the gamut of feeling we normally associate with aggressive, rebellious, and competitive tendencies. The option of moving away from others refers to a mental posture of emotional withdrawal and self-sufficiency. Normally the individual will need to adopt all three attitudes in order to deal effectively with his or her social world. In fact, if the relationship concerned is a close one, all three will usually be taken at different times with one and the same role partner.

For the child or adolescent afflicted by basic anxiety, gaining a feeling of security becomes of paramount importance, and this need tends to blind him or her to key features of interpersonal situations. According to Horney, the insecure young person will overreact to certain emotionally stressful situations, not unlike someone in a panic who jumps at the slightest sound. The specific triggers depend upon a number of different factors, including native constitution and local conditions, and so will differ from person to person. Under the right combination of circumstances, however, the afflicted party feels driven to find sanctuary, and this can take a great variety of forms, such as placing oneself under the wing of an intimidating parent through hero worship, or feeling powerful by dominating others, or simply escaping by emotionally turning one's back on difficult relationships. Whatever the specific strategy, the relief from anxiety it seems to promise often eclipses other desires nurtured by the self and creates pressure to think and act in a way that discourages a realistic and balanced survey of circumstances. Already feeling alienated from its social milieu, the child begins to grow alienated from itself.

If the unfavorable set of conditions persists, it is likely, according to Horney, that the young person will become neurotic, or, to use our terminology, develop a character disorder. The basis for the disorder has already been laid in the child's initial attempts to assuage its anxiety, and according to the degree to which these attempts have been renewed, the child will have already developed certain sensitivities, preferences, and interpersonal skills and weaknesses. Horney argues that the insecure youngster seeks a more permanent solution because it feels pulled in different directions by its own inner conflicts.[47] She points out that the child's early efforts to deal with anxiety typically lack coherence due to its immaturity, and that its immediate focus is upon its relations to others.

To these observations we could add the findings of Piaget and Kohlberg, which strongly suggest that the child's emotional immaturity is directly related to its cognitive immaturity. As we have seen, in advanced societies intellectual maturation includes developing the ability to conceive of oneself as a member of a complex social order. We have also seen that identity in such a society is more a matter of personal election than of cultural assignment, and that it involves the construction of a life narrative, which in turn entails an imaginative projection of the self into the future. It need hardly be said that the role of the imagination in forming an identity is by no means always limited to making sober assessments about oneself and realistic plans for one's future. Horney identifies the fateful step in the formation of a character disorder as the attempt by the individual to elevate himself or herself above others through an unwitting distortion of reality. By unconsciously idealizing his or her self-image, the insecure individual creates a sense of self-esteem based upon some type of supposed superiority. The actual form of superiority varies from person to person and covers all the typical objects of human conceit. It may range from the conviction that one is an unrecognized saint or sage, to the persuasion that one is the world's greatest lover. The unifying trait that these different types of self-conceit share, according to Horney, is their grandiose quality. The idealized self naturally soars into the realm of the superlative and unlimited, the superhuman and the absolute.

In its fully developed form the idealized self constitutes a type of secular idolatry. It is as if the modern individual has replaced the collective narratives of culture—the many myths and legends of religion and folklore—with a private fable tailored to his or her own person. Horney's theory suggests that the insecure individual's drive to the absolute is promoted by the presence of competition in so many different areas of modern life, both formal and informal. Where competition between individuals or groups sets the standards for good and bad performance, the proverbial bar is always at risk of being raised yet another notch. In a competitive society, records are duly recorded in order to be broken, and the limits of human performance and achievement are typically viewed as being quite flexible. The answers to questions about the nature of excellence and what is satisfactory are purely functional under a regime of competition: Since winning is everything, whoever comes out on top does the right thing almost by definition. Competition encourages the individual to think and desire in terms of unlimited possibilities, which may provide a useful goal to the exceptional few, but is often a recipe for disappointment for the average many.

In his classic study of suicide, Durkheim identifies a uniquely modern form of self-annihilation that he qualifies as "anomic," meaning that it results from the frustration of unbridled desire. He bases this classification upon the statistically founded hypothesis that economic crises generally lead to an increase in the suicide rate. Pointing out that poor regions actually have significantly lower suicide rates than affluent ones, Durkheim argues that the bare fact of economic need is not what leads people to take their own lives. The real culprit behind the surge in suicides that typically accompany economic upheavals is the sudden and drastic rupture that can occur between the individual's expectations on the one hand, and his or her concrete possibilities for realizing said expectations on the other. In other words, the anomic suicide is due to a violent clash between inner desire and outer circumstance.

The field of cultural anthropology has provided ample documentation of the plasticity of human desire and has established that people can be content living within very different types of social and material arrangements. Although all cultures must make some provisions for meeting certain physiological and biological requirements of the species, even such basic wants as those for food and sex have proven to be quite malleable. Durkheim argues that, taken by itself, the individual's capacity for desire is unlimited, restricted only by his or her power of imagination. Hence, he concludes, whatever bounds exist for human appetites are social in nature. In societies with a low degree of individualism, where social forms are relatively stable and slow to change, custom is usually a powerful force in the regulation of desire.

Hemmed in by tradition, the individual is constrained to articulate his or her wishes within a relatively narrow range of culturally predetermined options. Of course, the various practices and institutions of a given culture will not be equally congenial to all of its members, and there will even be those whose native propensities run directly against the grain of the cultural pattern. Every society, after all, has its share of eccentrics, rebels, and misfits. However, such persons are in the minority, human nature being pliant enough that in any given culture the majority of those reared in it feel themselves to be at home.

From the standpoint of modern individualism, the social codes of tradition-bound societies can often appear stifling. Dorothy Lee argues that what appears as a social constraint to an outside observer may in reality provide structure to the lives of those within the culture, and so be experienced by them as enabling. Instead of constituting an impediment *to* freedom, the custom or rule is actually a precondition *for* freedom. She likens such so-called constraints to girders in a skyscraper or to the skeleton of a vertebrate: they represent an underlying structure that furnishes "form and caliber and direction" and provides "meaning and limit to growth."[48] Lee is careful to explain that by "limit" she does not mean the cessation of growth per se, but rather a determinate shape that rules out some possibilities in order to realize others. Such limiting is a *delimiting* that provides definition and actuality to what was only potential and vague. Hence, social conventions and practices equip the individual with a basic orientation in the world and provide him or her with leading tendencies and suggestions for future action. Without such an orientation, the individual would find himself or herself adrift in the horse latitudes of mere possibility. Even such a supposedly innate, physiological given, like hunger, often requires a social context in order to be correctly interpreted. As Lee points out, if one has a rumbling stomach at three thirty in the afternoon, it is the overall structure of daily life that helps determine if the feelings are to be viewed as legitimate grounds for a meal, as mere pangs that should be quelled by a snack or simply ignored until they pass, or as the first signs of an impending illness.

The growth of modern individualism has often left the modern individual rather bereft of such constraints. For those who have entered into common social roles—such as husbands, mothers, political activists, and priests—there usually exist generally accepted moral standards (and sometimes even laws) that set forth various dos and don'ts for the officeholder. There's typically much less agreement, however, about what constitutes a good rationale for assuming such offices in the first place. The individual is aware that there are nearly countless roles and relationships to which he or she could commit, and the question naturally arises as to how he or she can best choose among them. The standard rationale for entering into the moral reciprocity constituted by a social role is that the performance of the role's function will contribute to the individual's happiness. Happiness, however, is a notoriously vague notion, and to the extent that the individual seeks to make intelligent choices, he or she must work out, however roughly, his or her personal vision of the good life. Such a guiding ideal, in turn, requires the individual to have some conception as to what sort of person he or she is, or at least should strive to become, since the character of one's preferences and sensibilities will obviously play a role in determining the conditions needed to make one happy. Hence, the individual would appear to be caught in a sort of catch-22, since in order to elaborate an identity it would appear that one already needs an identity.

Fortunately, closer inspection reveals that, under normal circumstances, the construction of an identity occurs piecemeal, through a trial-and-error process of discovery. Given the many possibilities and unknowns confronting the individual, it could hardly be otherwise. What seems appealing in the mind's eye sometimes turns out to be less than satisfying in practice, and what we imagine to be relatively easy for ourselves may prove to be insurmountable. Life is full of such surprises, but the well-adjusted person is able to treat them as "par for the course" and learn from them. In a society in which personal choice and judgment play a significant role in guiding the affairs of the individual, such learning is vital. Since tradition and custom have lost much of their authority to set us bounds and goals, it is often up to us to determine realistic aims and limits for ourselves. This is a difficult enough task under the best of conditions, but for those who suffer from a character disorder it is often well-nigh impossible.

Perhaps the most significant disability engendered by a character disorder is a relative inability for personal and moral growth. Not unlike the person who tells a lie and then is obliged to continue lying in order to cover up the original falsehood, the erection of the idealized self sets in motion a series of developments that make it quite difficult for the individual to learn from his or her mistakes. In order to protect his or her inflated self-image, the afflicted person is obliged to unconsciously adopt any number of strategies for deforming reality at those points which threaten to burst the bubble that is the idealized self.

Horney maintains that one of Freud's most important contributions to psychology was his discovery and description of the defensive strategies unwittingly employed by the individual to shield his or her idealized self from unhappy encounters with fact. Although she rejects the overall theoretical framework proposed by Freud, she argues that he accurately described the unconscious processes involved in self-interested and biased interpretations of interpersonal situations.

Horney essentially adopts the Freudian repertoire of defense mechanisms, such as reaction formation, projection, and rationalization, but without the accompanying psychic architectonic of id, ego, and superego. Rather, she treats the defenses in a way that suggests their close relationship with the "informal" variety of fallacious reasoning that has been an interest of logicians ever since Aristotle first founded their discipline. Instead of conceptualizing the unconscious in terms of the interplay of various psychic agencies, Horney implies that its real source lies in the perspectival nature of individual awareness. We all know from personal experience that an event can take place right "under our nose," but that if our attention is elsewhere we may only barely register its occurrence. Consciousness has a focal point and a periphery. The very act of paying attention reveals the selective and fragmentary nature of awareness. If something in our surroundings catches our eye, we may turn our head, focus our gaze, listen attentively, or even approach for closer inspection. By virtue of bringing some aspect of our environment into sharper relief, we inevitably consign the rest of it to the background of awareness.

It may be objected that while perception is certainly perspectival, the same does not hold for knowledge. The limited firsthand experience each of us has with the planet, for instance, is construed through and greatly enriched by ideas provided to us by the physical sciences. If I were to theorize about the shape of the earth based solely on my personal experience of moving about on it, it might seem reasonable to conclude that the planet is actually flat. However, I don't let myself be misled by immediate experience since I've been taught that really it is round(ish). Furthermore, insofar as I accept this scientific pronouncement as true, I believe that it accurately describes a condition that holds for everyone, regardless of whatever view a given individual happens to subscribe to in the matter. This appeal to objective truth would seem to be a far cry from perspectivalism. By grounding its claims through the systematic use of the experimental method, science provides significant safeguards against the often narrow and biased nature of conclusions drawn from personal experience. Nevertheless, the history of science clearly reveals that even the conclusions of inquiries carried out by communities of professional researchers are fallible and open to revision in the light of new experience. The very heart of the scientific method—experimentation—is ultimately selective and partial, and the results of any given experiment are always potentially open to challenge through future ones. Hence, even science fails to achieve a "God's eye" perspective on the universe.

More importantly as regards our topic, the comparison to scientific knowledge suggests that a substantial problem faced by the individual in search of self-understanding is the absence of an equivalent to the community of scientific investigators. There is no recognized authority to whom one can turn for a realistic appraisal of one's character and potential. Certainly, there exist persons who would be capable of giving us a just estimate of our strengths and weaknesses, but locating them is no easy matter. While we may encounter such persons among our family members, friends, or acquaintances, the mere fact that someone is our mother, best friend, teacher, or family physician is no guarantee that the role occupant in question will have the insight and good judgment needed to help us. While those who know us best are usually those who are most likely to offer their advice, it is also often the case that their counsel is skewed due to the fact that they, too, suffer from personality problems. Indeed, one of the factors that Horney identifies in the genesis of character disorders is family members too involved with their own inner conflicts to be able to provide genuine love and insightful support to the young.[49] Because their personalities lead them to distort certain aspects of their human environment, their ability to achieve an unbiased and empathetic understanding of others is limited.[50]

Another hurdle to self-knowledge is the uncertainty that naturally accrues to knowing any person's potential for achievement and excellence in any given domain. While there are some cases in which it is relatively easy to evaluate an individual's chances for success (e.g., the short man whose career goal is to be a center on an NBA team), in most instances it is difficult to determine someone's limits. As Horney remarks, it is virtually inevitable that we set our goals either too high or too low.[51] However, those who do not have character disorders are more likely than not to benefit from the trials and errors of life, and thus learn to recognize and accept their limitations, while those with character disorders are often condemned to doggedly pursue the Holy Grail of the idealized self.

On Horney's view, an attitude or tendency operates unconsciously to the degree that the individual is unaware of its general role in his or her life. That is, one may be cognizant of being, say, hypersensitive to criticism, but remain oblivious to the origins of this attitude and to its relation to the overall structure of one's character. Indeed, one may even view the hypersensitivity as a mark of distinction that shows one's naturally noble nature; one simply can't settle for what satisfies the run-of-the-mill crowd because one is called to greater things. The individual unknowingly adopts a self-serving interpretation that blinds him or her to certain key features of a given circumstance and remains committed to the characterization because it satisfies a need. From the standpoint of informal logic, the individual's reasoning is fallacious because it involves one or more unexamined presuppositions. Since such assumptions have worth for the individual above and beyond their purported truth-value, there is often considerable resistance to changing or even critically exploring them.

Horney gave her most complete statement regarding the unconscious in *New Ways in Psychoanalysis*.[52] Although her view represents a considerable departure from the orthodox position, in *New Ways* her exposition tends to downplay the differences between her understanding of the unconscious and Freud's. Indeed, she even indirectly presents herself as a defender of the Freudian standpoint by complaining that the standard objections to the psychoanalytic conception are made from a perspective that is "too formalistic."[53] It is true that if one accepts Horney's more commonsensical version of the unconscious, the difficulties arising from the idea of an "unconscious conscious" psychic censor disappear, but of course one has also thereby abandoned the Freudian machinery of repression. Horney's tendency to soft-pedal her differences with Freud in *New Ways* needs to be seen in the context of the politics of the psychoanalytic establishment at the time she was writing. Although she eventually wound up in the role of the psychoanalytic rebel, it had been her long-standing intention to function as a reformer, and *New Ways* was authored during a period when she could still reasonably hope to be accepted as a psychoanalyst in good standing.

Horney's view of unconscious processes indirectly suggests that part of the difficulty in recognizing the important role of unconscious motivations in personal behavior is due to an oversimplified understanding of consciousness. Human awareness is often popularly conceived of as a sort of window on the self and the outside world. For instance, the capacity for intellectual objectivity is frequently grasped in negative terms, the idea being that if one were to simply remove the distorting influence of feeling and interest, perspective and interpretation, what would remain would be an accurate view of the facts. Like the sculptor of lore, who forms a human figure by simply cutting away everything that does not look like one, the would-be knower is counseled to remove everything that is not a fact. The main objection to this type of naive realism is that facts are themselves theory-loaded. In other words, any characterization of a given state of affairs inevitably includes some assumptions about the nature of the world, or least about a part of the world. Without such guiding ideas the so-called facts would be nothing more than an unstructured mass of data.

Observation of everyday life teaches that our capacity for learning is what allows experience to grow in meaning. Expertise in any field typically renders a firsthand experience of the subject matter in question more meaningful to the expert than it is to the novice. Hence, a hike through the forest reveals more and suggests more to the trained senses of the seasoned woodsman than it does to the proverbial city slicker. Although it is often assumed that the individual is expert about his or her own inner life, such an assumption has little warrant. There is no more reason to suppose that most of us are endowed with special powers of self-understanding than to assume that most people are "natural born" baseball players or corporate managers. As counterintuitive as it may sometimes seem, the single greatest source of inspiration for self-insight is the social dimension of human experience. The very words the individual employs to analyze his or her own states of consciousness are, after all, part of a cultural heritage. We've seen that Hallpike and other social scientists have found evidence that supports the contention that the individual's social environment plays a decisive role in determining the degree and nature of his or her self-awareness. As concerns self-knowledge, the rule of thumb is that we come to know ourselves by developing the capacity to see ourselves as others see us. The objectivity that is available to us as individuals is not that of an absolute standpoint but rather that which arises by carefully sifting through different perspectives and weighing their respective pros and cons. Intellectual objectivity is a dialectical acquisition, if by "dialectic" we broadly understand the formation of belief through communication and reasoning. For the person who has achieved a degree of objectivity in a given area, the perspective and methodology that he or she brings to the subject matter in question are themselves the fruit of inquiry.

Given the special value that beliefs about oneself have for the individual, we can readily understand why objectivity is hard to achieve when it comes to understanding one's own motivations. After all, we begin forming ideas about ourselves long before the capacity for critical thinking matures. Although the construction of a self-image implicitly involves making truth claims, the child or adolescent often fails to distinguish between the factual basis for a particular belief about himself or herself, and the affective value the belief may hold as a source of comfort or self-esteem. As a rule of thumb, the more insecure the individual feels, the greater will be the temptation to find assurance through accepting unrealistic but gratifying opinions about himself or herself. If a person's self-esteem and identity is predicated upon skewed beliefs, the emotional investment in maintaining them can become such an impediment to clear thinking and rational decision-making that the individual will require outside help in order to achieve insight into the true nature of his or her problems. Horney's greatly revised version of Freud's "talking cure" was formulated to offer precisely such assistance, and she conceives of the therapeutic situation as a unique type of human relationship that, through the everyday miracle of authentic communication, can enable the analysand to achieve a new perspective on his or her interpersonal difficulties.

Although her original therapeutic focus was on neurosis, Horney eventually came to hold that her theory and technique could be of benefit to anyone interested in achieving greater self-understanding and personal growth. The fact that personal preference and judgment play such an important role in human affairs in societies where individualism has taken root lends a specifically moral aspect to knowing oneself in the modern world. Where the claims of custom and tradition are submitted to the approval of individual conscience, failure to recognize one's true motivations can compromise one's ability to make intelligent decisions. Morals become the prerogative of the individual at the price of perpetual self-examination. The notion that the path of virtue requires continual exertion is not new, and Hallpike points out that in addition to being a familiar feature of Greek moral philosophy, it can also be found in the teachings of early Confucianism and Buddhism.[54] In what follows, we shall argue that Horney's version of psychoanalysis represents a powerful new tool in the ancient quest to know oneself.

Notes

1. Hallpike, *The Evolution of Moral Understanding*, 199–200.
2. Ibid., 190.
3. Dorothy Lee, *Valuing the Self: What We Can Learn from Other Cultures* (Prospect Heights, Illinois: Waveland Press Inc., 1986), 53–63.
4. Ibid., 56.
5. Ibid., 68–69.
6. Hallpike, *The Evolution of Moral Understanding*, 254.
7. Ibid., 122.
8. Ibid., 65–67.
9. Ibid., 119.
10. Ibid., 124.
11. Rose Laub Coser, *In Defense of Modernity: Role Complexity and Individual Autonomy* (Stanford, CA: Stanford University Press, 1991), 93.
12. Ibid., 22.
13. Ibid., 92–93.
14. Ruth Benedict, *Patterns of Culture* (Boston: Houghton Mifflin Company, 1934), 23–24.
15. Dorothy Lee, *Religious Perspectives of College Teaching in Anthropology* (New Haven, CT: The Edward W. Hazen Foundation, 1951), 9.
16. My remarks on the birth of the market economy are indebted to the discussion of this subject in Robert L. Heilbroner and William Milberg, *The Making of Economic Society*, 11th ed. (Upper Saddle River, NJ: Prentice Hall, 2002), 45.
17. Jack Goody, *The Domestication of the Savage Mind* (New York: Cambridge University Press, 1977), 44.
18. Bronislaw Malinowski, "The Problem of Meaning in Primitive Languages," included as Supplement I in C. K. Ogden and I. A. Richards, *The Meaning of Meaning: A Study of The Influence of Language upon Thought and of The Science of Symbolism*, 8th ed. (New York: Harcourt, Brace & World, Inc., 1946), 312.
19. Goody, *The Domestication of the Savage Mind*, 44.
20. Hallpike, *The Evolution of Moral Understanding*, 162.
21. Ibid., 161–162.
22. Coser, *In Defense of Modernity*, 84–85.
23. Ibid., 78.
24. Lawrence Kohlberg and Carol Gilligan, "The Adolescent Philosopher: The Discovery of Self in a Postconventional World" in *Twelve to Sixteen: Early Adolescence*, ed. Jerome Kagan and Robert Coles (New York: W. W. Norton and Co. Inc., 1972), 158–159.
25. Michael Maccoby and Nancy Modiano, "On Culture and Equivalence: I" in *Studies in Cognitive Growth*, ed. Jerome S. Bruner et al. (New York: John Wiley & Sons, Inc., 1966), 267.
26. Sylvia Scribner and Michael Cole, "Cognitive Consequences of Formal and Informal Education," *Science* 182 (9 November 1973): 553–559.
27. Hallpike, *The Evolution of Moral Understanding*, 161.
28. John Dewey, *Democracy and Education* (New York: The Free Press, 1944), 293.

29. Scribner and Cole, "Cognitive Consequences of Formal and Informal Education," 555.
30. For an extended review of the relevant literature up to the late 1970s, see C. R. Hallpike, *The Foundations of Primitive Thought* (Oxford: Clarendon Press, 1979), 174–195.
31. George Herbert Mead, *Mind, Self and Society from the Standpoint of a Social Behaviorist*, ed. Charles W. Morris (Chicago: University of Chicago Press, 1932), 157–158.
32. Ibid., 260.
33. For a discussion of a number of empirical studies that have documented the deleterious effects of competition on human relationships, see Alfie Kohn's *No Contest: The Case Against Competition*, rev. ed. (New York: Houghton Mifflin Company, 1992), especially chapter six, "Against Each Other: Interpersonal Considerations."
34. For a sustained analysis of the predicament of the modern individual under capitalism, see Dewey's *Individualism Old and New*.
35. Peter L. Berger, Brigitte Berger, and Hansfried Keller, *The Homeless Mind: Modernization and Consciousness* (New York: Random House, 1973), 79.
36. Ibid.
37. Emile Durkheim, *The Division of Labor in Society*, trans. W. D. Halls (New York: The Free Press, 1984), 13.
38. Amitai Etzioni, *The Spirit of Community* (New York: Crown Publishers, Inc., 1993), 30.
39. Ibid., p. 37.
40. Robert D. Hare, *Without Conscience: The Disturbing World of the Psychopaths Among Us* (New York: The Guilford Press, 1995) 34.
41. For the terms "customary morality" and "reflective morality" I am indebted to Dewey and Tufts' *Ethics*.
42. John Dewey, *The Later Works, 1925–1953, Volume 12: 1938*, ed. Jo Ann Boydston (Carbondale, IL: Southern Illinois University Press, 1986), 180–181.
43. Malinowski's essay is included as a supplement in C. K. Ogden and I. A. Richards, *The Meaning of Meaning*, rev. ed. (New York: Harcourt, Brace & World, Inc., 1946), 296–336.
44. John Dewey, *The Later Works, 1925–1953, Volume 8: 1933*, ed. Jo Ann Boydston (Carbondale, IL: Southern Illinois University Press, 1986), 138.
45. Karen Horney, *Neurosis and Human Growth: The Struggle Toward Self-Realization* (New York: W. W. Norton & Company, 1950) 18.
46. Ibid., 18.
47. Ibid., 20.
48. Ibid., 67.
49. Ibid., 18.
50. Of course, the type of therapy developed by Horney is an attempt to correct this circumstance by instituting an effective form of professional help for persons suffering from personality disorders.
51. Horney, *Neurosis and Human Growth*, 37.
52. Karen Horney, *New Ways in Psychoanalysis* (New York: W. W. Norton & Company, Inc., 1966), 18–21.
53. Ibid., 20.
54. Hallpike, *The Evolution of Moral Understanding*, 311.

3

Dewey's Metapsychological Alternative to Freudianism

On the Danger of Throwing Out the Baby with the Bathwater

In his comparative study of Freud and Dewey on human nature, Morton Levitt cites a personal communication from Sidney Hook in which Hook discusses Dewey's attitude toward the work of Freud. Hook notes that he and his mentor found themselves in agreement that the Freudian architectonic of the human psyche, with its mental compartmentalizations and reifications, was, in essence, "mythology."[1] However, Hook also emphasizes the fact that Dewey repeatedly insisted upon Freud's gift for making close observations of human behavior. Once, when Hook suggested that Freud would have made a wonderful novelist, Dewey agreed.

Generally speaking, philosophers probably tend to underestimate the intellectual significance of new observations. Innovation within the field has traditionally been held to depend more upon analytic acumen and speculative imagination than on improved descriptions of what is already familiar or on the discovery of new phenomena. To the philosophical purist it may well seem that the task of observation should fall to science, concerned as it is with the nitty-gritty of measurement and experimentation. Of course, such a view, positing as it does a metaphysical cleft between theory and practice, was anathema to Dewey, who conceived of reflective thinking as an organic process in which observation, deliberation, and judgment constitute integrated phases of human action. Given his understanding of the fine art of observation as essential to the intellectual enterprise, Dewey's compliments on this score to Freud should not be taken lightly.

After all, the temptation for Deweyans and other pragmatists to simply dismiss psychoanalysis as a pseudo-science is considerable. With the 1922 publication of *Human Nature and Conduct*, some of the key metapsychological assumptions informing Freud's thought came under direct fire from Dewey. In the book in question Dewey provides an extended argument against the notion of instinct as employed by Freud and others as too rigid to do justice to the diversity of human behavior across cultures. He also judges Freud's focus upon sexual instincts as the prime movers of human behavior to be reductive. In addition, *Human Nature and Conduct* offers an alternative conception of the unconscious that is more fluid and less doctrinaire than the famous Freudian "machinery of repression" (to borrow a phrase from Hook).

As if all this were not enough to nourish a healthy pragmatist skepticism as regards the pronouncements of psychoanalysis, the latter history of the analytic tradition has done little to restore confidence among the pragmatically minded. Even before Freud's death, the psychoanalytic community began to schism in a fashion reminiscent of a religious or political tradition. To all appearances, psychoanalysis was as much a matter of creed and confession as it was of scientific proof. In fact, the major similarity among Freudian dissenters such as C. G. Jung, Alfred Adler, and Wilhelm Reich was the highly speculative and unsubstantiated nature of their own views. In truth, it was Freud himself who sowed the seeds of analytic apostasy by repeatedly grounding his own assertions on insufficient evidence. To this day the scientific reconstruction for which psychoanalysis is so long overdue is still on hold. Instead of embracing the techniques and findings of the new sciences of mind, such as cognitive psychology, many of the various analytic communities have tended to turn in on themselves. The popularity of the thought of the French analyst Jacques Lacan can perhaps be taken as a sign of the times. Lacan's brand of obscurantism has captivated both the analytic establishment and laity and even given European analysis an oddly academic emphasis. Under the influence of Lacan and his followers, some psychoanalysts have moved further away from the spirit of genuine scientific inquiry than ever before.

If the intellectual tradition launched by Freud is so fraught with error, why not simply make a fresh start? Whatever valuable observations Freud made ought to be available to contemporary investigators, and if his observations were actually insightful, their worth will not wholly depend upon being nested within a psychoanalytic framework of interpretation. Although much speaks in favor of making a clean sweep, such a move would be premature because it would overlook or discount the valuable work that has been done in the psychoanalytic tradition since Freud. Among the many analytic schismatics, there have been some who have addressed the flaws in Freudianism and sought to reestablish psychoanalysis upon a more solid theoretical basis. To simply lump all psychoanalytic and neo-psychoanalytic schools together and collectively condemn them as "fruit of the poisonous tree" would be to dismiss some very important insights into the human condition. Freud has inspired not only radicals bent upon outdoing their master, and devotees concerned to maintain and promote orthodoxy, but also thoughtful men and women who have sought to improve psychoanalytic theory and practice. For the most part these analytic moderates are less well known than the radicals. Thinkers who clearly stake a claim to originality and rebellion tend to draw attention to themselves in a way that theorists who choose the subtler "middle path" of judicious reform usually do not. There is perhaps more intellectual appeal in the clash of diametrically opposed doctrines than in the qualified yeses and noes of balanced criticism. In any event, analytic mavericks like Jung, Adler, Reich, and Lacan have generally enjoyed greater popularity than the more restrained "cultural" psychologists such as Erich Fromm and Karen Horney.

The work of reform-minded psychoanalysts deserves serious consideration from philosophers due to the fact that among the various schools of psychology, psychoanalysis still represents the most comprehensive attempt yet made to scientifically study mind in relation to selfhood, personality, and motivation. Beliefs about human psychology obviously play an important role in such major areas of philosophical inquiry as ethics and social and political philosophy—not to mention a whole host of more specialized philosophical disciplines in which assumptions about human nature and behavior are inevitable, such as philosophical anthropology and the philosophy of punishment. In an epistemologically ideal universe, philosophers would only rely on those psychological theories that have been scientifically proven. If the only sorts of assumptions concerning human psychology made by philosophers were those involving physiological psychology, it might even be possible to maintain such a rigorous standard. The problem, of course, is that when it comes to the description and explanation of more complex forms of human behavior, disagreement often constitutes the norm among professional psychologists.

It should go without saying that the mere presence of controversy within a discipline by no means disqualifies it from being scientific. Despite a relatively high level of dispute among the experts in psychology, the field as a whole has, over the course of the last century, gradually been replacing speculation with assertions funded by experimentally verified findings. Contemporary psychologists have shown themselves to be receptive to new ideas and methods and have been particularly innovative in fashioning research tools out of cutting edge technologies. Even schools of thought with a significant humanistic or literary component, such as some of the psychoanalytic schools, are in principle open to verification through the experimental method of inquiry. To some limited extent, this process of experimental testing has been carried out for psychoanalysis. Freud's theory of the Oedipus complex, for instance, has received much attention from anthropologists, who have sought to evaluate his conjectures through the comparative study of cultures. However, given the complexity of human behavior, and the dogmatic attitudes of some analysts, it is understandable that much work remains to be done on this score.

Since its very inception, psychoanalysis has been as much a therapeutic practice as it has a theory. The pragmatist will naturally want to know to what extent psychoanalysis has been successful in achieving its therapeutic aims, and how it stacks up against other psychotherapies in terms of treatment effectiveness. The answers to these questions are disconcerting. A body of research exists which suggests that a wide variety of psychotherapies—many of which have disparate theoretical perspectives and/or therapeutic techniques—tend to perform equally well in the field.[2] Of course, the appropriate method for the evaluation of psychotherapy is itself a matter of debate. At what point during or after therapy is the patient to be evaluated? After all, length of treatment has long been a controversial issue among analytic—not to mention nonanalytic—therapists. Furthermore, how are the self-reports of patients to be weighed? Are we to assume that a given patient abandoned a particular course of treatment because it was unfruitful, or because it was threatening to unearth some disquieting truths? A potentially even more fundamental problem for the comparison of different psychotherapies lies in the fact that they do not all share the same therapeutic goals. Whereas some approaches set their sights on psychic "normalcy," others are guided by an ideal of human flourishing. Although there is no reason to believe that these and other issues cannot eventually be resolved, for the time being the research on psychotherapeutic effectiveness has provided little in the way of validating any one approach over its competitors.

Given the speculative and even controversial nature of many personality theories, it might seem that skepticism would be the most prudent stance for the non-expert to take on such matters. As long as one could suspend belief about the psychological analysis of character without significantly affecting other theoretical commitments or practical concerns, skepticism about this subject would surely be warranted. The obvious difficulty confronting any skeptic of contemporary personality theory is the pervasiveness of psychological assumptions in everyday life. In our sundry pursuits—private and public, recreational as well as occupational—we continually make assumptions and inferences as to why people do the things they do. Beliefs about human psychology are an inevitable feature of life in a human community. As already noted, to this body of everyday assumptions the philosopher often adds a professional interest in some branch of human affairs. Since beliefs about motivation, personality, and other psychological subjects are often impossible to avoid, a general attitude of mistrust toward the claims of modern psychology would leave the skeptic ill equipped to intelligently confront a great many problems in theory and practice. Fortunately, there is a viable alternative to a blanket skepticism vis-à-vis psychology: We can acknowledge the imperfect nature of the contemporary study of mind, and still recognize the relative value of its findings. As W. V. O. Quine argued about knowledge in general, the most we can do, epistemologically speaking, is to adopt the best theory available to us at any given time.[3]

When it comes to evaluating the relative merits of different personality theories, the hitch to Quine's dictum should be apparent: On what basis are we to select the superior theory? At the present time the issue cannot be decisively settled by an appeal to the results of experimental research. Investigators of such complex psychological phenomena as character, decision-making, and dream life enjoy little direct control over their respective subject matters. The unconscious and subconscious factors at work in day-to-day human behavior are difficult to isolate and analyze under conditions that would exclude subjective influences. For the most part personality theorists must still depend upon introspection and the self-reports of volunteers or patients. In the absence of firm and unequivocal facts upon which to ground personality theory, competing interpretations have flourished. To make matters worse, the psychotherapeutic applications of the various personality theories have led to highly ambiguous results (a point to which I have already alluded).

Given the dearth of conclusive empirical evidence for any one view of personality, the metapsychological assumptions informing different personality theories take on added importance from the standpoint of theory assessment. In *New Ways in Psychoanalysis*, the book in which she presents a major revision of psychoanalytic theory, Karen Horney summarizes her misgivings about Freud's teachings by observing that in them, as a rule, "underlying observations of great keenness and depth are robbed of their constructive value because of their integration into an unconstructive theoretical system."[4] Judging from his references to psychoanalysis in *Human Nature and Conduct*, Dewey would have concurred with Horney's dictum. In this and subsequent chapters, I will argue that Dewey and Horney, working from different ends of the same problem, arrive at solutions that are fundamentally compatible and, indeed, complementary.

In her introduction to *New Ways*, Horney explains that her doubts about Freudian doctrine arose out of difficulties she encountered as a practicing psychoanalyst. Over the course of fifteen years she found that nearly every patient she treated suffered from problems that were simply not addressed by orthodox analysis.[5] Her focus is primarily therapeutic, and Horney's revision of psychoanalysis takes the form of a new theory of the neurotic personality. Her discussion of metapsychological issues is mainly limited to a rejection of some of Freud's guiding assumptions. When necessary, she offers new suppositions to replace the old ones, but in general her attention is devoted to matters of individual psychology. Horney's relative silence on the broader theoretical issues in psychoanalysis may come as a surprise to those readers who know that she is typically viewed in psychoanalytic circles as a "culturalist," a moniker reserved for psychoanalytic thinkers who emphasize environmental and cultural factors in lieu of Freud's biological orientation. Although her mature theory certainly reflects the conviction that personal psychology is inherently interpersonal, Horney did little to develop the wider theoretical implications of her cultural turn. Most of her theoretical contributions were directly grounded in her therapeutic work with neurotics and her own self-analysis,[6] and her writing rarely veers from its orbit around this set of experiences.

As a philosopher, Dewey's natural interest in psychoanalysis was meta-theoretical, and his published remarks concerning psychoanalysis generally deal with its underlying assumptions. In what follows, I hope to show that Dewey offers an original metapsychology, and one that constitutes an attractive alternative to Freud's instinct-based approach to the psyche. In a subsequent chapter I will extend my argument by showing how Dewey's philosophy could serve to ground and enrich Horney's version of psychoanalysis.

The Self

In his discussion of modern selfhood, Hallpike notes that the self has commonly been viewed as the primal source of rationality and freedom.[7] Historically, the inner self has variously done duty as the seat of reason, the wellspring of free will, and the agent of moral actions. In fact, until the modern social sciences began to take form in the late eighteenth century, "self" was considered to be essentially synonymous with "mind," and the self served as the setting for all manner of philosophical investigations. For instance, the Enlightenment's optimism regarding the potential for social and political reforms was premised upon belief in an inner self that included an innately rational part but whose growth to intellectual maturity was easily stunted by an inhospitable social environment. The faith of the *philosophes* was that if untoward influences such as superstition and the yoke of tradition could be weakened or eliminated, then the individual would be free to follow the light of his or her own reason.

Relying primarily upon introspection and everyday observations, the faculty psychologists cataloged key features of consciousness, such as the capacity for long-term planning and the ability to forgo the immediate satisfaction of desire. However, in addition to the obvious limitations of any psychology based mainly upon introspection, they were handicapped by a teleological worldview. The very idea of the faculty psychology—that is, a compartmentalized conception of mind in which each department fulfills a specific function according to a clear division of labor—assumed that the universe was the neatly ordered product of intelligent design. Of all the animals in creation, only humans were capable of reason. It followed that if the special office of humanity was to be rational, then mind was primarily the seat of reason and other rational faculties, such as understanding and judgment. What emerged was an epistemological version of self in which various mental functions operated more or less independently of one another according to a foreordained scheme.

At first glance, the teleological interpretative framework of the faculty psychologists may seem to involve only a minor inaccuracy. The most obvious source of inspiration for their approach was pre-Darwinian biology. Although it is technically incorrect from an evolutionary standpoint to talk about the "purpose" of a given organ when one wishes to discuss its function, the error appears slight at first blush. The mistake is merely semantic as long as we bear in mind that natural history can neither form intentions nor pursue goals. But, of course, for the faculty psychologists nature *was* informed by purposes. Since all life-forms were held to be the handiwork of a Great Designer, it was only logical to assume that each and every organism was perfectly adapted to its ecological niche. Extended to individual organs, this view resulted in the claim that direct evidence of intelligent design was available in the obvious perfection of certain anatomical structures, such as the human eye. In reality, though, our eyes provide evidence to the contrary, since they manifest the sort of structural weaknesses one would expect in an organ that has emerged through the haphazard process of natural selection. The blind spot in the field of vision and conditions such as retinal tears can be explained as inherent structural problems, which stem from the fact that the process of evolution is incapable of totally redesigning an organ in the manner of a human engineer. Evolution can only move forward, in the sense that it can only make modifica-tions to a preexisting basic plan, whereas engineers have the luxury of returning to the proverbial drawing board.[8]

The teleological view of mind suggested that the various mental faculties were perfectly suited to their respective functions: observa-tion, recall, reason, and judgment were designed to work efficiently in relative independence of one another. Given this set of teleological assumptions, the faculty psychologists tended to underestimate the impact of unconscious influences on consciousness. Although the existence of unconscious mental processes was hard to deny given the nightly fact of dreaming, they assumed that the unconscious had little impact on waking life. It stood to reason that those mental faculties that seemed to involve a heightened state of awareness—notably, the higher mental faculties—would be particularly immune to distortion by hidden forces.

The original sin of the faculty psychology was to identify the func-tion of mind with some of its most refined cultural products—namely, the techniques and bodies of knowledge found in scholarship and science. Abstract disciplines such as logic, mathematics, and physics were uppermost in theorists' minds as examples of correct reason-ing as they strove to understand the nature of cognition. Instead of recognizing that the theoretical sciences represent highly specialized forms of reflection, these disciplines were made to serve as models for thinking in general. As Dewey points out in his classic *How We Think*, the product of thought was mistaken for the process of thinking.[9] In consequence, the image of thought that emerged was overly formal and distant from typical instances of reflection: it was too abstract, too methodical, and too organized.

Despite the discrepancies between its description of thought and actual instances of thinking, the theory survived, largely due to the lack of an alternative to the underlying teleological framework of interpretation. When Darwin finally broke the hold of teleology in biology, he also indirectly created an alternative to the faculty psychology. Hitherto it had generally been assumed that the office of mind was to know and understand. Notwithstanding their famous differences over metaphysics and epistemology, continental rationalism and British empiricism had jointly held the assumption that the primary purpose of mind was to reason and acquire knowledge.[10] From the new perspective provided by the theory of evolution, the capacities for logical consistency and theoretical speculation seemed meager weapons indeed in the struggle for survival.

When humankind is considered as one among many species, subject during the greater part of its evolutionary history to the same process of natural selection as other life-forms, the capacity for abstract ratiocination appears as just one in a group of outstanding—if not always strictly unique—characteristics. In addition to the human status of being the rational animal, one could add bipedalism, the opposable thumb, language, and a greatly expanded ability for learning. Viewed from the perspective of animal behavior and psychology, what is most striking about the average representative of *Homo sapiens* is his or her capacity to acquire culture. Judging from the archaeological record, technological innovations during prehistory were rare. As we have seen, primitive societies provide their members with relatively few opportunities for abstract thinking or creative problem solving. What they do afford them is language and an integrated body of knowledge, belief, and behavior. The transmission of culture from generation to generation directly depends upon the human capacity for learning, and the rare innovations that took place during the many millennia of the Stone Age would have been lost without this essential ability.

Habit, Impulse, and Intelligence

In the wake of Darwin, probably no thinker did more than John Dewey to call attention to the fundamental role played by learning in human behavior. In fact, Dewey once pointed out that his philosophy took education as the "supreme human interest,"[11] and he is probably still best known today for his contribution to educational theory. Dewey's major work on the scientific study of human behavior was the 1922 *Human Nature and Conduct*, in which he presented an alternative to philosophical faculty psychology and to the instinct-based approach to mind commonly associated with Freud. Dewey's methodology in *Human Nature and Conduct* is behavioristic, in the sense that his access to mind is provided through different forms of comportment. He distinguishes three main types of behavior: conduct that is habitual, impulsive behavior, and active problem solving. These categories are by no means exclusive—for example, an act may incorporate both habit and reflection. Nevertheless, as different aspects of human conduct, habit, impulse, and intelligence are distinct enough from one another to be illustrated by actions in which one of the respective phases is clearly preponderant. Thus, the act of absentmindedly preparing one's bowl of cereal for breakfast is primarily habitual. A good example of an impulsive action is furnished by the employee who replies harshly and without forethought to his or her boss upon receiving criticism. Intelligence in action can be illustrated by any situation in which the individual is actively engaged in trying to solve a problem, such as the auto mechanic who attempts to discover why a customer's car won't start.

Although deceptively simple, Dewey's identification of the central aspects of human behavior is the result of a carefully crafted methodology. He hoped to avoid the mistakes of the faculty psychology and psychoanalysis by refocusing the human sciences on their actual subject matter—namely, human beings in the context of their natural habitat. Since we have always lived in groups, our habitat includes not only physical surroundings but also the cultural matrix of the social world. Dewey reasons that theorists who select an abstraction such as mind or the "pre-social" individual as their investigative starting point do so at the risk of losing the salutary restraint of fact. Potential observations that could serve to correct inaccurate preconceptions of the subject matter are lost, or at least rendered unlikely, since the field of observation has been preemptively and artificially narrowed.

Impulse

One of Dewey's central projects in *Human Nature and Conduct* is his reconstruction of the notion of instinct as it applies to human behavior. The term "instinct" commonly connotes that which is unlearned and elementary in conduct, and students of human nature have often assumed that instincts constitute the building blocks of all human activity. According to this line of reasoning, any adequate explanation of behavior will consist in analyzing complex pieces of conduct into their simpler instinctual components. Dewey argues that instinct-based psychologies have proven to be unproductive because their originators have failed to muster convincing evidence to support their conclusions. The list of the "universal" instincts has often differed from thinker to thinker in both composition and length, and in the most egregious cases theorists have simply introduced new instincts on an ad hoc basis. Ultimately, the failure of instinct theory to make good on its promises is due to the mistaken assumption that instinct is the primary factor in human comportment. If by "instinct" we mean the sort of unlearned, set patterns of behavior so common in other animal species, then it is impossible to explain the richness and variety of the anthropological universe in terms of either single or compounded instincts. At least, it would be impossible to do so without stretching the notion of instinct so far as to lend it a new meaning when applied to human beings.

To take the most influential instinct theorist as an example, Freud assumed that psychology, as a genuine natural science of the mind, would one day be able to translate psychic phenomena into neurobiological terms. Consistent with this perspective, he thought of the instincts as representing "the somatic demands upon mental life."[12] For Freud, any worthwhile psychology had to be elaborated within a neurobiological framework in which factors such as anatomy and heredity play the central role in determining psychic processes. Thus, the major thrust of his thought was to illuminate the transition from the organic to the mental, and he assumed that a better grasp of this shift would be tantamount to providing a causal explanation of behavior. As a logical consequence of this scheme, Freud viewed social and cultural phenomena as tertiary, since he believed that they were determined by psychological factors, which in turn were governed by biological ones.

Some defenders of Freud have argued that it is inaccurate to characterize him as an instinct theorist.[13] They point out that although German contains the word *Instinkt*, the father of psychoanalysis actually chose the term *Trieb* to denote the most elemental forces in the psyche. *Instinkt* is best illustrated in animal behavior, and, like its English equivalent, has connotations of a relatively fixed pattern of comportment that varies little from individual to individual. *Trieb*, on the other hand, connotes a mental force that pushes the individual in a general direction, but whose final expression is not necessarily predetermined; it is probably best rendered in English as "drive." In *Human Nature and Conduct*, Dewey proposes "impulse" as a replacement for "instinct" for precisely the same reason that Freud preferred *Trieb* to *Instinkt*—the latter is less determinate than the former.

Despite this similarity between Freudian drive and Deweyan impulse, the two notions are not equivalent. On Dewey's view, only the earliest phase of human life is dominated by impulse, since these primitive urges are soon swept up into the multitude of habits being acquired by the child. Habit not only incorporates native strivings and spontaneous desires but also mobilizes and transforms them. Through habit, an impulse can accrue new meanings and so differentiate into a variety of more complex forms. Feelings of anger—to borrow one of Dewey's examples—can range from a red-hot flash of rage at being embarrassed in public to a mild impatience with a needy individual. The very nature of the emotion at hand is dependent upon the human context of which it is a constituent element. In the life of every individual there occurs an *éducation sentimentale*, wherein general capacities for feeling and pathways for action undergo development. Were it not for this ability for emotional learning, the trademark self-control of the adult would be impossible.

In the toddler, anger and aggressive behavior are simply two sides of the same coin. Through interaction with others, the social significance of aggressive and violent behavior is impressed upon the child, and its anger becomes meaningful to it in a new way. Of course, depending upon circumstances, the new meanings with which the impulse is invested may vary considerably. For instance, a highly authoritarian parenting style may produce a pattern of conduct in the child wherein the main motive for obedience is fear of punishment. Such children often become unruly when they believe they can do so with impunity. Parents, on the other hand, who view discipline problems as opportunities for learning, and so provide their children with clear rationales for obedience, probably stand a better chance of raising offspring who will internalize the dos and don'ts of life with others.

As veritable titans of the psyche, Freud's drives—unlike Dewey's impulses—cannot be reformed. At most they can be restrained, and this restraint will always come at a price. The requirements of civilized life are such that our basic erotic and destructive urges must perpetually be held in check. Since they are wholly asocial, these drives would make short work of any compact, formal or informal, were they ever accorded free reign. Even the simplest social arrangements require a certain minimum of order and discipline, and the basic drives are oblivious to the very existence of such necessities. In *Civilization and Its Discontents*, Freud argues that there are better and worse ways of making our peace with them but warns us against nurturing high expectations. The inner peace we can realistically hope to achieve will never attain to a blissful tranquility. Rather, we must settle for a sort of uneasy—albeit sufferable—truce between our lower nature and our conscious self. Because it demands the frustration of our fundamental drives, civilized life, despite all its marvels, leaves us discordant with ourselves.

In an extended comparison of Dewey's and Freud's views of instinct, Philip Rieff has argued for the superiority of the latter's theory.[14] Although Rieff's objections to Dewey are mistaken, they are worth examining, since they are incorrect in a way that is instructive for our purposes. Rieff charges that Dewey is unable to account for instances of regressive behavior, unlike Freud, who can make sense of such conduct as an instinctual inundation that occurs when there is a breach in the levees of sublimation raised by culture. According to Rieff, Dewey treats impulse as a "neutral potentiality," a mere "reservoir of vitality" that lacks the socially disruptive nature of Freud's drives. Rather than label archaic pieces of conduct "regressive," Dewey prefers to talk about "disintegration" of a given activity into some other form of behavior. On Rieff's reading of *Human Nature and Conduct*, Dewey's analysis of human comportment is atemporal because he has made present experience the standard "to measure the success (health) or failure (sickness) of an individual or social institution."[15] In fact, on Rieff's interpretation, Dewey has essentially created an updated form of utilitarianism, since he construes Dewey as committed to the proposition that "human nature may be comprehended by its strivings to obtain pleasure and avoid pain."[16] Furthermore, Rieff implies that Dewey's social psychology clearly reflects the influence of political liberalism, especially Dewey's supposedly optimistic conviction that intelligent social reform can improve the human condition.

Rieff's criticisms of Dewey are premised upon several misunderstandings of the philosopher's actual views. In the first place, he misconstrues Dewey's reasons for preferring the notion of impulse to that of instinct. On Rieff's reading, Dewey embraces impulse as a value-neutral entity that promises to make human nature more malleable than the human nature of the instinct theorists. This explanation ignores the fact that one of Dewey's main reasons for the change of psychological vocabulary is methodological in character.[17] The subtitle to *Human Nature and Conduct* is *An Introduction to Social Psychology*, and Dewey points out in the preface that he did not intend the book to constitute an actual survey of the field of social psychology. He implies that his project is an introduction in the sense of a propaedeutic or grounding for social psychology. In *Human Nature and Conduct*, Dewey is concerned to take a preliminary survey of the territory that it is the job of social psychology proper to investigate. The discipline is in need of a new orientation, according to Dewey, because it is still unduly influenced by outmoded psychologies that primarily treat mind as an original, self-contained awareness. By inadvertently isolating mind from the world of social action that forms its natural environment, these psychologies relegate custom and habit to matters of secondary interest, when they ought to be of first importance for psychological inquiry. Dewey conceives of mind as a sort of field phenomenon—that is, a perceptual and cognitive process that arises in the interaction of the living human being with his or her physical and social surroundings. On his view, which owes its original inspiration to Hegel, culture is as much a part of mind as memory or the capacity for introspection.

As an experimentalist, Dewey does not attempt to prejudge the conclusions of scientific inquiry. He offers his views on human nature and society as useful working hypotheses for research and thought about human affairs, and it is in this spirit that his introduction of the concept of impulse should be interpreted. Instinct has become so associated with genetically fixed patterns of behavior that Dewey argues it is misleading to apply it to human conduct, which certainly manifests native tendencies, but tendencies that are expressed in a context that is itself largely the product of habit. Almost inevitably, even the simplest impulses end up incorporating elements of habit.

In a brief article he wrote on animal psychology, George Herbert Mead, one of Dewey's closest and most important collaborators, argued that the plasticity of impulse can be observed throughout the animal kingdom.[18] For instance, a chick's instinct to peck for food can be modified by certain unpleasant experiences, such as biting into a Cinnabar caterpillar. Mead argues that before the chick has actually tasted the caterpillar, it is simply stimulated by the sight of a moving object. The instinctive rejection of the caterpillar that follows upon tasting it actually serves to discriminate it from other moving objects, so that the pecking instinct is directly modified to include avoidance of moving objects with certain telltale markings. Of course, one could maintain that the chick actually learns to pick out Cinnabar caterpillars as identifiable entities in its memory, so that the next time it comes across one it recollects the previous unpleasant experience and decides not to peck. But, as Mead points out, there is little reason to suppose that chicks are capable of such a complex piece of cognition, which would imply a level of self-awareness that we do not normally attribute to them. It is much more likely that the chick's initial reaction to the caterpillar's unpleasant taste serves to directly sensitize it to the sight of future Cinnabar caterpillars.

Another example of the malleability of animal instinct that is even closer to the contemporary household is provided by canine behavior. It is a commonplace today among dog trainers that the high degree of sociability in the species stems from instincts that were originally adapted for life in a wolf pack. In fact, the well-trained dog's obedience to its owner is thought to represent a modification of an instinct to submit to the pack leaders, the alpha male and alpha female. According to specialists, a frequent cause of undesirable behavior in dogs lies in the owner's failure to establish alpha authority over his or her pet, and some dogs even end up behaving like dominant alphas!

Dewey treats *the degree to which* human instincts and impulses can be modified as an open question. Although Rieff charges that he is an overly optimistic social reformer, Dewey's position is consistent with his self-proclaimed experimentalism. In the 1929 foreword to the Modern Library edition of *Human Nature and Conduct,* he emphasizes that, despite the important place occupied by nurture in behavior, "there are always intrinsic forces of a common human nature at work."[19] It is not that Dewey denies a contribution to comportment from the side of nature, but rather that he believes that we do not yet know enough to say much about its exact character. By contrast, Freud's theory of the instincts is both more speculative and, at times, downright doctrinaire. Rieff himself points out that Freud's teachings about the fundamental instincts underwent several major changes throughout Freud's career, and Rieff admits in a footnote that "there is good reason for confusion" about this aspect of psychoanalysis.[20] In the same note, he observes that Freud once stated that his views concerning the instincts were the "most incomplete part" of the psychoanalytic project. Indeed, Freud appears to have even had some insight into the highly speculative nature of some of his pronouncements about the instincts. In his

New Introductory Lectures on Psychoanalysis, he makes the surprising confession that, "The theory of the instincts is so to say our mythology. Instincts are mythical entities, magnificent in their indefiniteness. In our work we cannot for a moment disregard them, yet we are never sure that we are seeing them clearly."[21] Given Freud's own skepticism toward this facet of his brainchild, why did he retain it as the very foundation of psychoanalysis?

The answer probably lies in Freud's positivist dream of explaining mental phenomena in the language of neurophysiology. In the nineteenth century the concept of energy constituted the natural point of entry for such a scientific reduction. It seemed clear enough that the body served as a sort of steam engine for the mind, and Freud assumed that a sufficiently scientific psychology would be able to analyze mental life in terms of the generation, conversion, distribution, and allocation of psychic energy. Hence he introduced distinctions between "free," "bound," and "cathetic" energy into the psychoanalytic vocabulary. In this mental economy the fundamental drives play the role of powerhouses, providing energy for the conscious processes. Although his theory has the virtue of stipulating a unity between mind and body, it does not go very far toward explaining what causes various mental events. In fact, its physiochemical orientation tends to draw attention away from the semantic dimension of mind that Dewey believes is the key to understanding so much of human behavior. It is interesting to note that the cognitive psychology of our own day, which certainly cannot be accused of ignoring the role of neurophysiological factors in mentation, has been able to make impressive progress without overly concerning itself with the issue of mental energy.

As we have seen, Rieff argues that Dewey reduces the standard for evaluating mental health to a sort of latter-day version of utilitarianism, in which psychological well-being depends upon a preponderance of pleasure over pain. Indeed, Rieff includes him in a tradition of intellectual liberalism that he traces to Jeremy Bentham, arguing that Dewey's major innovation to "liberal psychology" was to replace instinct with social organization as the major curb on the "perfectibility of human nature."[22] This close identification of Dewey's ideas with those of Bentham are surprising given that *Human Nature and Conduct* contains an extended criticism of utilitarianism. Dewey's critique stretches over several chapters and is probably the most detailed refutation of utilitarianism to be found in his writings, including his contribution to the *Ethics.*[23]

Although Rieff charges that Dewey attempts to place human nature on a hedonistic basis, the latter explicitly rejects hedonistic psychology. On Dewey's view, it is inaccurate to portray human behavior as primarily comprised of efforts to procure the pleasant and avoid the painful, because such a model inevitably oversimplifies the complex interplay of impulse, habit, and deliberation. The toddler who wreaks havoc in its mother's jewelry box does not do so *in order* to secure whatever pleasure is at hand, but because it is responding to a set of visual and tactile stimuli with a native impulse to manipulate and investigate its surroundings. That such exploration is usually enjoyable to the toddler cannot be denied, and the pleasure afforded by playing with the jewelry can serve to reinforce similar activity in the future. Nonetheless, the child's original act was spontaneous and impulsive, and pleasure was merely an accompaniment to the accomplishment of the action. The toddler's attention is not on its experience of pleasure, but on the baubles that awoke its curiosity in the first place.

In the adult, for whom we can normally assume that habit holds greater sway over impulse than in the immature, the shortcomings of the hedonistic psychology are even more evident. The exercise of most professions, for instance, demands its pound of self-denial, tedium, and routine. Yet habits can serve to lighten the burden of even the most onerous chore because, once well established, they have an impulsive force all their own. The teacher marking student papers may find the task disagreeable but nevertheless strive to do it well out of a firmly settled attitude of professionalism. If such a conscientious grader were challenged to justify his or her hard work, the rationale would likely include the assertion that a carefully marked essay with ample comments can benefit the student. In fact, we can readily imagine that our diligent teacher, having just completed a stack of papers after a long day of grading, feels a sense of accomplishment. The grading itself was monotonous and time-consuming, but the instructor did something worthwhile for his or her pupils. The psychological hedonist might object to this description by claiming that the sentiment of gratification for a job well done *is* the hedonistic payoff whose prospect originally served to motivate the activity of grading. If this were so, however, then how are we to explain how the rational agent came to choose grading over a myriad of other acts, like watching TV, that were potentially promising sources of pleasure?

Since Mill, a popular line of argument among utilitarians has been to acknowledge that pleasures can differ not only in quantity but also in quality, and then to assert that whatever activity was actually chosen by a given individual was the one characterized by the highest pleasure as evidence for psychological hedonism. In addition to begging the question, this argument misses the point. In other words, we can grant Mill's assertion that individual pleasures have different qualities without committing ourselves to psychological hedonism. The teacher may feel nobler for having spent the day working rather than lounging in front of the TV, but this sentiment is largely due to the instructor's belief that he or she has really done something useful that will help others. Insofar as the act was undertaken reflectively, it was performed to affect a change in the real world, and not just in order to secure pleasant feelings. It is perfectly conceivable that our painstaking grader may decide, after the fact, that although the grading involved a good deal of drudgery, it was worthwhile.

In *Human Nature and Conduct*, Dewey specifically criticizes the main premise of psychological egoism—namely, that self-interest constitutes the universal motive for human action.[24] Since psychological hedonism is closely related to psychological egoism, Dewey's argument against the former can be applied, with some relatively minor modifications, to the latter. Contra egoism, Dewey points out that simply because selves must act as selves does not prove that all human acts are self-interested. Since actions are always undertaken by individuals, through instigating action toward a particular end the actor is seeking to achieve or maintain a given state of affairs for which there is a corresponding desire. The fallacy of egoism, according to Dewey, is to hold that because every intentional act aims at the satisfaction of a desire formed by some self, all intentional action is motivated by self-interest. By a linguistic sleight of hand, the myriad distinctions between the deeds of sinners and saints suddenly vanish. Socrates is placed on equal moral footing with Stalin, and what is commonly meant by describing an act or person as "self-interested" is lost. If Socrates was just as bent as Stalin on satisfying his personal desires, weren't their motives ethically equivalent?

Yet it seems evident that we do make a meaningful distinction when we describe some forms of behavior or character types as "self-interested" as opposed to others. Consider our earlier example of two different styles of family vacation. One couple organizes a vacation that primarily interests them, with little regard for what their children would actually like to do. They assume that their young share their tastes, or, if they don't, that they should, and rationalize that the trip will have pedagogic value. The other couple makes an effort to include their children in the process of planning the vacation, and also takes pains to do activities that appeal to the children even if they are of little direct interest to the adults. Wouldn't we normally wish to describe the conduct of the first couple as more self-interested than that of the second, and wouldn't such a description be meaningful?

Similar considerations hold for psychological hedonism. Since waking life is characterized by purposeful activity, and since such activity invariably aims at the satisfaction of some sort of desire had by a self, this school reasons that all conduct aspires to obtain pleasure or avoid pain. It does this by supplementing psychological egoism with a premise to the effect that satisfaction must entail either the presence of pleasure or the absence of pain. In this variant of egoism, it is now the term "pleasure" which is distorted to the point that its new meaning would strike the average English speaker as alien. The category of the enjoyable becomes so broad that all acts of continence or self-denial, which we generally think of as entailing the renouncement of some form of pleasure, turn out to be hidden sources of pleasure themselves. So we are supposed to believe that the smoker who is trying to quit and in the throes of nicotine withdrawal is also experiencing pleasure. Though we can certainly recognize that the smoker's desire to quit is satisfied as long as he or she is able to refrain from smoking, what are we to make of his or her self-reported suffering? Instead of whitewashing the mind with enjoyment in the manner of psychological hedonism, it would be more accurate to distinguish between an immediately pleasant or unpleasant experience—say, being on a nicotine high or feeling the pangs of nicotine withdrawal—and the more abstract satisfactions associated with projected consequences. Many everyday activities, such as brushing one's teeth or taking out an insurance policy, are performed with future consequences in mind, and potential pleasures and pains are merely imagined. Of course, even the anticipation of future gratifications and advantages often creates a positive feeling, but such affective states are relatively fleeting and weak compared to the states of consciousness engendered by a chemical dependency.

Many decades ago, in a brief essay entitled "Emotion and Instinct," Mead argued that the key to the difference between passions and interests is to be found in the history of human evolution.[25] Drawing on the work of Darwin, he postulates that the basic emotions and desires, such as fear, anger, and sexual arousal, originally developed as elements of primitive acts. He points out that the passions are typically called into play in the phase of conduct that involves the appropriation of the object that has been sought after. Hunger and sexual excitement, for example, are called forth by the proximity of their respective objects. At first glance, anger and fear may seem to run counter to this rule, but Mead argues that they serve to prime the organism for direct encounters with objects that will require fight or flight. The more passionate the action, the more reflex-like and instinctive is its execution. By contrast, interests concern the multitude of intermediate phases of the act that have emerged in human behavior. Gratification must be delayed, but not forgotten, if appropriation or avoidance of the object necessitates a hunt for new means. Surveying the entire sweep of evolution in the animal kingdom, from unicellular organisms to *Homo sapiens*, Mead infers that the development of intelligence accompanied the growth of complexity in behavior. He observes that the degree of intelligence of an organism roughly corresponds to the distance and complexity of the path that lies between it and its food. The passions, he further reasons, served as the evolutionary "reservoirs" for the interests.

Contemporary research in neurobiology has lent support to Mead's views concerning the relation of emotion to interest. In his book *Emotional Intelligence*, Daniel Goleman, a behavioral and brain science writer for the *New York Times*, provides a nice overview of some of the most important recent findings on the neurobiology of emotion.[26] According to Goleman, neuroscientists believe that the appearance of emotional centers in animal brains preceded the development of the neocortex, which is constituted by upper layers of the brain found only in mammals and thought to be the site of higher-level cognition in human beings. In fact, researchers think that over a period of millions of years the neocortex actually evolved out of the emotional regions.[27]

Goleman also discusses recent discoveries about the functioning of the limbic system—the group of subcortical structures primarily responsible for emotion and motivation—that have resulted in a revised understanding of the relation of sentiment to cognition. On the conventional view, sensory information is sent to the thalamus, which then relays it to areas in the neocortex involved in processing sense perception. Once the signals have been sifted for meaning by the neocortex, they are passed on to the limbic system, which in turn provides a response that goes out to the body and the rest of the brain. Although this is still held to be the standard route for processing sense data, new discoveries have revealed a separate system in which the amygdala, a structure in the limbic system, plays a key role. In some instances, it

104

appears that a sort of emergency plan in the brain is activated through signals that the thalamus sends directly to the amygdala. Researchers have found evidence to support the conjecture that in crisis situations the amygdala can initiate very rapid behavior by completely bypassing the neocortex and, in effect, hijacking the brain. While the milliseconds saved by such hijacking could have conferred a significant advantage in the struggle for survival, today the instinctive response may be the mechanism at work in many crimes of passion.[28] In any event, the existence of such an ancient rapid response system in the brain lends credence to Mead's ideas concerning the origin of interests out of the emotions, because it provides neurological evidence for the close link between the emotions and primitive acts. Moreover, as our knowledge of the brain grows more detailed and nuanced through the work of contemporary neuroscientists, the oversimplified nature of the models of mind offered by psychological egoism and hedonism is becoming increasingly evident.

A final criticism leveled by Rieff at *Human Nature and Conduct* remains to be addressed. The reader will recall that Rieff contends that Dewey cannot account for instances of regressive behavior. Specifically, Rieff maintains that Dewey's position as regards cases of disintegrated conduct is tautological, because Dewey understands such behavior to constitute instances of a disturbed psychic equilibrium, and then Dewey explains them as resulting from a disturbance in the individual's psychic equilibrium. As it stands, this account indeed illumines little. However, Rieff's objection supposes that Dewey has proposed a theory of personality, and as we have seen, this was not his intention in writing *Human Nature and Conduct*. If Dewey's treatment of regression is vague, it is because regression was only peripherally related to the book's main mission, which was to provide a working theoretical framework or orientation for the psychological sciences and, more generally, for thinking about human affairs. Dewey's propaedeutic does not, of course, preclude a more detailed account of regression. As we shall see in a subsequent chapter, Karen Horney offers such an account as part of a personality theory whose underlying assumptions are ultimately much more Deweyan than they are Freudian.

Habit

The crucial fact of human life that has been assiduously elided by the psychologists of instinct, on Dewey's view, is the cultural or social dimension of human deportment. The evolutionary process that involved the transfer of behavior from a genetic to a cultural funda-ment left humankind with an unprecedented degree of malleability in its basic urges and strivings. Distilled into the individual member of the species, culturally transmitted custom appears as habit, and the vast majority of our behavior involves habit to some degree. In *Human Nature and Conduct*, Dewey provides the following defini-tion for "habit":

> The word habit may seem twisted somewhat from its customary usage when employed as we have been using it. But we need a word to express that kind of human activity which is influenced by prior activity and in that sense acquired; which contains within itself a certain ordering or systematization of minor elements of action; which is projective, dynamic in quality, ready for overt manifesta-tion; and which is operative in some subdued subordinate form even when not obviously dominating activity. Habit even in its ordinary usage comes nearer to denoting these facts than any other word. If the facts are recognized we may also use the words attitude and disposition.[29]

On Dewey's understanding, habit includes unconscious and subcon-scious processes. He stresses that habits are dynamic and projective, and that their influence on conduct extends far beyond their overt manifestations. Habit literally pervades human behavior because it plays a significant role in constituting the context in which human beings act. Objects in the environment are not simply given fully formed to consciousness, but accrue meanings through the vehicle of habit. The individual comes to "know" his or her surroundings by pursuing the myriad activities of daily life.

Even in societies that have formalized education into a specific social institution, the greater part of learning remains informal. Both as children and as adults, we learn by doing. Through interaction with their physical and human surroundings, toddlers learn to walk, talk, and relate to others years before they find themselves in the formal setting of the classroom. The toddler's inborn curiosity—that is, its penchant for exploration and repeated manipulation of its surroundings—has the effect of seeding its environment with meaning. Many everyday objects gradually take on roles as ends or means relative to specific activities. Clad in the cloth of habit, what was formerly a nondescript entity eventually presents itself to the individual as something to be applied or enjoyed, cherished or avoided. The mere sight of familiar objects is often enough to call forth suggestions as to future courses of action.

Through the miracle of habit, things have a tendency to show themselves to us in a way that directly relates them to our interests and aims. They often come to us value-loaded, announcing themselves as potential allies or foes in our various campaigns.

In the old faculty psychology this human contribution to experience was portrayed in terms of the association of ideas, a concept that was somewhat misleading since it implied a sort of dualism between the cognitive and the somatic. In fact, the habits that vest our surroundings with meaning often involve not only particular organizations of ideas and feelings but also certain bodily sets, as anyone knows who has ever learned how to swim or ride a bike. Through the trial and error of everyday experience we discover how much pressure to apply to doorknobs in order to turn them, and how to appropriately modulate our voice in close quarters. Such discoveries are, for the most part, acquired by us more or less subconsciously and remain at the fringes of awareness. Although the environment in which human beings operate is steeped in meanings, many of them never become focal points of interest. Meanings need not occupy the center stage of awareness in order to exert an influence on behavior.

Another unfortunate aspect of the earlier doctrine of the association of ideas was its implication that all meanings are objects of consciousness.

In fact, many of the meanings that shape and guide habit remain in the background of action. A peripatetic professor teaching in an unfamiliar classroom may absent-mindedly sit for a moment atop a desk while he or she is lecturing. Although the instructor has never before seen the desk in question, it has acquired the meaning of a place to sit on the basis of past experience with similar objects. Since the professor is caught up in the activity of lecturing, the meaning of the desk appears in only the most fleeting and peripheral way in his or her awareness. In order to be grasped as distinct entities, objects must occur in situations where they function as vehicles for meanings that point beyond whatever is immediately given to sense perception. To the extent that they come to our explicit attention, the things of this world largely exist for us as the horizon of a mediate or distant future.

In a famous line from *Human Nature and Conduct*, Dewey describes objects as "habits turned inside out."[30] Insofar as the habits in question involve our needs and desires, the perception and understanding of objects is naturally value-weighted. Con artists rely on the fact that often we are only partially aware of the meanings implicit in a given situation. They orchestrate circumstances specifically designed to bring our ulterior motives into play by dangling objects before us that in all probability already exist as goods in our behavior and then propose interpretations of the situation that intentionally leave out explicit reference to our desire for these goods. They rely on the fact that some people will try to achieve the ends in question without clearly telling themselves what they are doing, and without stopping to reflect before acting. In fact, the skilled con artist may even be able to confuse his or her marks by getting them to accept a flattering but misleading portrayal of their own motivations.

The activity of driving a motor vehicle can provide a further illustration of the manner in which habit makes a contribution to the *Lebenswelt* of the individual. It is common knowledge that safe and courteous driving is largely a question of acquiring the right habits. Many drivers fail, however, to form habits that take into account meanings that lie outside of immediate and everyday experience. Such prosaic but nevertheless from time to time deadly violations like failing to use seatbelts or turn signals, speeding, and tailgating often bespeak of a breakdown in the integration into daily conduct of meanings that are distant and only potential. Drivers understand the whys and wherefores of traffic laws but often treat them as abstractions that, beyond representing legal nuisances, have little to do with their own behavior behind the wheel. The more immediate considerations of comfort and convenience, as well as the temptations stemming from aggressive and competitive impulses, are allowed to crowd in and overpower the dictates of common sense and foresight. Actions or situations that should call forth corrective attitudes are engaged in blithely, due to the dampening effect of routine on attention. In other words, poor drivers function in a driving environment that is impoverished or skewed in direct meanings. The good driver does not merely employ a better strategy for driving (i.e., being a proactive or defensive driver): he or she acts within an environment that is richer in immediate meanings that can serve as useful reminders and warnings.

In *Human Nature and Conduct*, Dewey praises psychoanalysis for serving as a corrective to the outdated "psychology of conscious sensations, images, and ideas."[31] The psychoanalytic postulation of the unconscious is tantamount, he notes, to a practical acknowledgment of the central role played by habit in conduct, and of the influence of custom upon habit. By recognizing the significance of unconscious factors in human behavior, psychoanalysis has pointed to "facts of the utmost value" for the study of mind. Nevertheless, Dewey qualifies his praise by observing that Freud and his followers have usually assumed the existence of a "separate psychic realm" that operates independently of habit and custom. In positing such a dimension, psychoanalysis has fallen victim to the influence of the longstanding dualism in the Western intellectual tradition that asserts a metaphysical divide between body and soul, matter and mind. On this view, argues Dewey, individual consciousness is taken as a given whose nature is metaphysically distinct from all things physical. The essence of mind turns out to be an inner "knower" or "mind's eye" that constitutes the seat of consciousness, and the fact of individual awareness is deemed a necessary and undifferentiable starting point for psychological inquiry. Translated into the idiom of psychoanalysis, the logic of this perspective gave rise to the "unconscious consciousness" of hidden mental censors. Freud tended to assume that the "knower within" would see and hear all, if it were not for the covert activities of other mental agencies such as the id and superego. Dewey, however, proposes that an account of mind that starts with the fundamental facts of habit and custom and gives them their due dispenses with the need for positing the existence of dubious mental entities. The phenomena of self-consciousness and reflection lose their implicit claim to an absolute awareness of the inner space of mind, and emerge as aspects of an awareness that is selective and goal-directed. Even casual observation of human beings and animals shows the limited and discriminating nature of consciousness. They have heads that are equipped with sense organs and that can be readily adjusted in orientation in order to focus on select features of the environment.

Custom is the collective form of habit, and the respective food cultures of France and the United States can serve us as an example of the way in which custom, through its translation into the habits of the individual, can unconsciously influence behavior. In the French context, the act of eating is strongly overlaid with social significations that serve to regulate personal conduct by obliging the individual to integrate the satisfaction of his or her own nutritional needs with the satisfaction of such needs by others. The activities of eating and drinking normally call for social interaction. In other words, alimentation carries a normative aspect that dictates that it should ideally involve others. French culture has incorporated eating as its primary catalyst and centerpiece for family life and socializing. Guests are greeted with the mandatory *apéritif,* holiday celebrations and other social occasions are largely constructed around elaborate, multicourse meals that last for several hours, during which dining etiquette is carefully observed; even table conversation often focuses upon food. Unscheduled snacking is a cause for concern, as it is usually held to be indicative of illness, faulty upbringing, or discontent with household meals. Under normal circumstances, eating by oneself is seen as asocial and undisciplined. Attention is paid to the appreciation of food, and culinary criticism is encouraged and constitutes a common topic of conversation. Alimentation and its associated activities—such as shopping and cooking—are experienced less as sheer necessities than as natural parts of the art of living well. Thus, eating exists as a markedly multivalent social act in French culture, an act whose communal and aesthetic values are by no means secondary to its physiological function.

The judicious balancing of nutrition, good taste, and community in French culture leaves relatively little room for the culinary individualism characteristic of the American scene. From within the matrix of French custom, the average Frenchman knows that when it comes to cuisine there is often a clear right and wrong. Although he may not be explicitly aware of everything that he appreciates about his native cookery, when placed in a cultural context in which some of those goods are missing he will readily register their loss. (It should be noted that this description refers to the role of food in *traditional* French culture. Due to the entry of increasing numbers of women into the workforce and the pressures of an evolving global economy, American-style cuisine has begun to find a considerable market in France.)

The American relationship to food is, in contrast to the French arrangement, more utilitarian; put quite simply, Americans set much more store by convenience in eating than do the French. American cuisine is also far less under the controlling influence of custom and so tends to vary much more from family to family. Although the art of dining is certainly present in American culture, it exists more as a hobby for a minority than as a national way of life. Food and its associated values are less integrated into a body of custom and tradition, and, in consequence, the door has been left open for the growth of culinary idiosyncrasy and extremism. The American culinary landscape is full of either/or choices—junk food versus health food, high cuisine versus fast food, convenience versus home cooking, price versus quality, quality versus quantity, and so forth. The relation of the individual to what he or she eats is particularistic: the one is a health nut, the other a junk food junkie, while yet another puts on the airs of a European gourmet.

The chronic American problem of obesity, an issue of public-health dimensions in the United States, is arguably related to American cultural laxness concerning eating habits. In the absence of dominant cultural practices, with their sophisticated complex of goods and standards, tastes tend to sink to the lowest common denominator. Americans are generally at more liberty than the French to snack and to decide how, when, and where they will eat. The American overeater is not necessarily aware of how the social environment plays a role in his or her diet, and there is a marked tendency in American society to attribute overeating to personal factors, such as a proclivity for sweets and a lack of self-discipline. Nevertheless, the very technology of food, such as beverage and snack-food vending machines, fast-food drive-throughs, and microwaveable meals, help to make possible a lifestyle in which the activity of eating is readily detached from social interaction. If an individual develops a craving for food as a sort of emotional security blanket or as a substitute for deprivations in other areas of his or her life, there are fewer countervailing forces in American culture than in the French to hold such tendencies in check. In the American context, the desire to eat often calls out an expectation of personal and immediate gratification. Hunger in the French context is more likely to summon dispositions that either inhibit the impulse or channel it into social activities, such as preparing a meal for oneself and others, which in effect would delay the act of eating.

In a subsequent chapter we shall return to consider the unconscious influence exercised by habit and custom on conduct. For the time being, we note with Dewey that "Man is a creature of habit, not of reason nor yet of instinct."[32] The lion's share of meaning that our environment holds for us stems from habit; however, if habit were the only factor in human behavior, we would be little more than automatons. The natural office of impulse is to keep us alive to the present. Indeed, in situations where we confront what is novel and hence unknown, impulse often serves as the forward feelers of action. Instinctive reactions can allow us to forge ahead when our store of habit comes up short. In the absence of any natural tendencies and sensibilities in conduct, the sway of habit would be absolute, and could blind us to important changes in our circumstances. Established attitudes and dispositions would impose themselves mechanically on new situations, instead of bringing the self into the rapport of action-assessment-modification that is characteristic of all true organic growth. Impulse, in short, is the safeguard of spontaneity and openness to experience, without which useful habits would degenerate into outmoded routines. Dewey of course recognizes that impulsive behavior can often be shortsighted and disastrously ill adapted to conditions, and he stresses that the real value of impulse is as a brake on habit. Frustrated inclinations naturally bring poorly functioning habits to the forefront of awareness, and so provide the fodder of reform. Perhaps even more importantly, conflicts between impulse and habit can engender the inhibition of overt behavior that is a prerequisite for reflective thinking.

Intelligence

While Dewey's treatment of human conduct does not include an evolutionary account of the development of mind, it certainly suggests one, at least in broad outline. Instinct dictated the behavior of the most primitive organisms, and, long before the appearance of the first mammals, habit emerged as a way of adapting instinct to better fit the circumstances of the individual life-form. In the human species— nature's habit-forming animal *par excellence*—the multiplication of habits and the diversification of impulses paved the way for the emergence of intelligence, if by "intelligence" we understand a general cognitive capacity for problem solving. The very complexity of human behavior promoted the development of reflective thinking by sometimes inhibiting an immediate response to a given situation, thus leaving the individual hesitant and vacillating, in a state of doubt or confusion. The inhibition of action could result from a conflict between impulse and habit or a conflict between competing habits, or could simply be the product of a habit that failed to function well in a new situation.

Dewey coins the condition of stymied activity "the problematic situation," and sees in it the original stimulus to reflective thought. One of his most elementary illustrations is that of a man striding across a field who unexpectedly encounters a deep ditch blocking his path. Recognizing the ditch as a possible source of danger, the man comes to a halt. The act of walking is frustrated, but the intention that guided the walking remains active, and so serves to initiate a new phase of behavior in which thought plays a key role. The subject must properly assess the nature of the predicament at hand in order to have a reasonable chance of arriving at an effective solution. Is the ditch actually wide and deep enough to make walking across it unfeasible? If a double take confirms the original impression, then the problematic situation graduates to the status of a well-delineated problem—namely, how to cross the ditch—and a search for solutions can ensue.

Dewey's theory implies that the active problem solving of reflective thought constitutes a distinct form of conduct. Although reflection incorporates both impulse and habit, it is neither primarily impulsive nor habitual in character. Unlike impulse, it involves the assessment of various courses of action by imagining their potential consequences. And whereas a habitual activity often requires little concentration on the part of the actor, reflective thought demands our attention because to some degree all problems confront us with what is perplexing or unknown. Habit works well for the tried and the true, but what is genuinely novel requires careful investigation.

Despite the distinctive features of reflective thinking, Dewey rejects the once common belief in an underlying unique faculty or power of thought. Knowing is accomplished through the coordination of various habits, such as those involved in observation, recall, and reasoning. The familiar fact of expertise in so many areas of human inquiry and endeavor testifies to the central role played by habit in human intelligence. The expert has more at his or her command than just a specific body of learning. True mastery implies that the knowledge and techniques of a given field have transformed the perceived environment of the advanced practitioner. Due to the pervasive influence of habit, the expert and the novice experience the same subject matter differently. Identical phenomena are more meaningful to the former than they are to the latter, in the sense that they are richer in relations to the rest of the world. The trained eye perceives a myriad of potential consequences and employments to which the untrained eye is blind. In *How We Think*, Dewey describes reflective thinking as "the *way* the vast multitude of objects that are observed and suggested are employed, the way they run together and are *made* to run together, they way they are handled."[33] Add to this description an awareness of habit's contribution to the constitution of objects in the individual's experience, and we get a better picture of the overall role of habit in reflective thinking.

We have already alluded to the fact that Dewey offers an extended criticism of utilitarianism in *Human Nature and Conduct*. Against psychological hedonism, he proposes the view that deliberation is born out of a problematic situation, and represents an attempt to resolve the difficulty at hand. Choice is not based on a weighing of pleasures and pains, but rather on the effort to find the solution that satisfies the impulses and desires that form the backdrop to the problem. Deliberation proceeds by considering different scenarios and their implications for the various goods that stand to be affected. Choice has a better chance of being reasonable, Dewey argues, when reflection takes into account all the relevant values that are at stake. Note that such deliberation is usually not a rule-guided procedure, particularly when it entails selection among competing goods. Decisions involving the evaluation of values are common in practical affairs, and the particular features of any given situation are so variable as to render any sort of calculus, hedonistic or otherwise, futile. For instance, nearly every student of history knows that although the past can be a good guide to understanding the present, its study at best provides useful tips, and not algorithms, for making contemporary choices. Strictly speaking, history never repeats itself, and every historical situation is just as unique as the individuals who act within it. Our past, present, and future are so fraught with epistemological uncertainty that often we must expend considerable energy merely in order to accurately ascertain the nature of given conditions. In a world in which the straw of probability is replaced by the brick of certitude, something like a hedonistic calculus might be feasible. However, as Dewey points out, in actuality we even have difficulty estimating what will give us pleasure in the future.[34] Enjoyment is so wrapped up with mood, spontaneity, and the unexpected, that our future pleasures cannot be controlled; at best they can be cultivated. Hence, our attention should not be on pleasures per se, but on the conditions that tend to give rise to what is pleasurable and desirable.

Dewey holds that good decisions are generally those in which competing impulses and habits are intelligently harmonized, and that such harmonization often involves the sublimation, redirection, and even transformation of desire. On his view, the evaluation and criticism of inclination constitutes one of the most important offices of reflective thinking. Given his contention that our strongest desires draw their sustenance from the elemental forces of the id, Freud is much less sanguine than Dewey about the human capacity to rationally shape desire. Although the father of psychoanalysis certainly recognizes intelligence as a factor in human affairs, he tends to limit it to scientific and instrumental reasoning. In fact, he conceives of his brainchild as an applied science. Like medicine, psychoanalysis is a healing art, but besides its obvious end of mental health, Freud maintains that psychoanalysis is neutral as regards value judgments, and he urges its practitioners to cultivate an attitude of tolerance and surgical dispassion in treating their patients.[35] While consciousness includes the capacity for careful observation and logical thinking, Freud is skeptical of the individual's ability to consciously mold his or her desires through reasoning and decision-making. For instance, in the conclusion to *Civilization and Its Discontents*, he asserts that "man's judgements of value follow directly his wishes for happiness—that, accordingly, they are an attempt to support his illusions with arguments."[36] Freud's statement appears to imply that all value judgments merely represent various ways of window dressing desire. In a private conversation with his student Theodor Reik, Freud once even voiced the belief that in issues involving deep-seated desires, reason should bow to the unconscious.

Reik recounts that one evening he accidently encountered his teacher on Vienna's Ringstrasse, where the latter was taking his daily walk. At the time Reik, a young man of twenty-five, was struggling with some important life decisions, and he asked Freud for advice. According to Reik, Freud offered the following:

> I can only tell you of my personal experience. . . . When making a decision of minor importance, I have always found it advantageous to consider all the pros and cons. In vital matters, however, such as the choice of a mate or profession, the decision should come from the unconscious, from somewhere within ourselves. In the important decisions of our personal life, we should be governed, I think, by the deep inner needs of our nature.[37]

While there is certainly something to be said for taking one's intuitions seriously, the sentiment that Freud expresses in Reik's recollection goes beyond this bit of common sense. In the cited passage, Freud implies that critical thinking has little to contribute to those private issues about which we care the most. The best we can do, in such instances, is to be attuned to the demands of our unconscious.

Freud notwithstanding, the intelligent reconstruction of ends is one of the modern hallmarks of emotional maturation and growth in character, and becoming an adult in the moral sense of the term always involves a reordering of values. In many traditional societies the major transitions in the life cycle are accompanied by rites of passage. Some of the most dramatic changes undergone by the individual call forth a communal response, and his or her reactions are channeled into the socially approved forms of ritual. In the rite of passage, ceremony and symbolism serve to create a stage for a sort of structured psychodrama in which the involved parties can find both a vehicle for the expression of their feelings and a technique for dealing with change. Strong emotions, such as grief or anger, that could be socially disruptive are provided with an outlet and, indeed, actually stimulated into a controlled enactment of real life. Many rites and ceremonies are, in fact, cathartic. Aristotle used "catharsis" to describe the purgative or purifying effects of tragedy on theatergoers, but the term originally had medical and religious connotations. There is some evidence that Greek drama originated in the context of religious festivals, and, given the presence of dramatization in all ritual and ceremony, this would not be surprising. The Greek creation of drama may well have represented an elaboration and intensification of the elements of play-acting and catharsis already present in ritual.

Even in modern societies, ceremonies such as weddings and funerals have retained many of their traditional functions and continue to assist individuals in negotiating the difficult transitions often imposed by marriage and death. The sublimation and redirection of desire, which Dewey sees as a hallmark of good decision-making by an individual, has its collective parallel in the wedding ceremony. The many customs and local practices regulating events before, during, and after the celebration announce the public interest of the wedding. Much of its contemporary value is as a rite of passage that provides the bride and groom with new social roles, symbolically bringing to a close that phase of life associated with being single. Although the couple's choice to marry is deeply personal, by so choosing they endow their relationship with a new legal and public status. There is much in the traditional wedding ceremony and marriage customs that promotes the adoption of the roles of husband and wife: the act of taking vows before assembled families and friends, the wearing of wedding bands, the change of last name, and so forth. Part of the value of such traditions is that they involve the community in the change of status, which in turn can facilitate the transition to the new role. The enactment of social roles does not take place in a vacuum, and the expectations of others toward us as role-bearers generally exercises an influence over how we fulfill our various offices.

In traditional societies the pattern of culture often provides for at least a partial integration and harmonization of the individual's desires. Where change is the exception to the rule, and the makeup of society relatively homogenous, the fate of the present generation will often follow the same muster as that of those bygone. Such conditions are conducive to the development of customs that shepherd the individual through life's various crossroads. In the modern setting, where different cultural traditions exist side by side, and social subsystems have emerged that function according to their own logic, the individual must often face role transitions and the adoption of new ends with little or no assistance from custom.

The explicit backdrop to the social psychology Dewey sketches in *Human Nature and Conduct* is the modern social order. While habit, impulse, and intelligence certainly exist as aspects of individual behavior in all cultures, it is only in complex societies that a significant proportion of the population takes prevailing customs and social relations as objects of reflection and criticism. Customary morality becomes reflective when intelligence is employed to evaluate the ends of custom and tradition, instead of just serving as an instrument to their realization. Rather than primarily being an academic exercise, the analysis and criticism of custom within modern society is a practical necessity created by contradictions and inconsistencies that confront individuals living within the prevailing social order. Unlike their primitive counterparts, modern civilizations do not manifest one clearly delineated cultural pattern. Under an advanced division of labor, social systems are maintained by conscious design for certain express purposes, and so constitute distinct spheres of activity that function with a considerable degree of autonomy from the general cultural heritage. In addition, modern societies have often absorbed different ethnic groups and incorporated cultural elements from other civilizations via commerce and conquest. Since complex societies are highly stratified, there are usually significant cultural differences between the various social classes. The complex interplay of these factors means that even specific social institutions often combine a wide variety of attitudes and beliefs. For instance, in most Western societies family life is conducted under the influence of local traditions, class mores, popular religious and ethical doctrines, and the various possibilities and constraints created by material conditions and legislative decree. The interaction of these manifold elements often results in a conflict between goods or norms. To cite a contemporary example, many people now marry partners who bring offspring from a previous relationship into the new household who are already adolescents or young adults. When the time comes for the stepchild to leave home, the stepparent may be confronted with deciding how much financial assistance he or she should provide for the young adult's continued schooling and living expenses. Monetary value must be weighed against the goods and duties associated with parenthood. Insofar as the stepparent tries to accurately gauge what is at stake, and to reach a solution that best satisfies the various values in play, the choice is a moral one. Moral conscience is born out of a conflict of norms, goods, and interests in which the individual must act as referee.

In simple societies, few occasions for moral deliberation arise because their members have little opportunity to cultivate interests that run counter to the groove of custom. The lack of differentiation in the primitive setting means that most social activities are integrated into the general cultural pattern. One and the same activity will often serve multiple ends. The classic illustration of primitive multitasking is mythology, which combines storytelling, cosmology, and ideology. At the risk of somewhat abusing a contemporary expression, myth is a jack-of-all-trades and master of none. Alternatively—and perhaps more to the point—from the modern perspective mythology fulfills all of these functions in the most vague and partial of fashions, albeit with a mix of emotional intensity, pageantry, and communal sentiment that is hard to convey in textbook accounts.

Of course, primitive cultures are not all integrated to the same degree, a point long ago established by the cultural anthropologist Ruth Benedict in her well-known *Patterns of Culture*.[38] However, even in primitive societies that lack a central leitmotif, and that simultaneously promote inconsistent values, reflective morality will find little foothold. In the primitive context there is no clear distinction between means and ends. Means are not sanctified solely or even primarily due to their instrumental worth, but mainly because they are part of "the way things are done," and are intricately enmeshed with goods that individuals feel to be fundamentally important. Social differentiation encourages the growth of instrumental reasoning, and, where the division of labor is sufficiently advanced, means and ends become distinct entities within the behavior of role players. In highly differentiated activity systems, evaluations of people tend to concentrate on the fulfillment of allotted functions, and not on the whole person, as is typically the case in particularistic societies where roles and audiences overlap. "There is no greater enemy of effective thinking," Dewey notes in *How We Think*, "than divided interest."[39] Squarely placing individuals before the demands of a particular task or set of tasks has the effect of crystallizing instrumental reasoning.

118

Within the context of a highly differentiated social system the individual also often has the opportunity to develop and expand a new set of motives. Absent a social environment that in some way corresponds to and nourishes an individual's desire, be it even for such perennial favorites as riches, fame, or power, the aspiration will gradually wither and eventually die. The "lead us not into temptation" of the Lord's Prayer is a frank acknowledgment of the fact that the most powerful stimulus to any desire is an actual opportunity to satisfy it. Members of advanced societies live in a social world that is home to an excess of goods, in the sense that no one person can pursue them all, and often the choice of one entails renouncing another. The life of adventure usually includes a substantial degree of discomfort and uncertainty, and those who strive to come out on top in their chosen field or profession must normally be willing to sacrifice time with friends and family. At best, the individual can carefully pick and choose among possible ends, examine their respective merits and drawbacks, and make personal assignments of relative weight. Insofar as such choices are reflective, they are moral, because they determine the framework of ends that informs the individual's social interactions. Especially as regards the impact of personal decisions upon others, we speak of conscience, and in the next chapter we turn to examine what this term implies.

Notes

1. Morton Levitt, *Freud and Dewey on the Nature of Man* (Westport, CT: Greenwood Press, Publishers, 1960), 156.
2. See, for example, Martin E. P. Seligman, "The Effectiveness of Psychotherapy: The *Consumer Reports* Study," *American Psychologist*, December 1995, 965–974.
3. Willard Van Orman Quine, *Word & Object* (Cambridge, MA: The M.I.T. Press, 1960), 22.
4. Horney, *New Ways in Psychoanalysis*, 185.
5. Ibid., 7.
6. The case for the critical influence exercised by Horney's self-analysis on her personality theory is convincingly made by Bernard Paris in his *Karen Horney: A Psychoanalyst's Search for Self-Understanding* (New Haven, CT: Yale University Press, 1994).
7. Ibid., 178.
8. *Evolution, Program 1:Darwin's Dangerous Idea*, a co-production of the WGBH/NOVA Science Unit and Clear Blue Sky Productions (Boston: WGBH Boston Video, 2001).
9. John Dewey, *The Later Works*, 1925-1953, Vol. 8: 1933, Essays and *How We Think*, Revised Edition, ed. Jo Ann Boydston (Carbondale, IL: Southern Illinois University Press, 1989), passim, Chapter 5: "The Process and Product of Reflective Activity: Psychological Process and Logical Form."

10. John Dewey, *Types of Thinking, including A Survey of Greek Philosophy*, trans. and ed. Robert W. Clopton and Tsuin-Chen Ou (New York: Philosophical Library, 1984), 114–116.

11. John Dewey, "From Absolutism to Experimentalism," reprinted in John Dewey, *On Experience, Nature, and Freedom: Representative Selections*, ed. Richard J. Bernstein (Indianapolis, IN: Bobbs-Merrill, 1960), 14.

12. Sigmund Freud, *An Outline of Psychoanalysis*, trans. James Strachey (New York: W. W. Norton, 1949), 19.

13. See, for example, the entries under *instinct* and *pulsion* in Jean Laplanche and J.-B. Pontalis, *Vocabulaire de la psychanalyse*, 3rd ed. (Paris: Presses Universitaires de France, 2002).

14. Philip Rieff, *Freud: The Mind of the Moralist*, 3rd ed. (Chicago: The University of Chicago Press, 1979), 30–34.

15. Ibid., 33.

16. Ibid.

17. It is also worth noting that in *The Principles of Psychology*, which imparted a considerable impetus to Dewey's thinking, William James provides a classification of instincts into three major types of impulse. The influence of *The Principles* can be seen elsewhere in *Human Nature and Conduct*: for instance, in the notion that inhibition arises through competing impulses that, at least momentarily, block one another. Compare James: "However uncertain man's reactions upon his environment may sometimes seem in comparison with those of lower creatures, the uncertainty is probably not due to their possession of any principles of action which he lacks. *On the contrary, man possesses all the impulses that they have, and a great many more besides.*" [*The Principles of Psychology*, vol. II (New York: Dover Publications, Inc., 1950), 393] with Dewey: "Man can progress as beasts cannot, precisely because he has so many 'instincts' that they cut across one another, so that most serviceable actions must be *learned.*" [*The Middle Works, 1899–1924, Volume 14: Human Nature and Conduct, 1922*, ed. Jo Ann Boydston (Carbondale, IL: Southern Illinois University Press, 1988), note #1, 75].

18. "Concerning Animal Perception" in George Herbert Mead, *Selected Writings*, ed. Andrew J. Reck (Chicago: The University of Chicago Press, 1964), 74–75.

19. Dewey, *Human Nature and Conduct*, 230.

20. Rieff, *Freud*, 30.

21. Sigmund Freud, *New Introductory Lectures on Psychoanalysis* in *The Standard Edition of the Complete Psychological Works of Sigmund Freud*, Vol. XXIII, trans. James Strachey (London: Hogarth Press, 1900–1953), 547.

22. Rieff, *Freud*, 33.

23. The chapters in question in *Human Nature and Conduct* are located in Part III: The Place of Intelligence in Conduct, and consist of Chapter 17: Deliberation and Calculation, Chapter 18: The Uniqueness of Good, and Chapter 19: The Nature of Aims.

24. Dewey, *Human Nature and Conduct*, 94–96.

25. First published posthumously in George Herbert Mead, *Essays in Social Psychology*, ed. Mary Jo Deegan (New Brunswick: Transaction Publishers, 2001).

26. Daniel Goleman, *Emotional Intelligence* (New York: Bantam Books, 1995).
27. Ibid., 9–12.
28. Ibid., 13–20.
29. Dewey, *Human Nature and Conduct*, 31.
30. Ibid., 127.
31. Ibid., 61.
32. Ibid., 88.
33. Dewey, *How We Think*, 156–157.
34. Dewey, *Human Nature and Conduct*, 141.
35. For numerous references to Freud's writings that provide evidence for this interpretation, see Erich Fromm, *Die Gesellschaft als Gegenstand der Psychoanalyse: frühe Schriften zur analytischen Sozialpsychologie*, Hrsg. von Rainer Funk (Frankfurt am Main: Suhrkamp Verlag, 1993), 41–43.
36. Sigmund Freud, *Civilization and Its Discontents*, trans. James Strachey (New York: W. W. Norton & Co., 1961) 92.
37. Theodor Reik, *Listening with the Third Ear: The Inner Experience of a Psychoanalyst* (New York: Farrar, Straus and Company, 1949), vii.
38. Ruth Benedict, *Patterns of Culture*, 223–228.
39. Dewey, *How We Think*, 137.

4

Conscience as Individual Judgment

Imagine being an employee in a poorly run workplace, one with a handful of Machiavellian managers who have helped to create a work environment fraught with office politics and intrigue. Furthermore, suppose that the staff includes an assortment of individuals who appear to be morally challenged, in the sense that they repeatedly fail to take a stand when colleagues are unfairly treated or professional standards are violated. For instance, there's the officemate whose compulsive need for affection and approbation makes him a pawn for unscrupulous superiors. He's a smart dresser who prides himself on staying up-to-date on the latest trends in fashion, music, and entertainment, and he's a natural born master of ceremonies who is good at putting others at ease. Witty and vivacious, he makes colleagues and clients feel that he likes them, although privately he disdains them for being so gullible. While he may catch occasional glimpses of his exploitive tendencies and general disdain for the unwashed masses, his self-image as a charismatic and gregarious person prevents him from recognizing evidence to the contrary. He generally takes great pride in his ability to get others to like him and even enjoys manipulating them, although he also scorns such behavior as egocentric and shallow. Moreover, he lacks confidence in his other abilities—which are not inconsiderable—and tends to overcompensate by exaggerating his skill at manipulating others. If he eventually encounters a conflict with his superiors and is sanctioned, he feels completely humiliated, devastated, and powerless. In general he tells himself that it is reasonable to be a good soldier in office politics, since to do otherwise would be to put his job at risk. Although it is true that siding with management in workplace conflicts carries with it increased job security, failure to do so would not necessarily mean loss of employment. Also, it is possible that he could find an even better position elsewhere. Ultimately, his rationale serves to hide from himself his emotional dependence upon the approval and amity of his superiors.

Then there's the ambitious employee who is burning to be recognized and promoted for what she is convinced are her outstanding skills and leadership qualities. She's a perfectionist who maintains a spotless office and prides herself on her meticulous organization, punctuality, and knowledge of company policies and regulations. Once passed over for an administrative position, she has now managed to convince herself that she didn't really want the additional responsibilities that would have come with the move up the corporate ladder. Although she often does not approve of her superiors' decisions, she manages to never be in open disagreement with the powers that be. In her own mind she's not a climber, but a natural born organizer and diplomat who is sensitive to the needs and concerns of both labor and management. A former officer in the military, she likes clear chains of command and believes that an automatic respect for authority is a precondition for organizational excellence and efficiency. On those occasions when she has found the decisions of her superiors to be questionable or even unjust, she has generally rationalized that it is simply not her place to challenge them.

Yet a third staff member is genuinely troubled by the machinations of his superiors and colleagues. He maintains to others that he could easily find employment elsewhere, and, if things ever become too unbearable, would simply quit. However, when confronted with workplace problems that threaten to bring him into direct conflict with others, he will suddenly and conveniently discover reasons for siding with and even assisting those in power. Corrupt superiors are not to be opposed but won over through love, since everything is part of a divine plan. In any event, the bad deeds they do will ultimately catch up with them on a metaphysical plane, if not on our temporal one. He sees himself as serenely avoiding the accumulation of negative feelings and spiritual turmoil, when in fact he is quite scared but has managed to repress the feelings of fear.

In his or her own unique way, each of these individuals is hampered by an underlying personality problem in properly assessing interpersonal conflicts and determining appropriate courses of action. Such personal difficulties are widespread in our civilization and have a direct impact on public morality, yet they have received scant attention from moral philosophers. In an article entitled "The Schizophrenia of Modern Ethical Theories," Michael Stocker pointed out nearly forty years ago that the leading contemporary moral philosophies tend to divorce their study of values and reasons from a consideration of personal motives and moral character.[1] Stocker argued that this failure to take the motivational structure of personality and character into consideration ultimately constitutes a failure of ethical theory to provide individuals with a genuine moral compass for conduct. Since the publication of Stocker's article, the field of moral philosophy has seen the appearance (or, rather, long belated reappearance) of "virtue ethics," a school of thought that takes its inspiration from Aristotle and his moral psychology of the virtues and vices.

Although the revival of interest in moral character is certainly needed in the study of ethics, few of those writing about the ethics of virtue have paid serious attention to the contribution that modern psychology has to make on the subject. Given Freud's tendency to conceive of analysis as a medical procedure in which value judgments are inappropriate, it is not surprising that psychoanalysis has not been very attractive to philosophers interested in moral psychology. I will argue that Horney's reconstructed version of psychoanalysis constitutes a moral psychology, and one that represents an advance over the moral psychologies of the past. She avoids both the inherent rationalism of the introspectionist faculty psychologies of the Western philosophical tradition, and the anti-rationalism of Freud. I aim to show that Horney's theory takes into account the unconscious and subconscious elements in motivation, yet also acknowledges the individual's capacity for genuine moral choice.

The Legislative Model of Modern Moral Philosophy

In his essay "The Schizophrenia of Modern Ethical Theories," Michael Stocker observes that modern moral theorists have tended to adopt a legislative standpoint.[2] The subject that most contemporary ethicists place under their analytic loupe is the so-called rational agent, whose specific social context is assumed to be irrelevant for the purposes of moral philosophy. This actor is obviously an abstraction who has been divested of all social ties in order to be rendered as generic as possible. Like the conscientious legislator, who works to create a law in the public interest that will apply equally to everyone, the modern moral philosopher assumes that ethics should be universal in its extent. Insofar as philosophy is a discipline based upon logical analysis and speculation, the assumption that it should address itself to all members of the universe of rational discourse is warranted. Such a supposition does not, however, necessarily imply that the ideal *subject* for moral analysis is identical to the rational agent to whom such analysis is addressed. Unfortunately, moral theorists have not always observed this distinction.

A human being entirely divorced from his or her social and cultural context is, of course, a human being lacking in both an identity and the resources required for constructing one. The contextless rational agent represents a considerably impoverished version of the average self, since it is deficient in normal human interests, motives, and aspirations. Stripped of loves and loyalties, it constitutes such a minimal version of the self as to be asocial, and one might well wonder what led it to have such a distinguished career as the ideal specimen of ethical analysis.

An important clue to the origin of the rational self in moral theory is contained in Stocker's observation about the legislative orientation of modern moral philosophy. The unstated—and usually unacknowledged—backdrop to the birth of the rational agent is the emergence of the modern social order. Stocker himself makes this connection, noting that the legislative orientation, with its emphasis on duty and its legalistic conception of morality, was indicative of "a time of diminishing personal relations; of a time when the ties holding people together and easing the frictions of their various enterprises were less and less affection; of a time when commercial relations superseded family (or family-like) relations; of a time of growing individualism."[3] While seventeenth and eighteenth century thinkers took themselves to be describing human nature per se, in reality they were largely describing the human condition as it existed in their era, and their conclusions tended to reflect the major social problems of the day. Rationality was essentially identified with the capacity for abstract thinking and the ability to act on behalf of whatever is in one's own interest. As we have seen, the ability to think abstractly is typically encountered in societies of the advanced type and is in short supply in structurally simple social orders. In addition, while what qualifies as being in one's genuine interest may appear to be straightforward, the answer rather obviously depends upon one's worldview, which in turn is largely derived from one's cultural setting, particularly in structurally primitive societies.

The emphasis in modern moral philosophy on the fundamental duties and rights of the individual originated primarily in response to a social transformation that occurred gradually but eventually had dramatic effects—namely, the construction of modern society out of the remnants of the medieval world. In several important respects, the latter would have qualified as a society of corporate order according to the criteria established by Hallpike, particularly during its early and middle phases. In his book *Escape from Freedom*, Eric Fromm offers a description of the medieval social order that clearly exhibits its corporate nature:

> What characterizes medieval in contrast to modern society is its lack of individual freedom. Everybody in the earlier period was chained to his role in the social order. A man had little chance to move socially from one class to another, he was hardly able to move even geographically from one town or from one country to another. With few exceptions he had to stay where he was born. He was often not even free to dress as he pleased or to eat what he liked. The artisan had to sell at a certain price and the peasant at a certain place, the market of the town. A guild member was forbidden to divulge any technical secrets of production to anybody who was not a member of his guild and was compelled to let his fellow guild members share in any advantageous buying of raw material. Personal, economic, and social life was dominated by rules and obligations from which practically no sphere of activity was exempted.[4]

In his discussion of corporate order societies, Hallpike notes that identity is mainly a function of the various social statuses held by the individual, and that there is little sense of a self that could be something more than simply the sum total of its social roles.[5] Concerning the members of medieval society, Fromm observes that "A person was identical with his role in society; he *was* a peasant, an artisan, a knight, and not *an individual* who *happened* to have this or that occupation."[6] In addition to the lack of individualism that is characteristic of corporate order, the other key features of medieval society, such as its symbolic underpinning through Christian cosmology, are generally consistent with Hallpike's taxonomy.

By the High Middle Ages economic development had begun to reintroduce elements of a complex social order into Western Europe. The great agricultural revolution of the twelfth century was accompanied by urban growth, the revival of trade and industry, and the return of a money-based economy. On the political front, the High Middle Ages saw the birth of national monarchies, the ancestors of our modern nation-states. Consequently, by the late Middle Ages, significant changes were evident in the structure of Western society. Comparing the modern era to the medieval world, Alasdair MacIntyre observes that

The state becomes distinct from society; in the Middle Ages social ties and political ties have a unity, just as they did for the Greeks, even if the unity of the πόλις were quite different. A man is related to the state not via a web of social relations binding superiors and inferiors in all sorts of ways, but just as subject. A man is related to the economic order not via a well-defined status in a set of linked associations and guilds, but just as one who has the legal power to make contracts. Of course this social process of transition from status to contract is not only slow and uneven, it never takes place once for all. Time and again, different sections of the community experience the shock of the dissolution of patriarchal ties; time and again, consciousness of the free market and the absolute state is sharpened. But in every case, what emerges is a new identity for the moral agent.[7]

By considerably liberating the individual from the constraints of ascription, the transition from the medieval world to modernity created the need for society to find new forms of social control. How was society to harness the unleashed energy of individual initiative and creativity without being torn apart by the appetites and ambitions called to life by the new freedoms? What was to replace the yoke of tradition, custom, and ignorance?

The tentative answer of the philosophers was to replace fear with understanding, and blind obedience with reflective choice. What was needed were arguments to demonstrate to the newly discovered rational agent that it was actually in his or her own best interest to observe at least the most basic moral rules, those without which organized social life would give way to anarchy and chaos. The social contract theorists provided such arguments and, by so doing, played a key role in making the ideas of strict rights and duties central to modern moral philosophy. The ancient Greek conception of ethics as concerned with the good life tended to be eclipsed by the new deontic emphasis, and, in fact, the sphere of ethics was gradually redefined. Genuinely moral issues came to be viewed as those that involve the consideration the individual owes others, or the consideration others owe the individual. Based on the assumption that an enlightened moral code was to provide the modern social order with its basis of legitimation and its guiding light in politics, ethics was primarily identified with rules determining right and wrong conduct. By default, personal choices to which the rules did not apply were not ethical but *merely* personal. From the standpoint of moral philosophy, the new elbow room enjoyed by the modern individual was primarily a private matter without moral standing. This implicit attitude anticipated the explicit stance of late-nineteenth-century liberalism: If an individual's conduct does not directly injure others, then it is none of their business.

In the nascent complex society of the seventeenth and eighteenth centuries, antiquity's preoccupation with character and virtue and vice seemed outdated. Under the conditions of modernity, individuals are called to a wide variety of employments, and what might constitute a virtue in one line of work could be a hindrance in another. The merchant's acquisitive drive would be inappropriate in the clergyman, and the latter's compassion a flaw in a judge or military leader. Indeed, one of the advantages of the market economy over its predecessor was greater flexibility in allowing the individual to find an occupation well suited to his or her particular temperament and gifts. Furthermore, Aristotle's catalog of the virtues and vices presupposes a unity of social life and a common cultural background that proved to be incompatible with the development of capitalism. In its early phase, capitalism transformed legions of agricultural laborers into urban factory workers and created an international market of trade and industry that drew the attention of the upper classes to the world scene, breaking down the mental borders of provincialism. In addition, the relatively rapid pace of social, political, and economic changes in the modern world tended to confound efforts to identify a fixed list of virtues and vices.

The deontological focus of modern ethics and the loss of interest in character set the stage for the separation of morals from psychology. Moral values were assumed to be grounded in a rational principle or law that was the province of philosophical speculation, whereas psychology, qua science of the mind, was strictly interested in the facts of mental life. This divide finds its most influential expression in Kant's philosophy, and he goes to considerable lengths to show that moral judgment has nothing to do with sentiment. Hence, at least as concerns the theory of moral value, Freud unexpectedly turns out to be the flip side of Kant.

In her well-known article, "Modern Moral Philosophy," G. E. M. Anscombe has offered an alternate account for the genesis of this division, tracing it to a memory lapse in the Western philosophical tradition. She argues that the "law conception" of ethics was derived from the Judeo-Christian belief in divine law, and that the concept of a moral absolute—absolute because mandated by God—managed to outlive its original theological framework. The special normative force identified by Hume in the concept of "ought" is actually the vestige of the divine law, *sans* the theological context. On Anscombe's analysis, the reason Hume and subsequent thinkers found the idea of absolute

129

moral obligation associated with words like "ought" and "should" puzzling is because the divine rationale behind the peculiar normative force of such terminology had been forgotten.

Although Anscombe's explanation is ingenious, it is difficult to see why Western philosophy suddenly became so absentminded about its own history. She points out that Protestants had given up the idea of divine law during the Reformation, but of course a powerful and vocal Catholic presence remained in Europe, and even someone with a cursory knowledge of the history of philosophy would have been aware that medieval thought was erected within the framework of Church doctrine (incidentally, in addition to being a philosopher, Hume was an historian). While being incorporated into a divine command would certainly suffice to lend special emotive force to normative language, such incorporation is not a necessary condition for feelings of obligation and awe to be aroused by a cultural injunction. For instance, even in modern, highly secularized societies, the prohibition against incest is capable of inspiring such sentiments in many people.

It is more likely that, as a number of writers have suggested, the is/ ought gap identified by Hume emerged due to the progressive loss of a teleological worldview. For both ancient and medieval thinkers, the universe incorporated natural purposes, and in light of these it was possible to evaluate things in terms of how well they actually performed their native tasks. The rise of modern science led to the demise of the teleological conception of the cosmos, since advances in the various natural sciences—first in astronomy and physics and later in chemistry and biology—replaced the objective hierarchy of beings and purposes with a world of valueless facts.[8] In the realm of human affairs, we've seen that a similar development took place in regard to the gradual breakdown of the medieval system of ascription. Modern moral philosophers found themselves dealing with a rational agent whose identity and social offices were indeterminate. Given such a minimalist version of the self, their problem was one of how to find a basis of motivation in this abstract individual strong enough to produce socially acceptable behavior. Predictably, one such basis was discovered in the capacity for reason, and another in the capacity for pleasure and pain. Kant championed the former approach, and utilitarianism the latter.

As concerns Kant's moral philosophy, Alasdair MacIntyre has pointed out that the categorical imperative does not provide direction to one's life but simply sets one certain boundaries, thus making Kantian ethics well geared to the emerging "liberal individualist society" of modernity.

Kant identifies a moral principle that leaves the individual free to choose his or her social roles and obligations.[9] When he adopts an anthropological point of view, he is in a position to acknowledge the self-interested nature of most human conduct, as when people engage in trade or respect the laws of the land. Such psychological realism, however, by no means prevents him from identifying a genuinely moral dimension within the self that serves to equip society with the rules it needs for the maintenance of its specialized activity systems. Of course, Kant himself denies that the moral law is founded upon any such practical consideration as the upkeep and furtherance of social order, but his attempts to justify the law on purely rational grounds are unconvincing. In a society of the advanced type it would be impractical to try to instill people with specific, context-oriented prohibitions and commandments, because one cannot know in advance the exact nature of the moral agent's future social circumstances. What is needed are guidelines that will guarantee at least a minimal safeguard to the social fabric. Any such principle or set of principles will necessarily take an abstract and universal form, like the Golden Rule, that can be used by any rational agent. It is just such a principle that Kant furnishes with the categorical imperative.

We've argued that it was the emergence of modern individualism that set the agenda for modern moral philosophy, and that this agenda was primarily concerned with the sort of social control necessary for the continued existence and smooth functioning of society. If this "end-of-the-world-as-we-know-it" fear sounds exaggerated or implausible, it is important to bear in mind that revolution was very much in the air in Western Europe during the seventeenth and eighteenth centuries. Nowhere is this more evident than in the case of social contract theory. Hobbes, the father of contract theory, wrote against the backdrop of the English Civil War. The version of the social contract advanced by Locke, his successor, was intended to justify the Glorious Revolution, and Locke's political theory also inspired a number of leading American revolutionaries. Although Rousseau did not live to see the French Revolution, his conception of the social contract exercised a considerable influence over many of its leaders.

Among modern moral philosophies, the two most influential have been Kantian deontology and utilitarianism, and both share in the underlying assumptions of the legislative model. Rousseau's notion of the general will directly influenced Kant's conception of the moral law, and in its earliest, Benthamite version, utilitarianism was primarily intended as a rationale for social and political reform. More importantly, both schools assume that moral judgments involve the application of a general rule to a specific case, and that the primary purpose of ethical theory is to discover the underlying moral algorithm and to determine its proper application. This assumption implies that ethics is a sort of science of morality in which the traditional truth-values of true and false are supplemented with the specifically ethical assessments of right and wrong.

The close correspondence between truth-values and moral values suggested by the legislative model tends to obscure several important differences between them. The former are generally construed as properties of statements that purport to describe a given state of affairs, and so primarily involve belief. Other sorts of values, whether aesthetic, moral, or social, principally involve a stance of approval or disapproval regarding some circumstance. Directly or indirectly, non-epistemic evaluations represent recommendations or exhortations for how we ought to act or for what attitude we should adopt in a given situation. On the other hand, insofar as statements involve descriptions of known states of affairs, their truth-value can be determined by comparing them to whatever relevant evidence is available. Non-epistemic value claims, however, inherently imply an option in conduct or attitude, and enjoin us to elect or avoid a given alternative. There's often "more than one way to skin a cat," that is—more than one way to achieve a certain end—and different paths to the same end frequently have different advantages and disadvantages that need to be weighed against each other in order to determine the best available option. We are also often confronted with the necessity of choosing between competing goods, which likewise requires an assessment of their respective merits and liabilities. Regardless of whether evaluation involves the selection of means or ends, the outcome of such reflection rarely invites description in the strict terms of right versus wrong, since in situations in which the alternatives fall into such a stark dichotomy there is usually little need for inquiry. Selection between competing means or ends is typically a matter of ranking relatively better and worse options. Truth-values, on the other hand, generally involve a more black-and-white determination of descriptive accuracy since they are assessed in virtue of a given state of affairs. There's no corresponding set reality that could serve to evaluate non-epistemic value claims because in their case the decision-making process is undertaken in regard to the future.

The legislative model that informs modern ethical theory has tended to hide from view the relative leeway enjoyed by the individual in finding solutions to some moral problems. Its emphasis has been upon creating a rational basis for public consensus about ethics, instead of on navigating the choices between private goods. Thus, the irony of modern moral philosophy is that it largely ignores the territory of individual conscience and choice that was liberated by the very social order it has often served to legitimize.

We should mention in passing that although the legislative model has tended to dominate moral philosophy in the English-speaking world, it has exercised less of an influence on French thought. Since their classical period in the seventeenth century, French letters have had a marked orientation to a combination of psychological analysis and moral critique. Inaugurated by the sixteenth-century essayist Montaigne, the seventeenth century witnessed the golden age of the *moralistes*, among whom the best known are La Rochefoucauld and La Bruyère. These French writers inherited their genre from Greek and Latin predecessors, and their art consisted in making pithy and often witty observations concerning contemporary mores and character types. The connection between the psychological and the ethical is still directly suggested by the French word *moral* and its cognates, which, in addition to having an ethical sense, possess strong connotations of character and intellect.

Due to their Christian culture and historical situation, the *moralistes* brought a new point of view to the ancient pagan literary form. The Christian virtues of humility, love, and charity provided a rich critical perspective from which to evaluate moral character, since their idealistic nature virtually guaranteed a considerable gulf between theory and practice in an aristocratic social sphere increasingly dominated by secular aims. The *moralistes* were united by their interest in investigating not only the gap between moral ideals and daily practice but also the gap separating the individual's self-image from his or her actual self.

This focus on moral psychology is particularly evident in La Rochefoucauld's *Maximes*, where the author identifies a powerful and largely subconscious force at work in the personality that he calls amour propre. The French term has no exact synonym in English, but in La Rochefoucauld's usage combines the meanings of self-esteem and self-interest. It is the hidden influence of amour propre that dupes the individual into taking his or her vices for virtues, that compels him or her continually to engage in secret calculations to maximize profit to the self in all actions, and that ultimately renders the individual a house divided. As we shall see, La Rochefoucauld's observations concerning amour propre anticipate some of the major themes of Horney's depth psychology, and it is regrettable that his work has not received more attention from contemporary moral theorists.

Non-linguistic Meaning and the Nature of Goods

In the 1997 film "The Game," Michael Douglas plays Nicholas Van Orten, a highly self-centered businessman who has been so successful in his career that he can allow himself the best of everything. The problem is, Van Orten seems incapable of enjoying anything. He moves through splendid surroundings in a sort of tragically splendid state of detachment. His business strategy of cool calculation and control seems to have infected all of his interpersonal relationships. Whether dealing with a secretary, maid, ex-wife, or brother, his wealth inevitably gives him the upper hand; he is the man who is always in charge. We as viewers are quickly led to understand that Van Orten suffers from much the same affliction as King Midas of lore: both men are doomed by their special gifts. Van Orten's fortune gives him so much autonomy from others that he is cut off from the normal give-and-take of human relationships. No one is in a position to tell him the things he doesn't want to hear but really needs to. Although he vaguely senses how empty his life really is, this intuition never rises to the level of genuine insight.

Enter Van Orton's ne'er-do-well brother, Conrad, played by Sean Penn. Conrad's immediate problem is what to give his brother, the man who has everything, for his birthday. Fortunately, Conrad has just the ticket: A gift certificate for something called "the game" run by a company named (blandly enough) Consumer Recreation Services. Nicholas takes the bait, and after a barrage of physical and psychological tests, is ready to play. Without warning, his world begins to fall apart as the unseen personnel of CRS systematically sabotage his highly organized existence. A faulty pen and briefcase that suddenly won't open become preludes to homelessness and even violence against his person. The game is finally pushed to such a point of intensity that Nicholas breaks, losing the last vestiges of his cockiness and self-control: This, it turns out, was the whole point of playing. By being defeated, Nicholas has actually won back his life. The game provided him with precisely those experiences he needed in order to reestablish emotional contact with those around him.

Now one could argue that the game revealed truths to Van Orten of a moral, spiritual, or psychological nature that could not be communicated by means of language alone. Before the scales could fall from his eyes, Nicholas had to undergo a series of emotionally charged experiences in which he was confronted with his own human limitations and dependence on others. The game that was tailor-made for him constituted a sort of modern rite of passage. Is it, however, accurate to hold that the game transmitted truths that could not have been communicated discursively? One's response to this question largely depends upon one's assumptions concerning the nature of truth. Many philosophers within the Continental tradition would presumably be comfortable with the notion of such a non-linguistic truth. For those of us who take our lead from Dewey, however, I believe that the short answer is no. In other words, technically speaking, there are no truths which are non-linguistic, only meanings.

Dewey was particularly critical of claims for the existence of special truths unavailable to scientific inquiry. On his view, such claims often involve a conflation of meaning with truth. Although there are no truth-values without meanings, there do exist meanings for which truth-values are largely irrelevant. In *Experience and Nature*, he writes

> But the realm of meanings is wider than that of true-and-false meanings; it is more urgent and more fertile. When the claim of meanings to truth enters in, then truth is indeed preeminent. But this fact is often confused with the idea that truth has a claim to enter everywhere; that it has monopolistic jurisdiction. Poetic meanings, moral meanings, a large part of the goods of life are matters of richness and freedom of meanings, rather than of truth; a large part of our life is carried on in a realm of meanings to which truth and falsity as such are irrelevant.[10]

The sweep of significant experience includes realms in which descriptive accuracy is either irrelevant, or at least not immediately germane. In most affairs in which the aesthetic dimension of experience is dominant and conduct is oriented toward appreciation and consummation, meanings are configured in terms of intensity, depth, harmony, vivacity, and the like. The arts and applied sciences often incorporate such aesthetic considerations into the ends they pursue. However, perhaps the clearest examples of meanings with regard to which the logical categories of truth and falsity do not apply come to us from language. There exist various forms of meaningful speech, such as questions, commands, and exclamations, which are neither true nor false. The swear word I utter when I stub my toe may be inappropriate depending upon who happens to be within earshot, but normally it cannot be true or false in the sense of being consistent or inconsistent with the facts. And while it may be a matter of some debate among educators whether or not there is such a thing as a bad question, logically speaking, there are no true or false ones.

The varieties of meaning are at least as numerous as the different ends toward which individuals act. When knowledge is the end-in-view, cognitive meanings come to the fore that convey information and can be evaluated in terms of truth value. However, as Dewey points out, human life is rife with situations in which truth and falsity are only indirectly pertinent or even largely irrelevant to the involved meanings. A good political speechwriter is concerned not only to convey a message to the audience but also to persuade and inspire it. To these ends words are selected with an ear for their emotive meanings. Church services are just as much geared to make explicit moral values and create fellowship as they are to provide instruction in doctrinal matters. For the musician a note in a musical score derives most of its significance from its placement in the arrangement and the overall nature of the piece to be performed.

Logicians generally agree that only statements—that is, declarative sentences—can be assigned truth-values. After all, something must be asserted about the world in order to be affirmed or denied. Discourse is, therefore, a prerequisite for the existence of truth, and truth always involves a symbolically mediated relation to the world. Truth-value is a primary consideration when we are interested in the prediction and control of a given subject matter, and when we are trying to secure rational agreement with others about some disputed issue. It may be objected that the truth can also be pursued for its own sake, and not simply for the sake of the better manipulation of nature. Although people can, and do, treat truth as an end in itself, if pragmatism is correct, then in practice even the most disinterested scientific inquiry can do no better than to test its hypotheses through experimentation. And experimentation amounts to screening our statements about the world by checking how accurately they allow us to predict and manipulate the subject matter with which they are concerned. Regardless of the specific nature of the phenomena involved—whether they be biological, historical, or literary—when truth is a major consideration, statements are involved that point toward events and consequences not contained in the statements themselves.

This view of truth implies that any given truth can be stated. But what, then, are we to make of the case of Nicholas Van Orten (or, for that matter, of Dickens's Scrooge)? The bald statement of a truth, of course, does not guarantee that it will be understood. The intended audience must have sufficient previous acquaintance with the meanings presupposed in the statement in order to grasp its import. Before their transformational experiences, neither Van Orten nor Scrooge thought of himself as missing out on life. Only by being forced to undergo passionate experiences does each man begin to reevaluate his former conceptions and standards. As Dewey argues in his well-known essay "Qualitative Thought," each universe of discourse presupposes a situation that serves as a backdrop to statement, and that does not appear in the given discourse:

> The situation as such is not and cannot be stated or made explicit. It is taken for granted, "understood," or implicit in all propositional symbolization. It forms the universe of discourse of whatever is expressly stated or of what appears as a term in a proposition. The situation cannot present itself as an element in a proposition any more than a universe of discourse can appear as a member of discourse within that universe.[11]

A scholarly discussion of the different uses of light by French impressionists will probably hold little meaning for the congenitally blind. Truth involves a relation between discourse and the non-linguistic or extra-linguistic world that can only be pointed to through the use of symbols.

Many of the difficulties in the theory of meaning stem from the assumption that linguistic meaning encompasses all genuine forms of meaning. Linguistic meaning, however, is a highly refined form of meaning, and taking language as the point of departure for an explanation of meaning unnecessarily obfuscates the subject. As in the biblical account, nature is made to appear wholly dumb, blind, and directionless until humans bestowed significance upon their surroundings through the act of naming. The emergence of the spoken word is left seeming miraculous and mysterious, an event for which nature was completely unprepared. Although philosophers have often treated meaning exclusively as a sort of linguistic entity that adheres to words, Dewey understood that the world was meaningful for many different animal species long before our ancestors first began to confer names on it. In fact, the human discovery of language could only have occurred in an environment that was already replete with meaning.

The very recognition of objects as specific, enduring entities distinguishable from the environment in which they exist imputes characteristics to them that exceed what could be given in a world of pure qualia. In the lower life-forms, such as the earthworm, the environment is probably experienced largely in terms of relatively unembodied or simple qualities such as darkness and light, wetness and dryness. More complex life-forms, like mammals, are able to perceive and act toward objects such as prey, predators, and offspring. Because the perception of an object implies a background from which it is distinguished, there can be no object without a context. Hence, the object arises in a world of relations. The perceptual and mnemonic organization of phenomena into objects that can be at hand or absent allows complex organisms to operate in a present experience that includes a near future. From a biological standpoint, time emerges as the medium in which objects subsist. Object-oriented conduct is intentional, at least in a rudimentary sense. Being able to act toward a specific goal or end is what introduces the dimension of meaning to existence. *A thing or event is meaningful insofar as it serves as an indication or instrumentality for something else not immediately given in perception.* Things become significant to the extent that they are incorporated into the organism's behavior. The house cat on the prowl is especially attuned to sights, sounds, and smells which could serve as indications of suitable quarry. Once it has hit upon a clue of something worth stalking, the cat displays behavior that is obviously exploratory in nature: it may narrow its search, attempt to flush out its prey by batting about with its paws, lie motionless in ambush, and so forth. Granted, the cat cannot abstractly exhibit its surroundings to itself in the medium of language, but its environment is nevertheless meaningful to it.

In our species, of course, the constitution of objects through habit and memory is powerfully supplemented by language. Consider, for example, the different experiences had by a human being and a chimpanzee gazing at the full moon. Visually, of course, both gazers initially have similar experiences, though the moon is so much richer in meaning for the human that even his or her simple act of looking may take on characteristics quite different from those of the chimpanzee's stare. What begins as a spontaneous glance on the part of the human may become an intentional second take in an attempt to determine if the moon is completely full, or to distinguish its largest topographical features. Such searching behavior is based on the knowledge that the lunar phases are cyclical and that the lunar surface is marked by craters, knowledge that is a cultural artifact and whose medium is language.

Through language experience is seeded with symbolic meanings that permit the mapping of a great variety of different relations between things. Via the atlas of language, the world, which is never present as a totality in firsthand experience, can be constituted as an abstract object and given general contours. Like a lost stranger in a strange land who suddenly chances upon a useful map, the individual endowed with language is equipped with handy abstractions that can be employed to synthesize the natural series of local and often fragmentary experiences into a greater and more meaningful whole. For the disoriented wanderer with his or her newfound map, what had been a nondescript hill becomes a landmark full of indications for his or her actual location. Likewise, for travelers in the universe of discourse, the different groups and relations which can be symbolically labeled lend their significance to that which is immediately experienced, and introduce a greater degree of organization into the transactions that take place between the speaker and his or her environment. Serving as a sort of chart of experience, language dramatically expands the horizons surrounding the linguistic voyager.

So great is the impact of language on human thought and perception that the view that abstract ideas constitute the true reality long enjoyed a considerable following in Western philosophy. Although idealism has taken a backseat to scientific naturalism ever since Darwin proposed the theory of evolution, one of its legacies has been the tendency to privilege mind over matter in theoretical descriptions and explanations. Contemporary moral philosophers have been particularly prone to commit what we may call the mentalistic fallacy, that is, to assume that a phenomenon that involves interaction between a live creature and its environment can be adequately understood by focusing on the mental aspects of said phenomenon. Thus, many discussions of values or goods have tended to treat them as primarily mental entities, thereby cutting them off from the non-linguistic meanings which give them life.

The contrary to this view enjoyed broad currency from late antiquity up to the eighteenth century. Known as the Great Chain of Being, this doctrine asserted that things inherently have different degrees of perfection or being, and so an objective ranking or value that stems from their specific nature. When Darwinism eroded confidence in the Great Chain of Being, the idea that value claims were identical with states of mind proved to be a popular alternative to the old belief. What wasn't physical must, it seemed, be mental. Even as mental entities, values were able to retain their authority as long as they were nested in various forms of idealism, since idealism asserted the ontological superiority of mind over matter. However, with the waning of idealism, this rationale was lost, leaving values as subjective mental states, thus paving the way for twentieth-century emotivism.

As George Herbert Mead argues in his seminal essay, "The Objective Reality of Perspectives," absolute idealism failed to fully appreciate the two forces that have revolutionized the modern world—namely, individualism and experimental science.[12] Hegel's assertion that Absolute Spirit constitutes ultimate reality inevitably tainted the finite self with a certain degree of unreality. In his essay, Mead points out that modern physics has provided indirect evidence for the shortcomings of absolute idealism in the form of the theory of relativity. On Mead's understanding, the new physics shows the impossibility of the main aim of Hegel's philosophy, which was to subsume nature into experience. Hegel's metaphysics relies upon the supposition that the physical universe is dependent upon mind or spirit as its substrate, whereas the theory of relativity reveals that all experience is perspectival. In order to make his case, Mead draws on the work of Alfred North Whitehead, who interprets the theory of relativity as positing a universe that is partially constituted by intersecting time systems. Einstein was able to show that no independent backdrop of absolute space or absolute time exists from which the sum total of nature could be considered. In other words, there is no perspective in the universe that would allow for a God's eye view of the universe. Rather, modern physics conceives of space and time as constituting a continuum, and Whitehead argues that the existence of the space-time continuum implies that nature is stratified into perspectives. Mead points out that these perspectives are as objectively real as the physical phenomena that take place within them.

Mead argues that the traditional dualism between mind and body is overcome by a metaphysics that directly incorporates experience into nature. According to the view he proposes, mind is not distinct from the physical universe but rather constitutes an emergent property that arises within it. Hence, human values are not purely subjective features of an individual's awareness but rather represent characteristics of a perspective or field of experience within nature. This experiential field involves the interaction between the human organism and its physical setting, when the latter is construed in its broadest sense, so as to include the social context. The individual's self-awareness develops through social interaction. Perhaps the most important precondition for the emergence of reflective self-consciousness is language, and language is inherently social, since communication through symbols can only occur if meanings are shared. The keystone of Mead's social psychology is his insight into the mental mechanism of all verbal communication: In order to be an effective vehicle for the transmission of meaning, the significant symbol must arouse the same response in the speaker that it calls forth in the listener. Thus, the very act of speaking embodies the notion of listening, and the speech act is guided by the response that it engenders in the speaker. The shared meanings presupposed by language are born within the common life of the group, and a mind informed by language is one that is inherently intersubjective. Hence, the experiential field, or, to borrow an older term from German, *Lebenswelt*, is both interactive and intersubjective.

In the essay "The Nature of Esthetic Experience," Mead applies his notion of the experiential field to an analysis of ends or goods. He writes of a "relativity of the living individual and its environment," in which objects reveal traits that correspond to sensitivities in the actor.[13] Things "present themselves" to us in terms of our specific patterns of action and constitute the horizon of the future:

> Physical things are not only the meaning of what we see and hear; they are also the means we employ to accomplish our ends. They are mediate in both senses. They constitute a meaning of all that lies between us and our most distant horizons, and they are the means and instruments of our consummations. They lie in this mediate fashion between the distant stimuli that initiate our acts and the enjoyments and disappointments that terminate them. They are the proximate goal of our sights and sounds, and they are the instrumental stuff in which we embody our ends and purposes.
>
> Thus on the one hand they constitute the hard physical realities of science, and on the other the material out of which to build the world of our heart's desire, the stuff that dreams are made of.[14]

Mead's view of ends contrasts sharply with the venerable philosophical tradition that would locate treasured goods in a supernatural or transcendent realm. By elevating such goods above experience, transcendental doctrines tend to stultify them, since once so ensconced these goods are effectively cut off from future change and development. Another consequence of this metaphysical promotion is that ends or goods are sundered from their non-linguistic meanings and so tend to wither into dry abstractions and vague generalities, which belie the actual richness of experience.

Mead's metaphysical and epistemological views constitute a standpoint often referred to as objective relativism. As concerns values, this theory clearly exposes the shortcomings of emotivism, the doctrine that ethical judgments merely reflect the individual's affective or emotional state of mind. Emotivism is premised upon the assumption that reality is synonymous with scientific fact, and that the only values with genuine logical standing are truth-values. It discounts the possibility that other value judgments could be rationally persuasive because it privileges the theoretical attitude over all other stances that can be adopted toward the world. Practical and aesthetic intentions, which cast things as means and ends, are not recognized as having any logical worth, and yet the subject matter of many arguments assumes or implies precisely such intentions. Indeed, many arguments even involve the criticism of ends (e.g., as in a debate over the goals of American foreign policy). Although truth can certainly serve as an end of conduct, there don't seem to be any compelling reasons to exclude other ends from critical examination and argument. On the contrary, intelligent decision making, both personal and public, would seem to demand it.

While value judgments often bring the emotions into play, to identify such judgments wholly with affect is to ignore the existence of the non-linguistic meanings that serve to elicit them. Emotional reactions take place in regard to events and objects that are replete with such meanings, and they constitute the subject matter in many practical pursuits and activities. In practices as disparate as wine tasting and stand-up comedy, or bird watching and opera, participants are united by a shared backdrop of meaning, in terms of which ends and standards are formulated. Sensitivity to the relevant goods must often be cultivated. In practices undertaken primarily for enjoyment and appreciation, and in which expertise in judgment is recognized, such acquired sensibility and the corresponding capacity for accurate assessment are known as good taste. Although taste is popularly understood to pertain only to aesthetic and artistic matters, in what follows we shall argue that it in fact enters into play whenever decision making involves the evaluation of goods or values.

Individual Judgment as Taste

Although an equivalent to taste in its abstract sense existed in neither ancient Greek nor Latin, the concept itself was not foreign to antiquity. That this was so is not surprising, given that ancient Greece and Rome were societies of the "transcendent" type according to Hallpike's scheme of social evolution. The increase they underwent in societal differentiation and structural complexity spelled a significant increase in the kinds of goods at the disposal of the individual. The old dichotomies between right and wrong were partially superseded by the predicaments that arose when goods came into competition and conflict with each other. Socrates and his successors inhabited a society whose activity systems had become differentiated enough to permit at least some of its members to pick and choose among different careers and lifestyles.

As Hans-Georg Gadamer has suggested, the ethics of Plato and Aristotle are "in a profound and comprehensive sense an ethics of good taste."[15] Perhaps taste's earliest forerunner was the Greek notion of *phronesis*. Originally associated with thought or understanding, *phronesis* was employed by Plato and Aristotle to refer to what we now think of as practical intelligence, wisdom, or prudence. Like taste, it enables correct decision making in situations for which there are no foolproof techniques or methods for arriving at solutions or judgments. *Phronesis* is an especially important idea for Aristotle, who relies on it as the linchpin of his ethics.

In Aristotle's moral psychology, practical intelligence or prudence constitutes the key intellectual virtue. In fact, Aristotle asserts that it is both a necessary and a sufficient condition to being fully virtuous.[16] He defines it as a reasoned disposition or state that involves the capacity to accurately assess actions as they relate to realizing human goods. Practical intelligence involves correct deliberation about how to achieve the best good available in any situation where two or more courses of action to the same said good appear choiceworthy, but it is not immediately obvious which course is superior. Aristotle understands deliberation to be purely limited to the consideration of means, since he views the various ends of human behavior as fixed (e.g., the goal of the physician is to heal, that of the statesman to produce law and order, etc.). He takes pains to make clear that *phronesis* is not limited to deliberating about what is good for oneself, but also extends to deliberation about what is good for people in general. Hence, those who have this intellectual virtue are good at managing groups, ranging in size from the family to the state.

In his description of practical intelligence, Aristotle stresses that it requires experience, since it involves an assessment of specific conditions. As opposed to abstract disciplines such as geometry or mathematics, whose objects are purely conceptual, the subject matter of practical intelligence includes goods that are concrete features of the human condition. As such, their measure can only be taken in full through first-hand experience. Aristotle refers to the particulars with which practical intelligence is concerned as "objects of perception," and his claim appears to be that as existential entities they cannot be known through language and reasoning alone. Whereas young people can fully grasp the subject matter of mathematics, they lack the requisite experience for good deliberation about the particulars of human affairs. In addition to involving deliberation about particulars, practical intelligence includes grasping universals. Since it is prescriptive and renders verdicts as to what we should do or avoid doing, the universals it incorporates are the set ends toward which humans ought to strive.

Taste in its abstract or metaphorical sense—that is, qua discerning judgment or appreciation—is a relatively modern word, first appearing in the languages of Western Europe during the Renaissance. Its earliest recorded use in connection with an abstract aesthetic assessment was made by the Italian author Filarete, who in 1464 wrote, "I also used to like the Moderns; but, as soon as I began tasting the Ancients, I came to hate the Moderns."[17] The term went on to be closely associated with beauty and pleasure during the next two and a half centuries but was by no means exclusively limited to purely aesthetic subject matter. Gadamer observes that, prior to Kant, taste was generally thought of in relation to morality, and that it represented an "ideal of genuine humanity."[18] Among earlier writers taste was repeatedly employed as a power of individual judgment that led to right decision in various aspects of life. The Spaniard Baltasar Gracián was one of the most influential of those authors who approached taste as a capacity of judgment vital to good living. In *El Discreto* (the gentleman or educated man) (1646), Gracián analyses the *gusto* or taste that characterizes the man of the world. This type of individual achieves his qualification as an *"hombre en su punto"* (as a man who has attained his perfection) through his *gusto*, which guides him to make the right decision in every department of life. *Gusto* is the result of broad experience and of deep and continual introspection. It permits the man of the world to escape his subjective deceptions, to see things as they really are, and to measure their true worth.[19]

Gadamer points out that Gracián made taste the starting pointing for an ideal of social education and cultivation (*Bildung*), which recognized that not only abstract reasoning but also judgment could be nurtured. In fact, on Gadamer's analysis, Gracián's new educational model of the gentleman was intended to replace the inherited, class-oriented ideal of the Christian courtier, which had received its most powerful expression in the writings of Count Baldassare Castiglione. According to Gadamer, it was no accident that the concept of a capacity for discerning judgment that could be fostered through education flourished in the age of absolutism:

> The idea of social *Bildung* seems to emerge everywhere in the wake of absolutism and its suppression of the hereditary aristocracy. Thus the history of the idea of taste follows the history of absolutism from Spain to France and England and is closely bound up with the antecedents of the third estate. Taste is not only the ideal created by a new society, but we see this ideal of 'good taste' producing what was subsequently called 'good society.' Its criteria are no longer birth and rank but simply the shared nature of its judgments or, rather, its capacity to rise above narrowness of interests and private predilections to the title of judgment.[20]

In France, La Rochefoucauld echoed Gracián's notion of taste as a power of judgment treating social, moral, intellectual, and aesthetic objects. Like Gracián, he envisioned a *bon goût* or good taste that transcends the limitations of individual judgments insofar as it correctly estimates the true value of its subject matter. The ability to measure something's objective worth requires a detachment that can normally only be achieved in decisions which do not personally concern the decision maker. The individual who can overcome personal preoccupations to impartially judge all situations is extremely rare according to La Rochefoucauld, owing to the primarily self-interested and emotional nature of human beings.

In his *Delle riflessioni sopra il buon gusto . . .* (1708), the Italian writer L. A. Muratori credits taste with significantly more autonomy than La Rochefoucauld. Far from being rule-guided, taste (for Muratori *gusto*, *giudizio* or *dritta ragione*) is the ability to judge individual situations that cannot be subsumed under universal rules.[21]

During the late eighteenth and early nineteenth centuries taste underwent its transformation into the more restricted aesthetic term we know today. Historians usually trace the word's original association with the "science of the beautiful" to A. G. Baumgarten, although Kant was ultimately responsible for the successful aestheticization of taste. In any event, Baumgarten's version of taste found its most cogent and lasting expression in Kant's *Critique of Judgment*, where it is duly integrated into the Kantian architectonic of mind. It is worth noting that in Hume's thought, which immediately preceded Kant's work and which was to be an important source of inspiration for the Prussian philosopher, taste is still treated as a mental capacity involved in *both* aesthetic and moral judgments.

For Kant, taste pronounces judgments of beauty that spring from indeterminate principles that are inaccessible to examination by reason, but nonetheless universal. Consequently, taste is effectively cut off from reason, in the sense that there can be no objective understanding of the principles informing its judgments. This is not to say, however, that taste's pronouncements express feeling only: Kant clearly rules out such an interpretation by insisting that taste is a function of judgment, which is one of the faculties of reason. On his view, taste can only genuinely operate when extraneous interests do not influence its estimation of aesthetic value, regardless of whether such interests be religious, political, moral, or psychological. Involving a sort of "disinterested satisfaction," taste is a faculty of judgment that deals with pure feeling as distinct from specific, empirical desires. Genuine beauty, teaches Kant, is a type of "purposeless purposiveness" that taste, as a formal and subjective species of teleological judgment, can alone detect. Great artists are guided by an innate genius that allows them to obey the rules which nature gives to art through the free exercise of the imagination. These rules can never be explicitly formulated by means of concepts, and our only real access to them is an indirect one—namely, through the appreciation of great works of art.

In retrospect, Kant's theory of taste, beauty, and artistic genius was well tailored to the art world of modernity, whose general outlines were already clearly visible by his lifetime. For our purposes, the two key features of this world are the emergence of art as an activity undertaken for its own sake and the emergence of the artist qua celebrity. Art as a largely autonomous social institution represents a fairly recent development, and originally artistic activity was so intimately bound up with different social practices and their magical, religious, and political dimensions that it was not conceived of as an independent entity. Indeed, throughout most of its history art was treated matter-of-factly as a servant to various masters, notably the spirit world, gods and goddesses, the city-state, the Church, the aristocracy, and the national state. Works of art typically lent public expression to communal viewpoints and attitudes, and before the modern era official styles, themes, and subject matters set the artistic agenda of the day. Consequently, until the birth of the cult of artistic genius in Renaissance Italy, artists were more often seen as skilled craftsmen than as eccentric virtuosos. Gadamer notes that following the decline of commissioned art, the artist was supposed to enjoy total creative independence, and he observes that the self-consciously bohemian lifestyle of some nineteenth-century artists was the outcome of this quest for complete artistic freedom.[22] Dewey makes a related point when he remarks that modern artists have often felt it necessary to signal their independence from the market by insisting that genuine art is a form of "self-expression" in which the artist remains true to his or her own aesthetic vision. The result, according to Dewey, is all too often a forced type of aesthetic "individualism" that produces self-possessed eccentrics.[23]

Kant's aesthetics allows him to accommodate the modern view that the rules of art are subjective[24] and, at the same time, avoid a thoroughgoing aesthetic relativism by relocating the old teleological structure of the universe to a supersensible dimension where nature's purposes can be felt or intuited, but not conceptualized. Because genuinely good taste constitutes a type of disinterested satisfaction, many—if not most—of the well-known differences of taste that people have in mind when they assert *chacun à son goût* turn out to actually involve conflicts of personal interest and inclination. Furthermore, since the attainment and maintenance of the properly aesthetic frame of mind requires a high degree of self-knowledge and self-discipline, one would expect that the aesthetically competent would be relatively few in number and constitute a sort of natural aristocracy. The cultivation of the fine arts by specialists, such as artists, museum curators, art critics, gallery owners, and private collectors, suggests as much. By making the rules of art non-conceptual and only indirectly accessible through masterpieces, Kant could approve of the essential conservatism of artistic traditions but also make room for occasional innovation at the hands of a Michelangelo or a Mozart. Hence, he indirectly furnished a philosophical justification for the on-going differentiation of the fine arts, and his restriction of taste to the aesthetic should be understood within this social context.

Kant's treatment of taste is ultimately very similar to his earlier treatments of metaphysics and morals. He begins by assuming the truth of a certain class of propositions or judgments, and then proceeds to infer the conditions that make them possible. His first two critiques expose the epistemological conditions that serve as the basis for our knowledge of scientific and moral laws, respectively.

In the third critique he proceeds in the same manner by assuming that judgments about beauty are either correct or incorrect, and he then posits the existence of a faculty of taste that makes accurate aesthetic judgments possible. The dangers inherent to such an ad hoc method are well known. Kant supposes that he is exposing the source for the social phenomenon of good taste in the mind of the individual, when in fact he is taking certain features of a social situation and lending them a parallel existence as a mental faculty. The reason taste exercises an almost purely aesthetic function in his thought is due in large part to the highly differentiated nature of the art world he observes, and to his assumption that this degree of specialization reflects a similar circumstance in human nature. The tidy division of labor that Kant finds in the mind is ultimately based on a teleological conception of nature in which the various mental faculties are the result of an intelligent design. Without the benefit of Darwin's theory of natural selection, he has no reason to entertain the alternative of a less tidy mental arrangement that would be the more likely product of chance and the interaction of blind forces.

Less than a century after Kant's death, Nietzsche revived the robust, pre-Kantian understanding of taste. Although this resuscitated version repeatedly surfaces in Nietzsche's writings, it never receives systematic development, and so generally remains a more or less indistinct sighting on the horizon of his thought. The following citation, taken from *Thus Spoke Zarathustra*, is probably as representative of Nietzsche's idea of taste as any:

> And you tell me, friends, that there is no disputing of taste and tasting? But all of life is a dispute over taste and tasting. Taste—that is at the same time weight and scales and weigher; and woe unto all the living that would live without disputes over weight and scales and weighers![25]

In addition to recovering taste as a general capacity of judgment and choice, Nietzsche regards it as a key aspect of individuality:

> A trying and questioning was my every move; and verily, one must also learn to answer such questioning. That, however, is my taste—not good, not bad, but *my* taste of which I am no longer ashamed and which I have no wish to hide.

> "This is *my* way; where is yours?"—thus I answered those who asked me "the way." For *the* way—that does not exist.[26]

One might assume that Nietzsche would be well disposed toward seeing in taste the individual's ability to reflectively shape and harmonize his or her preferences. Such a capacity could equip the self with some measure of control over the formative influences of nature and nurture, and so represent an increase of freedom. As it turns out, Nietzsche often conceived of taste as chiefly rooted in the unconscious or subconscious: In this sense, taste refers to one's general intellectual and moral disposition as determined by native temperament and physiology. Far from being the product of thoughtful cultivation, taste is principally a non-rational determinant of reason:

> *Changed Taste*—The change in general taste is more powerful than that of opinions. Opinions, along with all proofs, refutations, and the whole intellectual masquerade, are merely symptoms of the change in taste and most certainly not what they are still often supposed to be, its causes.[27]

Given this view of taste, it should come as no surprise that the idea makes its most vital appearance in the autobiographical *Ecce Homo* (Latin for "behold the man"). In this short book, Nietzsche presents us with a highly original—and often quite humorous—synthesis of intellectual autobiography, self-criticism, and psychograph. In the chapter on *Thus Spoke Zarathustra*, he notes that the inspiration for his great "present" to humankind was preceded by, and partially enabled through, an unexpected and mysterious change of taste, particularly in music. Nietzsche obviously construes this personal experience as evidence for his contention that there is more taste in reason than there is reason in taste.

In addition to providing brief analyses of his major works in *Ecce Homo*, Nietzsche sketches a psychological self-portrait that exhibits select details from his private sphere. Through this literary likeness the philosopher intends to equip his future critics with knowledge about his attitudes, habits, and preferences in the trivia of everyday life. By discussing his likes and dislikes in such seemingly irrelevant and prosaic matters as nutrition and exercise, he takes care to reveal the origin and character of his basic tastes. In a letter to Lou Salomé concerning her book about him, Nietzsche was enthusiastic about Salomé's project of interpreting the ideas of great thinkers as the intellectual expressions of their life histories.[28] The attention he pays in *Ecce Homo* to the subtle and not-so-subtle environmental influences upon his own thinking is consistent with his effort to bring reason down to earth from its castle in the sky, and to reintegrate it with the actual processes of life.

Nietzsche's view of taste is the affective counterpart to his epistemological stance. As concerns the latter, Kai-Michael Hingst has made a convincing case for interpreting Nietzsche as a perspectivist.[29] On Hingst's reading, Nietzsche employs the term "truth" in at least three different senses. First, there exists a class of popular "truths" accepted by many—if not most—people, but which are, in fact, erroneous. Secondly, Hingst identifies a group of "truths" that Nietzsche juxtaposes to the popular truths in order to expose them as false. Since Nietzsche's perspectivism commits him to the proposition that ultimately any truth arrived at by a human being is tainted by the limited perspective of the human condition, even these so-called truths are, at bottom, illusions and deceptions, though of a particularly persuasive nature (at least for the time being). Thirdly, Hingst argues that Nietzsche never fully abandoned the idea of absolute truth, although he held that such extra-perspectival verity was unattainable for human knowers. It is his assumption of the existence of this third class of truths—truths that hold universally and eternally—that lead Nietzsche to assert the flawed nature of all human knowledge. Rather than reconstruct his original criterion of absolute truth into something that would better correspond to actual mortal practice, Nietzsche opts for a sort of skepticism.

The truth of the matter is that Nietzsche did not really want to be constrained by truth, regardless of whether it was metaphysical or social and historical in nature. As a champion of free spirits in their struggle for survival among the *hoi polloi*, the prospect of the endless series of vistas held out by perspectivism must have possessed a certain charm for him. Here was indeed a promised land for authentic individuals who were their own philosophical lights. In these highlands the genuinely free spirit was beyond the reach of all authority. Neither tradition, social consensus, empirical fact, nor scientific law could limit the autonomy of the questing self. The true disciple of Zarathustra understood that he could never be a disciple, and in Nietzsche's mind authentic individualism and independence from others were virtually synonymous.

Nietzsche's focus on the inward and spiritual experiences of the self reveals the specific influences of his German cultural background by way of idealism and romanticism. George Santayana coined the preoccupation with subjectivity in German letters "egotism," and gave it the following description:

> The particular theory of egotism arises from an exorbitant interest in ourselves, in the medium of thought and action rather than in its

objects. It is not necessarily incorrect, because the self is actual and indispensable; but the insistence on it is a little abnormal, because the self, like consciousness, ought to be diaphanous. Egotism in philosophy is, therefore, a pretty sure symptom of excessive pedantry and inordinate self-assertion.[30]

Santayana argues that the original inspiration for egotism was provided by Protestant theology, which was subsequently rationalized by the German idealist philosophers. Dewey makes a similar argument in his *German Philosophy and Politics*, pointing out that Luther's theology assumed a world divided into two realms, the spiritual kingdom of the self, and the secular kingdom of society, and that these two realms were given elaborate metaphysical and epistemological expressions in German idealism.

Luther's doctrine of justification by faith alone is based on his understanding of original sin. As a consequence of the transgression of Adam and Eve, he holds that human nature became so depraved that even human will and reason are inexorably dragged into the service of desire, and so into the behest of sin. On Luther's view, the only legitimate source for morality is God's commandments, but, without the assistance of His saving grace, compliance with these laws is impossible. Left to their own devices people are too weak and corrupt to put God's will above their own egotistical desires. In the absence of divine grace, attempts at atonement through good works are doomed to failure, since such efforts are, at bottom, motivated by sinful self-interest. Salvation is accepted, not earned, and can only be had through faith. Because outward actions, such as alms giving, are disassociated from redemption, the individual's acceptance of God's love and mercy becomes a wholly personal and private affair.

Although Luther believed that God expects the good Christian to follow His ethic of love, the reformer also held that this moral code was frequently infeasible in the secular world of lost and all too often vicious souls. Furthermore, Luther viewed government by secular leaders as a divine creation intended to maintain law and order; consequently, he accepted the basic legitimacy of the social and political status quo in Germany, in spite of its injustices and shortcomings.[31] Without at least a minimal degree of social stability, Luther reasoned, it would be impossible to sustain the Church. In light of these considerations, he concluded that Christians, in their various secular roles as citizens and officials, were duty bound to help keep the peace, even if this meant the employment of force and manipulation. Hence, the faithful were to operate with two moral codes: an ideal ethic of love and forgiveness that was to be internalized by the self, and a practical code of law and order for dealing with the public world where egoism, pride, and sin set the agenda.[32]

Dewey points out that among German historians it was virtually a truism that Kant elucidated the philosophical significance of the Lutheran reformation.[33] In drawing a metaphysical divide between phenomena and noumena, Kant was able to undermine the traditional arguments for religious belief in order, in his own words, "to find a place for faith." The result of Kant's critique of traditional theology was to show that the heart of religion was faith, and that although such faith was not irrational, its role could never be wholly devolved to reason. In his ethics, Kant provided a philosophical apology for Luther's two moral realms by revealing an ideal moral law that the self legislates to itself of its own accord. He distinguished conduct willed in virtue of such a law from behavior based on appetite, desire, or the prudent calculations of self-satisfaction. As Dewey remarks, the "inner realm" of rational ethics turns out to be ideal and free, whereas the "outer realm" of empirical ethics or anthropology is presented as physical and necessary.[34] Kant and the post-Kantian idealists tended to grant pride of place to the inner realm, whether as reason, absolute spirit, or will. Nietzsche, for instance, acknowledged that it was Schopenhauer's metaphysics of will which constituted his philosophic shore of departure, and the two realms of the idealist tradition are preserved in Nietzsche's thinking to the extent that he privileges the inner one. The clearest example of Nietzsche's preoccupation with the inner realm is his *Zarathustra*. Although the narrative follows the hero through a series of adventures, the action is so freighted with symbolism and metaphors as to lend a dreamlike quality to many of the scenes, and it is obvious that the story's real action is inward and personal.

In addition to idealism, Santayana identifies romanticism as a major German cultural influence on Nietzsche:

> he knew no sort of good except the beautiful, and no sort of beauty except romantic stress. He was a belated prophet of romanticism. He wrote its epitaph, in which he praised it more extravagantly than anybody, when it was alive, had had the courage to do.[35]

Despite Nietzsche's critiques of romanticism, there is much in his work that is fundamentally in tune with its spirit. Many of his favorite motifs are profoundly romantic: the whole orientation toward the *Übermensch*, the high honors accorded to self-overcoming and genius, the lonely tribulations and glories reserved for those who dare to voyage beyond popular wisdom and social convention, the disdain for all that is common and merely average, the praise for those willing to sacrifice their happiness for "higher" ideals, the notion of treating one's life as a work of art; in short, the entire aesthetic of the sublime and awesome, with its acute appreciation of adventure, challenge, risk, and the *Sturm und Drang* of success and failure. The plot of *Thus Spoke Zarathustra* mirrors the heroic psychological and spiritual quests of the romantic *Bildungsromane*, not to mention the eerily romantic quality of the latter part of Nietzsche's own life, when the philosopher, engaged in an agonizing and lonely struggle against the progressive ravages of a chronic disease, spent his days writing and hiking in various Alpine locations throughout Switzerland and northern Italy.

In a sense, Nietzsche's greatest philosophical virtue is also his worst intellectual vice. As Josiah Royce observed in 1917:

> The central motive of Nietzsche seems to me to be this. It is clear to him that the moral problem concerns the perfection, not of society, not of the masses of men, but of the great individual. . . .
>
> There is no doubt that, from the point of view of a more systematic idealism, Nietzsche appears as entirely failing to see the organic character of the true life of coöperating individuals. The great problem of reconciling the unique individual with the world-order is simply not Nietzsche's problem. One must not go to him for light upon that subject. Therein lies his perfectly obvious limitation.[36]

Much of the poetic power of Nietzsche's writing stems from his focus on the inner life of the self; His *Zarathustra* is as much artistic communication of an inward journey as it is philosophical analysis. Perhaps no other philosopher has done as much as Nietzsche to convey the meaning of modern subjectivity, and his influence on later philosophical movements such as phenomenology, existentialism, and deconstruction has been, and continues to be, considerable. Nevertheless, it is precisely Nietzsche's preoccupation with the individual—his egotism—that prevented him from sufficiently appreciating the inherently social nature of truth. The instrumental character of truth is most easily seen in the life of communities, and

Nietzsche understood himself to be the advocate of the great individual who has managed to largely free himself or herself from the constraints, concerns, and moods of group life. The underlying egotism of Nietzsche's approach and his perspectivism lead him to underestimate the contribution objects make to value. Rather than comprehending valuation as an existential relation that crops up between humans and some aspect of their social and physical environment, Nietzsche conceives of valuing as a private affair which mainly takes place within the forge of the self, where assessments are caste through smelting together will, perception, and intellect. There is an undeniably romantic flavor to this view, since it implies that every attempt to get to the real significance of things leads not outward but inward. Everyday experience, however, reveals that we expect the objects we value to reinforce our desire to attain them, and that if they fail to do so, they run the risk of being reassessed.[37]

Our language and metaphysical tradition would have it that taste is a sort of faculty or agency, located somewhere in our brains. Insofar as it identifies the brain as a material precondition for the existence of taste, this view is not entirely mistaken, but it tends to exceed this observation and suggest that taste is entirely enclosed within the subjective inner space of the self. Once conceived of as a feature of this mental realm, the problem becomes how to characterize judgments of taste, and historically the two most popular options have been to construe value either as an objective feature of things or as a subjective emotional glow added to the dull facts of the world by mind. In reality, taste designates an ability to evaluate that relies on reflectively acquired attitudes of approval or disapproval. It is not subjective in the sense of somehow being trapped inside persons but is rather objectively relative to certain perspectives that exist within nature—namely, the perspectives of people who have been free to develop as individuals, according to their own informed preferences and judgment.

Like Nietzsche, Dewey rejects the Kantian delimitation of taste to the aesthetic. However, whereas Nietzsche tends to treat taste as a largely unconscious or subconscious influence on reason, Dewey conceives of it as a reflective phase of conduct:

> Instead of there being no disputing about tastes, they are the one thing worth disputing about, if by "dispute" is signified discussion involving reflective inquiry. Taste, if we use the word in its best sense, is the outcome of experience brought cumulatively to bear on the

intelligent appreciation of the real worth of likings and enjoyments. There is nothing in which a person so completely reveals himself as in the things which he judges enjoyable and desirable.[38]

By allowing for the refinement of feeling and sentiment through learning, Dewey revives an important aspect of the pre-Kantian conception of taste. Like the pre-Kantian theorists, he holds that taste is a general capacity for judgment of value that includes—but is not limited to—the realm of the artistic and aesthetic:

> The word "taste" has perhaps got too completely associated with arbitrary liking to express the nature of judgments of value. But if the word be used in the sense of an appreciation at once cultivated and active, one may say that the formation of taste is the chief matter wherever values enter in, whether intellectual, esthetic or moral. Relatively immediate judgments, which we call tact or to which we give the name of intuition, do not precede reflective inquiry, but are the funded products of much thoughtful experience. Expertness of taste is at once the result and the reward of constant exercise of thinking... The formation of a cultivated and effectively operative good judgment or taste with respect to what is esthetically admirable, intellectually acceptable and morally approvable is the supreme task set to human beings by the incidents of experience.[39]

As Dewey observes, the term "taste" is often used to refer to instances of individual inclination or preference that seem to be the result of mere whim or happenstance, such as choices involving the selection of one's favorite color or basketball team. Another popular meaning of taste, however, is that of discerning judgment in aesthetic matters, as when someone is said to have good taste. Unfortunately, taste in the sense of arbitrary liking is frequently confounded with taste in the sense of sound aesthetic judgment, perhaps because the latter is commonly viewed as being ultimately subjective. Since both spontaneous and reflective tastes are popularly thought to be subjective, they often end up being lumped together in the public mind.

Dewey largely assimilates good taste to expertness in judgment. Broadly speaking, such expertise is characterized by depth, coherency, and a firsthand knowledge of excellence in the relevant subject matter. A cornerstone of good taste is direct experience and awareness of what is fine in a given domain. The determination of excellence in any given field is a matter of comparison, and so relative to whatever has been attained or achieved in the area in question. As a rule of thumb, the court of appeal for what counts as superlative is constituted by a working consensus—insofar as one exists—among the competent practitioners in the given domain.

It is important to bear in mind that the assessment of something as innately superb—that is, as outstanding on the basis of its actual characteristics—presupposes an underlying interest in the thing or activity for its own sake. Such an interest on the part of the participant often arises quite naturally and need not exclude his or her self-interest or even the potential value of the thing or activity as a means to some other end. To value something for its own sake is simply to regard it with a general attitude of approbation and care, even in situations in which the object in question offers the self no immediate or clear personal advantage. Such attitudes are often acquired through the exercise of social roles that require the individual to adopt the standpoint of the group.

Kant pointed out the balanced and dispassionate nature of good taste, but assumed that selfless disinterest was its necessary precondition. In fact, good taste draws its distinctions not based on the mere absence of self-interest but rather through the acquired capacity to grasp social meaning. To illustrate this point, let us consider Aristotle's claim that certain actions, such as heroic deeds, are inherently fine. What, of course, arouses respect for such acts is their social meaning, the appreciation of which presupposes a general regard and concern for others. So widespread is the attitude that others merit our consideration that Aristotle takes it for granted. However, it is likely that the psychopath, who does not share this sentiment, identifies the worth of heroic actions exclusively with whatever reward they happen to confer to the hero.

Taste generally benefits from being cultivated, and the appreciation of fine things requires being exposed to them. This is no less true for morals than it is for art, music, or cuisine. As Aristotle notes about virtue, the study of ethics will only be beneficial for those students who come to the subject already equipped with the capacity to appreciate what is truly fine and noble and to recognize that which is shameful and better avoided. Without previous experience of the genuine goods of human life, moral arguments are doomed to forever remain cryptic abstractions.[40]

Expert judgment reflects not only richness of experience but also the thoughtful assimilation of this experiential wealth. The preferences and interests of someone who has good taste reveal more than a passing acquaintance with the subject matter in question. That which is truly desirable and has lasting value has been identified and distinguished from that which is only superficially attractive. Popularly held or well-known opinions and estimations touching on the given subject matter have been examined, evaluated, and taken up into habit when deemed worthwhile. A heightened degree of impartiality has been won by lessons drawn from past occasions when judgment was unduly swayed by subjective or adventitious factors, such as a momentary mood swing or the infectious but ill-placed enthusiasm of a companion. The development of good taste involves a process of self-discovery through which the individual learns how to pay close attention to the object to be evaluated by distinguishing the relevant from the irrelevant. In coming to know the object as an ongoing possibility for certain types of experience, the self is confronted with its own idiosyncrasies, dispositions, and biases. We can achieve a better understanding of the unique nature of our own personality by becoming acquainted with the personality of others, of our own language by learning foreign ones, and of our own country and culture by going abroad.

In addition to incorporating richness and depth of experience, good taste is characterized by a coherency of aims within the overall conduct of the individual. Specific prizings have been systematically organized into a functional hierarchy in light of their long-term consequences and interrelationships. Likes and interests in different subject matters and activities have been harmonized so that the self does not work at cross-purposes. When possible, different values and ends have been brought into such a relation with one another as to create mutual support. Such a harmonization of desire within the self is the hallmark of rationality, and is apparent in a type of individuality that is distinguished not simply by a unique personality but also by a distinctive personal style.

It may well be that the idea of taste has been too closely associated with aesthetic judgment to do useful service as a concept in moral psychology. Decisions of conscience, many may feel, are too serious an affair to be linked to the notion of personal preference. From this point of view, morality is indispensable for the continued survival of society, whereas taste involves what is merely optional and superfluous. Although I've tried to show that the contemporary understanding of taste that informs such objections is by no means either an intellectual or historical inevitability, it is certainly true that the theoretical definition I've suggested runs counter to popular usage. To readers who fear that characterizing conscience as a form of taste will lead to too many misunderstandings of the view I've been defending, I offer "individual judgment" as an alternate descriptor. Nevertheless, I believe "taste" to

157

be the preferable term because it better captures the nature of such judgments by connoting the creative space or latitude often had by the individual in fashioning solutions to moral dilemmas. In addition to conveying a sense of moral pluralism, taste has the advantage of indicating the affective component in valuation, a component that is not innate but rather has been shaped through thoughtful experience.

Ultimately, the conviction that morals must be grounded in a rational law or principle independent of feeling grows from the assumption that moral duty leads an autonomous existence, an assumption central to Kant's standpoint. In his *Ethics* Dewey identifies the greatest shortcoming of the deontological approach as the metaphysical disconnect Kant inaugurated between the idea of the good as what is enjoyed and prized, and the rules that serve to promote and maintain the good.[41] Dewey rightly points out that the ultimate raison d'être for moral rules and duties lies in their instrumental relationship to goods: they constitute a sort of shorthand for general measures undertaken to sustain and promote what is valued. He notes that the crucial difference between goods and duties is that we do not experience the immediate attraction for the latter that we do for the former.[42] While goods often appear as happy discoveries in the adventure of life, duties commonly emerge as afterthoughts, as the results of foresight or in response to the claims that others make upon us.

What about the individual who decides that the fulfillment of even elementary duties is offensive to his or her taste, and so simply resolves to ignore them? In other words, doesn't the notion of moral conscience as a form of taste justify ethical egoism? If the range of human goods were strictly limited to necessities and enjoyments that concerned only the individual, then ethical egoism would arguably follow from psychological egoism. Most people, however, develop genuine affections for others: They form strong attachments to their family members, they make friends, and sometimes they even fall in love. Social sentiment in the human species is by no means limited to face-to-face relationships, and the individual's affections can be extended to include neighborhood and nation or even future generations. The evidence for the social nature of many if not most human interests is patent.

Admittedly, psychopaths constitute an exception to this general rule. Scientific studies of psychopathy have revealed a mind-set that actually corresponds quite closely to an unadulterated version of the condition traditionally described by psychological egoism. For the psychopath, other people are usually just the means to the satisfaction of private desires and not ends in themselves. The psychopath understands that others have their own inner lives and value their own existence, but he or she does not care. Psychopaths are able to take the standpoint of others, and, indeed, some of them become skilled manipulators, but they lack empathy and compassion. While it is to be expected that the view that conscience is a form of taste will do little to deter the psychopath from immoral behavior, there is no reason to believe that other moral theories would fare any better. As Dewey once pointed out:

> Why attend to metaphysical and transcendental ideal realities even if we concede they are the authors of moral standards? Why do this act if I feel like doing something else? Any moral question may reduce itself to this question if we so choose.[43]

The best guarantee for morally acceptable behavior is not knowledge of moral laws but the presence of social goods in the individual's awareness and conduct.

One of the most puzzling pronouncements attributed to Socrates by his successors was the declaration that "virtue is knowledge." Socrates purportedly believed that if one truly knew how one ought to act, one would act as one should. This teaching seems to fly in the face of everyday experience, which provides us with an endless stream of examples in which individuals fail to do the right thing due to a moral deficit in the form of apathy, cowardice, impulsiveness, want of self-discipline, and so forth. In our criminal proceedings, only defendants who are judged to be insane or to have some serious mental defect are recognized as not understanding the difference between right and wrong, and the whole legal notion of responsibility assumes that it is possible to be cognizant of what should or should not be done and yet fail to act appropriately. However ambiguous and infelicitous his wording, perhaps the point Socrates wished to make depended upon the sort of distinction we have just drawn between duty merely apprehended as a demand for compliance, versus duty grasped as a social good. Virtue truly is knowledge if we construe knowledge to include the habits and desires that indicate the presence of a good in conduct. After all, we would rarely neglect to do the right thing if we not only could identify it as the best course of action but also actively desired it over the alternatives.

Assuming that the view of taste we have offered is substantially correct, does characterizing moral conscience as a form of taste constitute just another form of utilitarianism? After all, in his reconstruction of Bentham's utilitarianism, John Stuart Mill emphasizes the fact that pleasures can differ between each other not only quantitatively but also qualitatively. Mill argues that a difference in quality between two pleasures is detectable through the change it makes in human behavior. All considerations of moral obligation aside, there are some pleasures we find to be so innately valuable that even if they are rarer and more difficult to attain than lower pleasures, we still prefer them to lesser but more readily procured enjoyments. Mill observes that the collective experience of those people capable of both base and fine pleasures shows a marked preference for satisfactions that involve the higher human faculties. He famously claims that almost no one who has experienced lower as well as higher pleasures would exchange the lot of an unhappy Socrates for that of a happy pig.[44]

The metaphysical and psychological underpinnings of Mill's position limit him to grasping goods almost exclusively from the side of feeling. What lends different pleasures their distinctive character, however, is not just bodily sensation but the nonlinguistic meanings incorporated by the object of desire. Mill erroneously assumes that it is possible to accurately address the valuational aspect of human conduct exclusively in terms of sensation and sentiment. This supposition ignores the fact that value arises directly from the relations that pertain between the living creature and its environment. While pleasure is certainly an important factor in determining what we prize as well as the degree to which it is prized, the inclination we feel toward any particular object originates not in an inward orientation toward our own subjective states but in the significance the object possesses within the matrix of the experienced world.

It is clear from Mill's insistence on the existence of qualitatively different types of pleasure that he does not wish to limit the definition of "pleasure" to bodily sensations. In fact, Mill maintains that the most worthwhile pleasures, such as the appreciation of literature and the fine arts, are generally those that require discipline and deliberate cultivation. That which makes the enjoyment of Shakespeare a higher pleasure than, say, eating chocolate is not as obscure as Mill would have us believe. Given his divorce of feeling from cognition, he can at best point to certain pleasures and proclaim them to be qualitatively superior to others. If, however, we admit that pleasure is an integral part of certain experiences that are meaningful in various and sundry ways, and that we can only isolate the actual sensation of pleasure retrospectively and in the imagination, then we see that it is the agreeable people, things, and events of life that we value, and not pleasure per se. The "pleasurable" does not exist in and of itself; rather, the term denotes certain experiences wherein pleasure emerges as an aspect of a particular situation or state of affairs.

Aesthetic criticism provides an important clue to the true role of pleasure in conduct through its focus on aesthetic objects. Professional critics take for their subject matter not pleasure but the things that elicit it. For example, although the literary critic will certainly use his or her overall affective response to a novel as a guide in analysis and evaluation, his or her primary focus is the literary work itself. The reviewer pays close attention to elements like plot, character, and writing style in forming his or her estimation. To talk exclusively of his or her own subjective states would severely limit the scope and depth of the critique's assessment. The best approach to the aesthetic is not through feeling but through that which evokes feeling.

A utilitarian could grant that meaning is, in fact, a feature of valuation as it actually takes place within human conduct but still defend the reduction of values to kinds and quantities of pleasure as a legitimate and useful type of shorthand for making public policy decisions. After all, utilitarianism was born as a method of social reform and, so, was designed for dealing with social and political issues. By weighing goods in terms of pleasure, the specific nature of various goods is somewhat blurred, but what makes them essentially desirable—namely, the pleasure to which they give rise—is brought to the fore. Like textbook approximations of the number π, the utilitarian could claim that his or her method is as accurate as it needs to be for the work at hand.

On the whole, of course, it is perfectly reasonable to hope that our considered decisions and well-laid plans contribute to our happiness and the happiness of others. Good decision making, however, largely relies on making accurate forecasts of future conditions and consequences, and our abilities for predicting the future are notoriously limited. By requiring us to estimate not only what will happen but also how we'll actually feel about it if and when it comes to pass, utilitarianism renders a highly difficult enterprise well-nigh impossible. Furthermore, due to its flawed hedonistic psychology, to consider value from the vantage point of utilitarianism is akin to persisting in naked-eye observation of the heavens after the invention of the telescope: Certainly one sees something of the subject matter to be investigated, but only in the most vague and indistinct fashion. Utilitarianism is inaccurate as a description of how valuation actually occurs, and is hence at best imprecise as a guide to conduct, and at worse downright misleading.

Finally, if it is fair to characterize moral conscience as a form of taste, then why doesn't such a conception figure in Kohlberg's stages of moral development? Although conscience in the form of individual judgment isn't explicitly incorporated into his scheme, its presence is actually implied at the post-conventional level. The fifth and final stage of moral development is entitled "Social Contract or Utility and Individual Rights," and the perspective incorporates the awareness of moral pluralism—that is, the consciousness that people living in the same society often have different values and incompatible moral views. While some values are seen as being relative to individuals or groups, others are held to have universal or nearly universal application, and these turn out to be the fundamental rights typical of the liberal social order. These same rights, of course, not only enjoy widespread moral authority but also usually have the force of law behind them. At the fifth stage the individual is viewed as having a duty to uphold the laws of the land as part of his or her social contract, and as having an obligation to respect engagements and relationships that he or she has freely contracted. These contractual commitments can be either formal or informal and include roles in the family, with friends, at work, and in the community. Much of the moral elbowroom accorded to the individual in modern society consists in the ability to choose such contracts and, at least to some degree, to determine the manner in which they are fulfilled. Kohlberg notes that individuals who have achieved the social contract standpoint often find it difficult to integrate the legal and moral perspectives. This isn't surprising given that moral convictions frequently serve as the inspiration for the repeal or modification of old laws or the creation of new ones, a fact that renders the borderline between the legal and the ethical somewhat fluid. Political and social activism, which often involves the attempt to impact legislation, is yet another sphere in which the modern individual enjoys a considerable degree of freedom and, hence, moral latitude.

The reader may recall that Kohlberg originally include a sixth stage in his scheme, which bore the title "Universal Ethical Principle Orientation," and which was later abandoned due to the fact that longitudinal studies in the United States, Turkey, and Israel failed to reveal subjects who had actually achieved it. As announced by its title, the sixth stage designated a type of advanced moral understanding based upon the identification of an abstract ethical principle or law:

> Right is defined by the decision of conscience in accord with self-chosen *ethical principles* appealing to logical comprehensiveness, universality, and consistency. These principles are abstract and ethical (the Golden Rule, the categorical imperative); they are not concrete moral rules like the Ten Commandments. At heart, these are universal principles of *justice*, of the *reciprocity* and *equality* of human *rights*, and of respect for the dignity of human beings as *individual persons*.[45]

Kohlberg's conception of the highest stage of moral awareness is clearly influenced by the legislative model. We have, of course, argued that this model fundamentally fails to capture the nature of conscience in the modern individual, so the fact that Kohlberg's empirical work turned up insufficient evidence for the existence of this perspective can be interpreted as corroborating our claim.

Although the idea of conscience as a form of taste entails a certain degree of ethical pluralism, it by no means implies that all moral judgments are equal. Decisions and estimations based upon false premises are obviously flawed, because the warrant that has been provided for the judgment is, in fact, at least partially illusory. Although such judgments can still lead to good results, when this is the case the happy outcome depends, at least to some extent, upon dumb luck. In reasoning about interpersonal affairs, self-deception represents a major source of false belief and skewed values. Chronic self-deception usually indicates an underlying character disorder, and in order to better understand how such deformations of personality can warp the individual's capacity for rational judgment, we turn in the last two chapters to a consideration of Karen Horney's depth psychology.

Notes

1. Michael Stocker, "The Schizophrenia of Modern Ethical Theories," *The Journal of Philosophy* 73, no. 14 (August 12, 1976): 453–466.
2. Ibid., 465.
3. Ibid.
4. Erich Fromm, *Escape from Freedom* (New York: Holt, Rinehart and Winston, 1941), 41.
5. Hallpike, *The Evolution of Moral Understanding*, 240.
6. Fromm, *Escape from Freedom*, 41–42.
7. Alasdair MacIntyre, *A Short History of Ethics* (New York: Collier Books, 1966), 124.

8. W. T. Jones, *Hobbes to Hume*, vol. 3 of *A History of Western Philosophy*, 2nd ed. (New York: Harcourt Brace Jovanovich, Inc., 1969), 1–4.
9. MacIntyre, *A Short History of Ethics*, 197.
10. John Dewey, *The Later Works, 1925–1953, Vol. I: 1925*, ed. Jo Ann Boydston (Carbondale, IL: Southern Illinois University Press, 1981), 307.
11. John Dewey, *Philosophy and Civilization* (Gloucester, Massachusetts: Peter Smith, 1968), 97–98.
12. Mead, *Selected Writings*, 306.
13. "The Nature of Aesthetic Experience," in Mead, *Selected Writings*, 277–278.
14. Ibid., 294.
15. Hans-Georg Gadamer, *Truth and Method* (New York: Crossroad, 1984), 38.
16. Aristotle, *Nicomachean Ethics*, trans. Terence Irwin (Indianapolis, IN: Hackett Publishing Company, 1985), 171.
17. Philip P. Wiener, editor in chief, *Dictionary of the History of Ideas*, vol. IV (New York: Charles Scribner's Sons, 1973), s.v. "Taste in the History of Aesthetics from the Renaissance to 1770" by Giorgio Tonelli.
18. Gadamer, *Truth and Method*, 33.
19. Part of this paragraph was paraphrased from Joachim Ritter, ed., *Historisches Wörterbuch der Philosophie*, vol. 3: G–H (Darmstadt, Germany: Wissenschaftliche Buchgesellschaft, 1974), s.v. "Geschmack" by K. Stierle.
20. Gadamer, *Truth and Method*, 34.
21. Paraphrased from Wiener, *Dictionary of the History of Ideas*, s.v. "Taste in the History of Aesthetics from the Renaissance to 1770" by Giorgio Tonelli.
22. Gadamer, *Truth and Method*, 78-79.
23. John Dewey, *Art as Experience* (New York: Perigee Books, 1934), 9.
24. Peter Gay, *The Enlightenment: An Interpretation*, Vol. II: The Science of Freedom (New York: Alfred A. Knopf, 1969), 315.
25. Friedrich Nietzsche, *Thus Spoke Zarathustra*, trans. Walter Kaufmann (New York: Penguin Books, 1954), 117.
26. Ibid., 307.
27. Friedrich Nietzsche, *The Gay Science*, trans. Walter Kaufmann (New York: Vintage Books, 1974), 106.
28. Lou Andreas-Salomé, *Friedrich Nietzsche in seinen Werken* (Frankfurt am Main and Leipzig: Insel, 1983), 298.
29. Kai-Michael Hingst, *Perspektivismus und Pragmatismus: Ein Vergleich auf der Grundlage der Wahrheitsbegriffe und der Religionsphilosophien von Nietzsche und James* (Würzburg: Königshausen und Neumann, 1998).
30. George Santayana, *Egotism in German Philosophy*, 2nd ed. (London: J.M. Dent & Sons, Ltd., 1940), 162–163.
31. Gordon A. Craig, *The Germans* (New York: G. P. Putnam's Sons, 1982), 84.
32. This discussion of Luther's thought is indebted to Alasdair MacIntyre's synopsis of the same in *A Short History of Ethics*, 122.
33. John Dewey, *German Philosophy and Politics* (New York: Henry Holt and Company, 1915), 18–19.
34. Ibid., 20.
35. Santayana, *Egotism in German Philosophy*, 127.
36. Josiah Royce, "Nietzsche," *The Atlantic Monthly* 119, no. 3 (1917): 322, 327-8.

37. "The Philosophies of Royce, James, and Dewey in their American Setting," in Mead, *Selected Writings*, 384–385.
38. John Dewey, *The Quest for Certainty* (New York: Minton, Balch & Co., 1929), 262.
39. Ibid.
40. Aristotle, *Nicomachean Ethics*, 291–292.
41. John Dewey, *The Later Works, 1925–1953, Vol. 7: 1932*, ed. Jo Ann Boydston (Carbondale, IL: Southern Illinois University Press, 1983), 219–225.
42. Ibid., 229–230.
43. Dewey, *Human Nature and Conduct*, 57.
44. John Stuart Mill, *Utilitarianism*, ed. George Sher (Indianapolis, IN: Hackett Publishing Company, 1979), 8–10.
45. Lawrence Kohlberg, "From Is to Ought," in Jürgen Habermas, *Zur Rekonstruktion des Historischen Materialismus* (Frankfurt am Main: Suhrkamp, 1995), 73.

5

Horney's Depth Psychology of Moral Character

In this and the subsequent chapter, I will contend that Karen Horney's revision of psychoanalysis manages to outfit the best of Freud's observations and ideas with a greatly improved meta-theoretical scaffolding. Her work constitutes a form of analysis that is no longer susceptible to Dewey's criticisms of Freud's teachings; indeed, I will argue that her reconstructed version of psychoanalysis is essentially Deweyan in spirit. Her contributions have provided the basis for a deeper and more comprehensive understanding of personality than that offered by orthodox analysis, and I will show that her approach enjoys considerable support from the findings of other social sciences.

In addition to the fact that she developed a greatly improved version of psychoanalysis, Horney merits contemporary consideration for another reason. Her revision of psychoanalysis culminated in the creation of a highly original moral psychology that has been neither adequately recognized nor appreciated. As a "culturalist," she grasped the fact that personality and character are always partly the products of a particular social context, and that personal psychology can be accurately understood exclusively in terms of human biology no more than language can be in terms of the vocal chords. Horney criticized Freud for his essentially biological and acultural conception of human nature and sought to develop an individual psychology that would give cultural factors their due. In elaborating this line of thought, she recognized that a comprehensive understanding of the patient's personality structure must include a consideration of his or her values and moral fiber.

Whereas Freud conceived of conscious preferences and wishes as determined by the unconscious, Horney maintained that, although such cases exist, they are not universal but rather indicative of a personality disorder (or "neurosis," in her terminology). She rejected Freud's instinct theory and instead adopted a less doctrinaire view of unconscious mental processes that stresses the relative and partial nature of the individual's perspective as well as the general human tendency to selective emphasis and self-interested interpretation. While she allowed that the individual can develop and maintain a personal moral code, she believed that those who suffer from personality disorders are generally impaired in their ability to deal in an honest and forthright manner with themselves and others. Such persons have fallen victim to a private fantasy that endows them with a grandiose sense of self-worth and an exalted mission in life. The elevation of the self through wishful thinking comes at the price of a balanced and sober view of oneself and others. In order to prevent his or her pretensions from clashing with reality, the neurotic is obliged to develop unconscious strategies that inevitably skew his or her perception of the human environment. By privileging an idealized vision of the self, the afflicted individual loses touch with his or her own spontaneous feelings and reactions. The net result of this untoward development of the personality is a considerable degree of confusion over the true nature of one's own desires and values. The neurotic is torn between a more or less conscious catalog of "shoulds," which stem from the idealized self, and other attitudes and strivings whose existence is denied or downplayed because they contradict the former.

Although character disorders clearly constituted her main focus, Horney eventually argued that most people, including even those whom we would think of as psychologically "normal," could benefit from analysis. In addition to its use as a therapy, she believed that it could be fruitfully employed as an "aid to general character development."[1] As concerns this latter function, she held that the individual did not necessarily need a therapist in order to utilize analysis to good effect. To her way of thinking, psychoanalysis represented an important new contribution to the ancient quest to know oneself.

Horney repeatedly suggested that analysis was particularly valuable as a tool for self-knowledge and personal growth due to the complex and difficult nature of modern civilization. Although she left the social dimension of her theory relatively undeveloped, she clearly believed that the contemporary social world constitutes a confusing moral landscape, since it is home to activity systems, cultural patterns, and ideologies that make competing and sometimes even contradictory value claims on their participants. By equipping the modern self with a better understanding of its own subconscious motivations and desires, analysis could help improve the individual's ability to employ his or her own moral compass.

The implicit context of Horney's individual psychology is the modern social order, and, as concerns her theory, the most important feature of this order is individualism. If we grasp individualism from its social side and construe it primarily in terms of certain institutional and cultural arrangements, then we can say that it constitutes a necessary condition of the emergence of modern selfhood and what we typically think of as moral conscience. The former is characterized by a high degree of self-awareness and by a depth and complexity of feeling that springs from the multiple and varied social perspectives internalized by the modern individual. The latter arises when morals are no longer essentially just a function of custom but incorporate personal judgment and desire. The ethical standpoint of conscience is post-conventional, in the sense that the individual no longer automatically identifies goodness and justice with conformity to prevailing expectations and practices but seeks to arrive at right judgment through reflection.

These two features of the modern mind presuppose a self that is more than simply the sum of its social roles, and that is aware of this fact. It's a self whose identity is primarily achieved rather than assigned, and whose path in life typically involves a series of choices between competing goods. It is, in short, the sort of self whose natural habitat is a modern society in which there exists a high degree of structurally ensconced individualism. In what follows, I seek to establish that any personality theory that has the modern self at its center will inherently be a moral psychology, and that Horney grasped this fact, at least implicitly. By highlighting the unconscious dimension of personality, she made a significant advance over previous moral psychologies. That her achievement has been largely neglected is in part the result of an ill-conceived division of labor between psychologists and philosophers. As we have seen in previous chapters, the former have tended to assume that they could provide adequate accounts of personality divorced from a consideration of values, and the latter have often treated moral judgment as if it were independent of individuality.

Saving Psychoanalysis from Freud

It is my contention that Karen Horney's most important intellectual achievement was to have clearly indicated the path for saving psycho-analysis from Freud. Of course, she never portrayed her life's work in such unadorned terms; given Freud's authority among her peers, she could hardly have done so and hoped to remain within the psychoanalytic fold. Nevertheless, her personality theory was elaborated within a meta-theoretical perspective specifically constructed to overcome the limitations inherent in the Freudian framework, and she reached a number of conclusions pertaining to analytic theory and practice that differed substantially from Freud's.

Despite the fundamental nature of her objections, Horney clearly propounded the reform of Freud's brainchild, not its abandonment. Given the fact that she ultimately rejected his teachings on such crucial matters as the nature of the unconscious and the Oedipus complex, the reader may well wonder why she still considered herself a psychoanalyst. The answer, I believe, lies in a functional distinction she posited between analytic theory and practice. On her view, Freud's most valuable contributions lay in the latter realm. First and foremost among them, of course, was his instauration of the analytic session as a form of therapy for mental disorders. Although the idea of a "talking cure" did not wholly originate with Freud, no one was more instrumental than he was in establishing it as a widespread practice. In *New Ways in Psychoanalysis*, the book in which she presented a psychoanalytic alternative to the Freudian frame of reference, Horney asserts that the therapeutic relationship

> provides us with unheard-of possibilities in understanding these processes [i.e., the processes operating in human relationships]. Hence a more accurate and profound understanding of this one relationship will constitute the greatest contribution to psychology which psychoanalysis will eventually have to offer.[2]

Indeed, it was primarily her own experience as a therapist that provided her with a basis for calling fundamental aspects of Freud's theory into question.

In addition to having instituted the psychoanalytic relationship, Horney credits Freud with having furnished therapists with the valuable methodological concepts of transference, resistance, and free association.[3] However, in order to improve the effectiveness of these tools, she finds it necessary to divest them of their Freudian interpretations. On her view, for example, the idea of transference is most useful when construed as the guideline that the patient's relationship with the analyst is the best source of information for understanding the former's character structure and problems. Freud held that the analysand's emotional reactions to the analyst were essentially repetitions of modes of feeling acquired in early childhood and preserved in a sort of suspended animation in the unconscious. While acknowledging the importance of early childhood in the formation of personality, Horney argues that Freud's concept of the repetition compulsion is reductive. Instead of comprehending the personality as a dynamic system that integrates past experiences into an overall structure, Freud assumes that it is actually compartmentalized: Indeed, perhaps the most significant aspect of his famous tripartite division of the psyche is not the various roles he assigns to id, ego, and superego, but rather the fundamentally divided picture of mind he presents. The Freudian psyche is basically mechanistic, insofar as unconscious processes tend to determine conscious states, which amounts to making the frozen past of the unconscious the master of the waking, simmering present. As an alternative to this model Horney proposes a more dynamic, organic, and open-ended conception of self in which past and present interact and fuse in a myriad of ways, the diversity and profusion of which make each and every individual unique.

Generally speaking, she borrows more from Freud the descriptive naturalist of the human condition than from Freud the theoretician of mind. In fact, considered from the vantage point provided by her work, Freud's Achilles' heel turns out to be his attachment to preconceived ideas. Although he was gifted with subtle powers of observation—a talent noted by both Dewey and Horney—he tended to allow his theoretical commitments to overpower his empiricism. As an early student of psychoanalysis, Horney was perhaps better placed than the school's founder to appreciate the tremendous potential of the therapeutic situation for gaining new insight into individual psychology. Freud, after all, wore many hats and so had relatively little time to savor and fully explore the new vistas opened by his own discoveries. Critical appreciation and an eye for improvement are perhaps more easily acquired by those who follow than by those who lead the way. In any event, therapeutic experience figures more predominately as a check on theory in Horney's thinking than in Freud's.

Readers already familiar with Horney's writings may recall the high praise she accords Freud and object to the contention that her project involved saving the psychoanalytic movement from its founder. In *New Ways*, for instance, she writes that

> nothing of importance in the field of psychology and psychotherapy has been done since Freud's fundamental findings without those

findings being used as a directive for observation and thinking; when they have been discarded the value of new findings has been decreased.[4]

Clearly, Horney is keenly aware upon whose shoulders she is standing. However, closer examination reveals that the principles she adopts from Freud are actually quite broad in nature. In *New Ways*, she cites as the "most fundamental and most significant of Freud's findings" three interrelated ideas: the doctrine of psychic determinism, the notion that unconscious motivations may play a role in determining our feelings and actions, and the view that our strongest motivations are "emotional forces."[5] Long before Freud's day, many held that psychic determinism, or the postulate that mental events are strictly determined, was entailed by materialism. By the late nineteenth century, when Freud was beginning his career in psychology, both materialism and determinism were popular views among intellectuals (consider, for example, positivism and Marxism, both schools of thought that arose before psychoanalysis). It should also be noted that there is nothing particularly psychoanalytic about the doctrine: After all, one could subscribe to the belief that mental phenomena are determined and nevertheless reject psychoanalysis without fear of self-contradiction. As to Freud's teachings about unconscious motivations and the emotional nature of human drives, it has often been observed that these notions were largely anticipated in romanticism. Romantic art, literature, and philosophy are full of intimations of an inner dimension beyond the purview of reason and yet equal or even superior to it in terms of its human significance.

Of course, Freud created a unique synthesis out of these different currents of thought, and he considerably developed the idea of unconscious motivations. Nevertheless, viewed from her vantage point in the 1930s, many of Freud's underlying assumptions and teachings must have struck Horney as intellectual holdovers of a bygone era. Her adoption of the three doctrines in question actually does little to commit her to Freud's theory of mind. By Horney's day most psychologists accepted some form of psychological determinism, and for professional psychologists the real question became not *if* but *how* mental life is determined. In addition, Freud's view of the unconscious is so bound up with his instinct theory that one cannot consistently reject the one without also rejecting the other. Hence, as we shall see, Horney's conceptions of unconscious motivations and drives differ considerably from their Freudian counterparts.

The Strange Fate of Horney's Contribution

Horney's work has suffered an unusual fate. Far from having passed into obscurity, her personality theory is still mentioned and often discussed in many introductory textbooks in psychology and psychotherapy. Instead of languishing almost exclusively in university libraries, her books have enjoyed long careers as reprinted mass-market paperbacks and have reached a popular audience well outside the confines of the mental health professions and academia. Several of her volumes have been translated into a variety of languages. In addition to having popular appeal, her writings have influenced several generations of psychologists, an influence that is particularly evident in the thinking of the humanistic school.

And yet, oddly enough, the very psychoanalytic establishment out of which she emerged, and to which she devoted her career, has managed to largely ignore her. There has been a pronounced tendency in psychoanalytic circles to dismiss Horney as an intellectual lightweight whose theories are too commonsensical and popular to be taken seriously.[6] As a result, there are currently very few analysts who identify themselves as working in her tradition. Although her ideas continue to serve as a source of inspiration for psychotherapists, relatively little has been done to advance her overall theory or build upon the new foundations she laid for psychoanalysis.

In his book, *Karen Horney: A Psychoanalyst's Search for Self-Understanding*, Bernard J. Paris suggests several different reasons for the relative neglect of Horney's work. He argues that her fiery resignation from the prestigious New York Psychoanalytic Institute badly damaged her reputation among some professional analysts, marking her as a fringe figure.[7] He also points out that the clarity of her texts and her down-to-earth approach to individual psychology has been very much out of step with the psychoanalytic *Zeitgeist* that has prevailed since her death in 1952. In roughly the last half century, psychoanalysis has repeatedly come under the influence of contemporary European philosophy and has tended to be quite speculative and to emphasize intellectual tastes and values. In Europe, France has been the cultural center of psychoanalysis since the fifties, and many of the most recent developments in the field are due to French thinkers such as Jacques Lacan and Jacques Derrida, whose writings are recondite and highly technical. For analysts who have been weaned on a steady diet of Heidegger, Lacan, and French postmodernism, Horney's sober and matter-of-fact treatment of depth psychology must seem like the musings of a country bumpkin. As Paris points out, her very assumption of the self as an object of study flies in the face of much contemporary Continental philosophy, which has called the reality of selfhood into question.[8]

In his penetrating biography of Horney, Paris uncovers another probable factor behind the waning of her influence. He reveals with greater frankness and in more detail than her previous biographers the fact that Horney herself shouldered a considerable degree of the responsibility for the decline of her movement. The painstakingly researched and extensively documented portrait he presents of her in a leadership role is dispiriting.[9] After founding her own association and institute, she soon proved to have the full complement of vices for someone in her position and proceeded to alienate many of her closest and most talented collaborators. According to firsthand reports from former students and colleagues, Horney tended to be autocratic and intolerant of viewpoints that differed from her own. In addition, she was apparently motivated by a deep need to be adulated, and openly (though perhaps unconsciously) played favorites based largely upon an individual's capacity to be her devoted follower. She was also not above abusing her authority and power to punish those by whom she felt slighted, or to seduce a series of younger men entrusted to her as analysands as part of their training (a penchant which evidently began long before she resigned from the New York Psychoanalytic Institute). In short, her approach to institutional politics and management seemed to be Machiavellian, in the sense that in order to achieve her personal ends she used and discarded people with apparent abandon. More than a few of her associates were ultimately driven off by this shabby treatment, and Paris concludes that Horney damaged her own intellectual legacy by alienating precisely those individuals who would have been the best equipped and the most inclined to promulgate and further develop her reconstructed version of psychoanalysis.[10]

Such dysfunctional interpersonal behavior in a theorist who once wrote that "the essence of all human psychology resides in understanding the processes operating in human relationships"[11] is obviously cause for concern, and more than one reader will be reminded of the saying "Physician, heal thyself." Does Horney's failure to overcome her personal difficulties indicate that something is fundamentally flawed in her theory? Paris takes up this question as one of the central themes of his study and answers it in the negative. As the title of his book suggests, he argues that throughout her life Horney's single greatest source of insight into human psychology came from grappling with her own problems. By citing her juvenile diaries Paris shows that as an adolescent she was already engaged in intense introspection, and by reconstructing key phases of her private life he makes a convincing case for his claim that she borrowed abundantly from her private difficulties in her mature writings, thinly veiling their true source by attributing them to fictional patients. Although she certainly retained serious character flaws up to her death, her struggle for self-knowledge and transformation was not wholly without success. Paris's biography reveals a woman who, despite significant personal shortcomings, was able to engage in highly creative work, who took deep satisfaction in at least some of her relationships, and who was capable of fighting for her convictions. Given the hurdles that fate dealt her in the form of an unhappy early home environment and subsequent academic and professional settings in which women constituted a distinctly disadvantaged minority, such achievements should be paid their proper due. Although she was only partially successful in treating herself, Horney ultimately led a highly productive and vital life.

Yet another reason for Horney's lack of what Paris terms "cultural presence" can, I believe, be traced to her strategy of presenting herself as a reformer rather than a rebel. In matter of fact, the import of her ideas was to place psychoanalysis on radically new footing, but, due to considerations of institutional politics, Horney tended to soft-pedal the revolutionary nature of her approach. In *New Ways in Psychoanalysis*, which is largely an extended criticism of the "old ways" of Freud, she specifically disavows any intention of founding a new psychoanalytic school of thought.[12] As it turned out, the orthodox establishment at the time was not about to be coaxed into a radical departure from Freud, and Horney's strategy of reform from within failed. Unfortunately, her plan also meant that her theory lost some of the attractiveness it would have otherwise held for non-Freudians had she had been more forthcoming about the originality of her contribution. In reality, she actually transformed a very nineteenth-century instinct-based theory of mind into a highly innovative moral psychology, as I hope to demonstrate in what follows.

Before proceeding to a consideration of Horney's views, two points need to be made. The first is that my presentation of her ideas is not intended to be comprehensive. Several detailed overviews of her thought already exist, and for the reader interested in such an account Paris's intellectual biography is particularly recommended. My main intention in this and the subsequent chapter is to show how Horney brought the moral dimension of individual reasoning and judgment into depth psychology. In order to do so, I will primarily consider the final version of her theory as presented in her last book, *Neurosis and Human Growth*. Horney's ideas as expressed in her published articles and books developed considerably over time, but a chronologically ordered review of her work would exceed the scope of the present study, and has already been provided by Paris and her other biographers.

The second point that should be borne in mind involves Horney's reliance upon the term "neurosis" and its various derivatives. The word constitutes an important piece of standard analytic vocabulary, and it stands for a long-term mental and emotional disorder that does not involve a severe loss of contact with reality, whereby it contrasts with psychoses such as schizophrenia and bipolar disorder, which typically include hallucinations or delusions. Freud distinguished among several different types of neurosis, and later analysts have continued to identify new forms, so that contemporary psychoanalysis recognizes many different neurotic families and species. Outside of psychoanalytic circles the term has tended to fall into disfavor for being too closely associated with Freudian views and for being vague.

Horney's mature work was squarely focused on understanding the most prevalent kinds of mental affliction, those that we frequently encounter firsthand in our everyday dealings with family members, friends, and coworkers. Hence, neurotic processes constituted her theoretical bread and butter. Unfortunately, due to its Freudian implications and lack of precision, the term "neurosis" did not particularly well serve her thinking. Many contemporary psychologists no longer assume that typical neurotic symptoms such as sexual dysfunction or phobia originate in an underlying neurotic conflict. Several of the classic symptoms associated with the neurotic personality type are now classified as ailments in their own right, the so-called anxiety disorders. Some researchers believe that although these afflictions may occur in conjunction with a neurotic personality, neurosis does not constitute a necessary precondition for their existence. In addition, the tendency in contemporary psychology has been to abandon the language of neurosis in favor of "personality disorder" when describing what Freud thought of as the underlying conflict. Although Horney took careful note of neurotic symptoms, the central thrust of her thought was clearly to elucidate the structure of the submerged neurotic personality. Many of today's recognized personality disorders, such as dependent personality disorder or narcissistic personality disorder, find obvious parallels in Horney's theory. "Character disorder" is a common synonym for "personality disorder," and, I think, is the preferable of the two formulations to refer to Horney's work, since the word "character" carries a moral connotation that "personality" does not. Thus, readers who find that the word "neurosis" is antiquated or otherwise objectionable should keep in mind that Horney's description of neurotic personality types can be accurately translated into the more contemporary terminology of character disorders.[13]

Horney's Revised Version of Psychoanalysis

Simply put, Horney's main problem as a psychoanalyst was to discover how to throw out the bathwater without also discarding the baby. On the one hand, she believed she had inherited a revolutionary technique for helping the individual to recognize and overcome difficulties in which his or her own personality plays a leading role. On the other, her clinical experience as an orthodox Freudian therapist for over fifteen years convinced her that something was seriously amiss with psychoanalytic theory. By her own admission, she found that nearly every patient she treated displayed troubles for which orthodox analysis had no answers. In *New Ways in Psychoanalysis*, she recounts that her growing discontent with the limitations of standard analytic therapy constituted the initial impetus for a critical reevaluation of Freud's teachings. His views on feminine psychology, and his later doctrine of the death instinct, also served to feed her skepticism.[14]

It was Horney's signal achievement to have opened the moral aspect of individual judgment to psychoanalytic investigation. Of course, Freud had claimed to do as much, but under the loupe of orthodox analysis the individual's values are relegated to being little more than the visible tips of psychic icebergs, whose bulks are submerged in the dark waters of the unconscious. In *New Ways*, she points out that Freud in fact construed conscious preferences and value judgments as outcomes determined by the subterranean forces of the libido and the death instinct.[15] She regards his view as implying that values are merely surface phenomena whose inner nature is instinctual. In the Freudian scheme, reason primarily serves to furnish desire with a rational façade and has little power to redirect or fundamentally transform our feelings and passions.

In reducing preferences and value judgments to "more elemental 'instinctual' units,"[16] Freud was being consistent with his metapsychological assumptions, and these are precisely the assumptions that Horney criticizes in *New Ways*. She interprets his emphasis on instinct as part of an overall "biological" orientation to the study of psychology. On her view, Freud assumed that the psychoanalyst, as a genuine scientist of the mind, would conceive of psychic phenomena as "chemical-physiological" forces. Consistent with this perspective, he thought of the instincts themselves as restless "somatic stimuli" that forever seek release. For Freud, any worthwhile psychology had to be elaborated within a neurological framework in which factors such as anatomy and heredity play the central role in determining psychic processes. Thus, the major thrust of his thought was to illuminate the transition from the biological to the mental, and he assumed that a better grasp of this shift would be tantamount to providing a causal explanation for human behavior. As a logical consequence of this scheme, social and cultural phenomena were considered to be largely tertiary, in the sense that they were held to be primarily determined by the biological and psychic forces present in human nature. The human nature that psychoanalysis originally took for its object of study was assumed to be universal and pre-cultural, and Horney remarks that the minor role accorded by Freud to sociocultural factors reflected the common anthropological naïveté of the nineteenth century.

Horney also points out that the pride of place allotted by Freud to the instincts was of one piece with his "mechanistic" understanding of evolution. She characterizes the mechanistic model as one in which all change in nature is interpreted as being spatial in character. The new simply involves a repositioning or reorganization of the old, and the universe is incapable of generating novel qualities: Some qualities only appear to be original, but in reality have always been present, albeit in some latent and easily overlooked form.[17] She argues that key Freudian doctrines, such as the repetition compulsion, clearly reflect the influence of the metaphysical assumptions in question, as does Freud's "bottom up" approach to mind in general.

To the Freudian position she juxtaposes her own, which she refers to as "non-mechanistic," and which contemporary readers will readily identify as a version of emergent evolution. Like Dewey, Horney envisions the universe as constituting a process of open-ended development in which incremental quantitative change can usher in genuinely original characteristics and qualities that are more than simply the sum of their parts. Both Dewey and Horney conceive of mind as an emergent phase of nature whose unique traits are just as real as the physical features of carbon compounds or mammalian sexual reproduction.

According to Horney, Freud's metaphysics directly influenced his view of unconscious processes in at least two interrelated respects. She dubs the concepts in question the "timelessness of the unconscious" and the "repetition compulsion." By the former she means the view that repressed infantile memories and feelings are strictly segregated from the rest of the psyche and remain in a sort of suspended animation in the unconscious. Freud maintained that such repressed experiences are not integrated into the individual's waking life and retain the full force of their original intensity and quality deep beneath the turbulent surface of the ego. The hypothesis of repetition-compulsion posits an innate tendency in unconscious processes to seek repeated expression of the same event or reaction. The experiences the individual is unconsciously driven to repeat are not necessarily pleasurable and may even be quite painful and traumatic. So, for instance, the fact that a woman might be repeatedly drawn into relationships with domineering and abusive men could be chalked up to the influence of the repetition-compulsion. In *New Ways* Horney reviews the evidence that Freud mustered to support these contentions and concludes that the case he made for them is unconvincing.[18] Her own view is that childhood experiences are indeed fundamental to the formation of personality, but that they impact and are incorporated into the overall character structure. The repetitive aspects of neurotic conduct interpreted by Freud as the most visible effects of the repetition-compulsion—namely, clear patterns of disturbed relations to others—can be explained in terms of drives. Horney argues that it should come as no surprise that a specific constellation of drives tends to produce similar types of behavior. As we shall presently see, her notion of drive has much more in common with Dewey's conception of habit than it does with Freud's view of instinct.

In addition to making a general criticism of instinct theory in *Human Nature and Conduct*, Dewey specifically takes issue with Freud's views concerning the sexual instinct, or libido. In an analysis of the tendency toward psychological oversimplification in the social sciences, Dewey remarks that psychoanalysis is guilty of trying to reduce the vast complex of human behavior to a sexual motif.[19] Horney likewise rejects

Freud's conception of the libido, doing so on the grounds that it is based on the false premises of instinct theory, and that it is funded by "unwarranted and often gross generalizations of certain good observations."[20] She interprets Freud's teachings about the libido as boiling down to two basic doctrines, which she christens "the enlargement of the concept of sexuality" and "the transformation of instincts." According to the first doctrine, the libido does not dictate specific sexual behaviors in human beings but rather exists as an amorphous source of sexual energy that can be diverted into an exceedingly wide range of activities. In fact, on the orthodox analytic view, all physical pleasures are inherently sexual, including bodily functions normally thought of as nonsexual in character, such as digestion and defecation. The second tenet asserts that the libido extends its influence to virtually all areas of the individual's life via mechanisms such as aim-inhibition and sublimation. Every form of human affection is understood to be a refracted expression of libidinal desire, and behind every act of self-assertion lurks a sadistic striving. Horney points out that Freud's evidence for the sweeping use he makes of the libido is insufficient to shore up his claims and sometimes even seems to be frivolous. So, for instance, Freud notes that the contented facial expression of an infant that has just nursed is similar to that of an adult who has recently engaged in sexual intercourse. If this observation is to count as evidence for his contentions about the libido, it is a weak one indeed, since, as Horney points out, no one has ever doubted that many apparently nonsexual activities such as sucking and stretching are pleasurable.

Having concluded that the prevailing instinct theory in psychoanalysis is untenable, Horney proposes that the expression "neurotic trend" be used to designate personality features that Freud cast in terms of instinctual drives and superego. Neurotic trends are not rooted in the instincts but rather consist of largely unconscious or subconscious strivings and attitudes that are aspects of an entire personality structure. Such trends emerge as part of unconscious strategies to deal with anxieties experienced by the individual in his or her interpersonal relations. Unlike Freud, who thought that biology and neurology determined human behavior, Horney posits a social basis for selfhood. On her view, character formation occurs largely through the individual's interactions with others. Neurotic behaviors are unconsciously learned, and environmental factors play a key role in their development (although Horney does not rule out influence from inborn elements, such as a genetic predisposition to aggressivity or shyness).

In addition to denying Freudian instinct theory, Horney fundamentally reworks the idea of the unconscious. While always maintaining that her approach constitutes a depth psychology, she adopts a conception of unconscious processes that is more Deweyan than Freudian. In *New Ways*, she stresses that full awareness of an attitude includes not only recognition of the attitude's existence but also an understanding of its overall function in the personality. She observes that one may be vaguely aware of a given disposition within oneself without really grasping its strength, underlying causes, or global impact on one's life.[21] By "attitude" Horney essentially means what Dewey has in mind when he employs the same word in *Human Nature and Conduct*—namely, a habit not manifest in behavior, but active just beneath the surface. Dewey treats attitudes or dispositions as habits held in check by other tendencies.[22] For instance, an individual with a predisposition to exploit others may be unaware of this inclination if it is usually restrained by an even more powerful desire for affection from his or her fellows. However, in a relationship in which such a person is confident of holding sway over the other party's love or admiration, the exploitive tendency may rise to the surface and take relatively direct and undisguised forms.

Horney focused her work upon the arrangements of habit that furnish individuals with distinctive personalities, though in her writings she typically refers to these groupings as personality structures involving specific drives or trends. Her approach assumes that habits do not exist in isolation but form functional systems in which various dispositions modify one another. For his part, Dewey terms this feature of mind the "interpenetration of habits," and equates it with character.[23] In the absence of such interpenetration, he reasons, the behavior of the individual would be deprived of that more or less cohesive pattern of choices, interests, and preferences that we think of as revealing personality. As he notes, sometimes a mere look or gesture may suffice to provide us with a sudden glimpse into an individual's inner self.[24]

On the whole, the interpenetration of habits is an unconscious process. Operating beneath the radar of awareness, neural networks allow us to perceive and transact with a world of enduring objects. The basic recognition of identity and difference in the manifold of phenomena, as well as the very unity of individual consciousness, depend upon these pathways in the brain. As concerns the development of sensorimotor capacities, the interpenetration of habits takes place more or less involuntarily. A similar process governs the formation of character.

In neither case should the interpenetration of habits be confused with their successful integration. Most habits can be adjudged as superior or inferior, depending upon their specific functions and respective qualities. A poor posture, for instance, may have a wide range of harmful effects on an individual's health. In much the same manner, a negative character trait usually makes itself felt across the entire personality. Horney argues that neurotic processes are the results of inner conflicts between incompatible but nevertheless compulsive "drives," or between unhealthy drives and normal healthy strivings toward self-realization. In her later writings (i.e., after her break with orthodox analysis), she does not employ the term "drive" in the sense of an instinctual process but rather uses it to highlight the obsessive and primarily emotional nature of certain attitudes. On her view, the dispositions that play a key role in the development of neuroses are those responsible for providing the individual with a feeling of identity or sense of self. The attitudes in question involve a fundamental orientation of the self to specific goals and ideals. These are the ends and values that the individual internalizes and adopts as his or her own, and they are always accompanied by an intense emotional attachment, although such affective associations are not necessarily conscious.

In the neurotic personality, the identifications are incorporated into what Horney coins the "idealized self," an imagined and unrealistic identity. Although the neurotic "search for glory" may take many forms, it usually entails a quest for the superlative: a compulsive need to excel in some socially recognized domain—to be an artistic genius, a moral saint, a Don Juan, or even a Napoleon. The attitude that the neurotic takes toward his or her idealized self varies from person to person. Some individuals suppose that they actually possess the magnified qualities of their fanciful self-images (a personality type that Horney regards as narcissistic), while others view the desirable traits as goals that they can, *and must,* achieve. In both cases inner conflict is preprogrammed, due to the unrealistic nature of the accomplishments and qualities attributed to the idealized self. The deformation of truth in the neurotic's relation to himself or herself leads to a variety of personal and interpersonal disturbances. By and large, reality is unkind to the neurotic, since it is ever confronting him or her with situations that threaten to expose the underlying pretensions. The fantastic nature of neurotic aspirations makes them brittle if they are brought out into the open air of the public arena, and a collision with the hard facts of life can spell disaster.

Individuals generally exhibit different degrees of psychological self-awareness, and everyday experience shows that we do not automatically make our own states of mind objects of scrutiny. In fact, the performance of many activities requires our undivided focus, and were we to split our attention between concentrating on the task at hand and watching ourselves at work, our acumen would be considerably lessened. There are numerous situations in which we are aware without being particularly self-aware. Although it is relatively exceptional that one "forgets" or "loses" oneself through especially deep engagement in some pursuit, self-awareness often constitutes no more than an indistinct backdrop to some other scene. The selective nature of attention even extends to sensations and feelings. In the throes of an intense experience, people often fail to register physical discomfort, and may only do so once the moment has passed and its heat has ebbed. Likewise, we may be oblivious to the true extent of our affection for someone until that person is absent from our lives for a prolonged period of time.

Horney hints that the "repression" of thoughts and feelings from awareness can be chiefly explained in terms of such motivated attention and selective emphasis. The various forms of self-deception so characteristic of neurosis, such as projection and reaction formation, are not the clandestine work of some "conscious unconscious" agency. Rather, they may be understood as subconscious strategies that individuals haphazardly hit upon as they try to deal with their particular difficulties. If a given stratagem repeatedly provides psychic relief, it may become ensconced as a habit without the individual necessarily being aware of having adopted a new behavior. Since the foundations for the neurotic personality are laid in childhood and often directly involve the neurotic behaviors of one or both parents, it is not hard to imagine how someone could unconsciously learn to dissimulate to himself or herself. An insecure child or adolescent, for instance, might develop a hypersensitivity to any form of criticism and interpret even the mildest and best-intentioned critiques as slights against his or her person. Reacting to such perceived censures with feelings of rage and humiliation, the juvenile's impulse might be to lash out in kind by pointing to deficiencies in the bearer of bad news. This strategy—which is, in fact, fairly common—not only serves as a vent to anger but often has the added advantage of deflecting attention away from the original criticism. Intuiting that the best defense is a strong offense, the young person may even succeed in placing the interlocutor on the defensive, particularly if the other party suffers from his or her own insecurities.

It is not at all unusual for some neurotics to develop a sixth sense for the weaknesses of others, since such a capacity can be of great practical value in coping with the problems engendered by character disorders.

Horney's revised form of psychoanalysis effectively demystifies the Freudian conception of the unconscious. On the orthodox view, the analyst functions as a sort of technical expert of the psychological depths, whose science and techniques are aimed at correcting underlying imbalances in the psyche. With surgical care the therapist must attempt to reroute destructive drives and reinforce the ego. Such work is clearly the prerogative of specialists, and orthodox psychoanalysis holds that genuine help to the patient can be provided solely through professional treatment. Only a qualified analyst will be able to identify and then diffuse the inner tensions created by submerged disturbances like the Oedipus complex. The premise implicit in the traditional view is that neurotic processes primarily result from instinctual conflicts that occur far beneath the range of awareness, where, unbeknownst to the individual, part of the mind actively works to block them from consciousness. Left to his or her own devices, an afflicted person would almost certainly be incapable of unearthing them.

Horney rejects this supposition in favor of the view that the neurotic fails to detect or correctly identify certain key desires and tendencies because he or she has a vested interest in not recognizing their presence; to do so would call into question his or her very identity and life project. It is not an unseen censor that prevents the neurotic from confronting his or her personal difficulties, but self-interest and psychological naiveté.

Critics of psychoanalysis have often compared it to Roman Catholicism. These detractors have pointed to the doctrinaire nature of analytic teachings and have likened the authority enjoyed by Freud in psychoanalysis to that possessed by the popes of the Church of Rome. In addition, few skeptics have missed the close parallels between the Catholic confessional and analytic therapy. In keeping with this metaphor, Horney's reworking of the Freudian view of unconscious processes amounts to a sort of Protestant reform of orthodox analysis. Where it was successful, the historical Reformation had the effect of desacralizing the functions of the priesthood. The cleric who officiated the Eucharist was no longer seen as possessing special powers necessary for the miracle of transubstantiation, but was instead understood to play a symbolic function in the accomplishment of a symbolic act.

Although most of the Protestant clergy continued to offer spiritual solace and support to their congregations, in the majority of Protestant denominations the confessional and its sacred power to forgive sin became obsolete. In an analogous development, under Horney's reform the analyst loses the special claim to be the gatekeeper to the unconscious. Her rejection of Freud's metapsychological scaffolding also results in a more complex view of unconscious processes, because the boundaries separating the unconscious and the subconscious from waking awareness become more fluid. However, the reader may recall that, despite her denial of some of his key concepts, Horney retains Freud's basic stance that the unconscious forces at work in the personality are mainly emotional in nature. In cases of severe neurosis, she holds that an individual can be so immersed in inner conflicts that professional treatment by an analyst may be the only available course of action with a reasonable chance of success. However, in less extreme instances Horney recognizes a variety of avenues by which a person may achieve insight into his or her own character. "Life itself," she writes, "is the most effective help for our development."[25] She also identifies a significant source of help in a relationship with a genuinely caring and generous individual—perhaps a relative, spouse, or friend—who is willing to combine concern with honest criticism. The third book she wrote, *Self-Analysis*, explored the possibility for the individual to serve as his or her own analyst.

Another of Freud's views that Horney explicitly rejects is his claim that psychoanalysis is value-free. The most obvious problem with Freud's position is that, qua therapy, psychoanalysis has certain practical goals toward which it strives. In order to be treated, patients must be evaluated in terms of their psychological condition, and such evaluation inevitably involves the use of a standard for what generally constitutes mental health. While the ideal of mental health may differ somewhat from analyst to analyst, therapy itself would be rendered ineffectual (if not impossible) without the employment of a guiding norm. Horney maintains that even Freud was unable to stay true to his vision of an analysis untainted by value judgments. His remarks about Victorian sexual mores and his emphasis upon the importance of being honest with oneself both involved estimations of worth.[26] In addition to the evaluative aspect of therapeutic practice, psychoanalysis inherently deals with moral values, since neurotic processes always affect character. In her last book, Horney describes the key features of neurosis as involving "a disturbance in one's relation to self and to others."[27]

Her version of analysis is based upon the premise that character and identity emerge through interpersonal relations.

Along these same lines, Horney identifies an instance of the free will/determinism dualism in the history of psychology. She notes that since antiquity two major schools of thought have proposed competing interpretations of mental disturbance. One has advocated a moral conception of mental illness. On this view, neurotic processes are grasped as personal failings that are treated as vices, and the primary solution to them is assumed to lie in the individual's native potential for self-discipline and moral reform. The other school has adopted a medical model of psychological ailments and sought to scientifically determine their causes and effects. Although Horney takes the side of the medical approach, she insists that a scientific account of mind should not blind itself to the moral dimension of neurosis. In fact, she argues that to some degree all neuroses involve moral problems because the unconscious pretensions in the neurotic personality give rise to what she terms "pseudo-morals." The neurotic's idealized self-image serves as a front that allows, for example, cynicism to masquerade as level-headed devotion to realism or an unconscious strategy of superficial living to disguise itself as a philosophical commitment to hedonism. In *Human Nature and Conduct*, Dewey provides a nice illustration of such duplicity in his discussion of the "ruder forceful natures" who rebel against conventional morals. In this connection he points out that in certain individuals, hypocrisy is not the result of a conscious design to cover up malicious intentions but rather the product of "an intensely executive nature" that has been paired with a deep desire for public approval.[28] He observes that such a combination is virtually a recipe for hypocrisy when the executive type is confronted with conventional moral demands or constraints that threaten to impede the attainment of his or her goals. Torn between the desire to achieve and the desire to be liked, such a person may fall victim to a self-deception that at least momentarily dulls the sharp edges of the conflict. One strategy that Dewey describes constitutes, in psychoanalytic terms, a classic reaction formation: the individual dissimulates his or her own misgivings about conventional morals through a show of praise for the "good" and condemnation of the "bad." Another path of escape from the dilemma Dewey discusses is the convenient rationale that one is called to a higher morality, so that one's moral missteps are only transgressions when viewed from the conventional standpoint.

If the underlying emotional attitudes in question are largely uncon-scious and compulsive, in the sense of being inflexible, the resulting tensions and inconsistencies in the individual's rapport with himself or herself and others can constitute what Horney calls a "neurotic conflict." The presence of such conflicts seriously impairs the individual's capacity for moral responsibility. A person caught in an inner bind may be left unsure about the nature of his or her own feelings; that is, there may be a deep confusion between what one thinks one ought to feel and one's actual sentiments. Furthermore, since the difficult moral choices invariably involve a selection that must be made between competing goods (an observation with which readers of Dewey will probably be familiar), morality requires the capacity for renunciation. Unaware of the full extent of his or her divided inner loyalties, the neurotic is often incapable of making the required sacrifice. Some neurotics are also hampered in their moral development by the use of unconscious defense strategies, such as projection and rationalization, which allow them to shift responsibility from themselves to other people or external circumstances.

Although she accepts Freud's principle of "psychic determinism," according to which mental processes are as strictly determined as their physical counterparts, Horney acknowledges intelligence as a real force in human affairs. Her psychology assumes that individuals have the potential to make genuinely reflective and rational choices between competing values. However, the human capacity for intelligence can be easily subverted by submerged emotional conflicts. In addition, even persons free of neurotic difficulties can—and often do—fail to take a clear stand when circumstances would otherwise warrant it. Shirking one's moral responsibility is not necessarily a sign of neuro-sis. Horney holds that many non-neurotic individuals fall short of full moral agency by simply failing to develop their own system of values. Such persons uncritically accept conventional mores and so may float along in the mainstream of society without attracting much attention to themselves. However, closer inspection would reveal that they have made compromises and acted inconsistently in ways of which they are wholly or partially unaware.[29]

By the time she wrote *Self-Analysis* (first published in 1942), Horney already had come to the conclusion that one need not be neurotic in order to benefit from psychoanalysis. In addition to its traditional office as a type of psychotherapy, analysis could serve the non-neurotic individual as an "aid to general character development."[30] Given the important role played by sentiment in cognition and judgment, virtually everyone could benefit from a better grasp of his or her own motivations and desires. She continued to develop this theme in the books that followed *Self-Analysis*. In her later work, Horney increasingly emphasized the innate human capacity for growth and the educational potential of psychoanalysis to assist individuals in the lifelong process of self-realization. Her view that the non-neurotic person is naturally inclined toward moral growth, and that neurosis represents a particularly unfortunate development of the personality in which the possibility for such growth is largely stymied, anticipated the major themes of the contemporary school of positive psychology. In the last decade of her life, Horney repeatedly pointed to the social and political ramifications of analysis. In seeking to liberate the individual from the bonds of inner conflicts, thereby freeing him or her for self-development, she held that analysis worked in the service of the open society.[31]

A Note Concerning Horney's Mature Theory

In our discussion of the integrative function of identity we have already briefly considered Horney's mature theory. As we noted earlier, several comprehensive accounts of her thought already exist, and to undertake another one would be to run the double risks of redundancy and digression. Nevertheless, a few remarks are in order as concerns Horney's final version of her personality theory. Among the major texts in psychoanalysis, Horney's books stand out due to their lack of technical jargon, their clarity, and their popular appeal. Since, as the saying goes, no good deed goes unpunished, there has arisen a decided tendency to oversimplify her thinking by equating her readily understandable prose with a foolproof guide to therapy. Despite her repeated warnings that her theory only offers general guidelines for analysis, and that each individual offers a unique psychological profile, some of those inspired by her work have tended toward a formulaic interpretation of her approach. This has been particularly true as concerns her triad of the major neurotic solutions—in the language of *Our Inner Conflicts,* the moves toward, against, and away from others. The classification of the three major types is deceptively simple, and it is easy to overlook the fact that each type actually represents a genus or family grouping whose membership is quite diverse. Being able to class a given person into one of the major divisions can certainly be an aid to grasping the structure of his or her personality, but it is only a step toward a fuller understanding, and should not be construed as filling in the last piece in the analytic puzzle.

In the book we have described as her magnum opus, *Neurosis and Human Growth*, Horney re-conceptualizes neurosis as comprising disturbed relations to oneself and others. In what turned out to be the last complete statement of her views, she clearly identifies the origin of neurotic processes with an untoward development of personal identity. Character disorders are constituted by a "central inner conflict" that pits the "real" or actual self of the individual against the idealized self-image. Explaining the genesis of her ideas, she notes that the thesis of *Neurosis and Human Growth* was born of the insight that the neurotic is bound to both despise and adore himself or herself. Although she had previously noted the coexistence of these diametrically opposed tendencies, her approach had been to treat them separately. Horney's final breakthrough was to grasp that they are simply different aspects of the same development. Prolonged self-idealization gives rise to a "pride system," by which she means the sum total of inclinations and attitudes that the individual inevitably acquires by measuring his or her actual self according to the standards of the idealized one. Given the woefully overinflated and wholly unrealistic expectations associated with the latter, the former is damned to always come up short. In Horney's words, *"the godlike being is bound to hate his actual being."*[32]

While from the afflicted individual's perspective the actual self constitutes a ball and chain that only serves to hinder the complete achievement of perfection, Horney maintains that it really harbors the seeds of rehabilitation. Try as the neurotic might, he or she can never entirely bring into line his or her merely human and imperfect self with the magnificence of its idealized counterpart. However, the very factors that continually betray the all too human nature of the individual who would be superhuman also constitute a potential source for spontaneous and genuine reactions and desires. Constructive growth is rooted in such unregulated features of the self, since their existence is actual and not merely premised upon a bundle of pretensions. These are the oddball and misfit elements that have escaped the narrow totalitarianism imposed by the blind faith in the idealized self. On Horney's view, the central conflict is the struggle that is waged between the self-imposed dictatorship of the neurotic ideal and the contrary elements that clamor for the freedom to simply be oneself. Since the therapist, in order to stand any chance of succeeding, must appeal to the forces

189

of constructive growth, the therapeutic goal of curing neurosis is tantamount to helping the individual toward self-realization.

Horney and Literature

We have argued that Horney's depth psychology is consistent with Hallpike's theory of social evolution, and that she recognized the highly individuated nature of modern selfhood. As a prominent member of what was eventually dubbed the "cultural school" of psychoanalysis, she also specifically acknowledged the role played by social and historical conditions in the formation of personality, and held that Freud had generally failed to take such factors into account. Given her belief in the relevance of historical context and sociological findings for depth psychology, it is only natural that Horney found a wealth of illustrative material in literature for her views. The so-called "modern novel" is, after all, the most psychological form of art, since in the traditional "omniscient" narrative style the novelist can depict and even dissect the subjectivity of his or her characters against the backdrop of an objective universe. Through the miracle of language the third person narrator can communicate the inner experience of a character, shift to consider the same character from the perspective of another individual or group, or even take measure of the entire interpersonal situation by contrasting it with the world of fact. Because the various shifts in perspective often necessitate that the author convey abstract ideas and information, the natural medium of the art that utilizes such epistemic transitions is language. While painting, music, and the other fine arts can express or evoke the personal aspects of an individual's experience, literature is arguably the form of art best suited for taking *inter*personal experience as its object.

Nietzsche was particularly sensitive to the psychological possibilities of literature and especially praised Stendhal and Dostoevsky as astute psychologists. For Nietzsche, both men qualified as psychologists in the sense that they functioned as naturalists of the human condition, that is, as perceptive observers and sketch artists of the psyche. Like many great writers, the two novelists were also attuned to the unique character of their time and place, and their works convey a sense of what life must have been like for themselves and their contemporaries. As witnesses of their respective eras, they brought to their fictional characters a richness, depth, and complexity often missing from the descriptions of subjects in social-scientific studies. Since their task as novelists didn't commit them to any particular school of psychology, they didn't have to worry about defending or supporting a specific theory and were free to record what they observed. Their observations point to the conclusion that individual awareness is conditioned by a variety of factors from both within and without.

Consider, for example, the following passages, taken from Stendhal's *The Red and The Black*. The quotations are from the book's seventh chapter, entitled "Elective Affinities," which recounts the budding love affair between the novel's protagonist, Julien, and Madame de Renal, in whose home the penniless young man is employed as a tutor to her children.

> In Paris, Julien's position with regard to Madame de Renal would very soon have been simplified; but in Paris love is the child of the novels. The young tutor and his timid mistress would have found in three or four novels, and even in the lyrics of the Gymnase, a clear statement of their situation. The novels would have outlined for them the part to be played, shown them the model to copy; and this model, sooner or later, albeit without the slightest pleasure, and perhaps with reluctance, vanity would have compelled Julien to follow . . .

> Madame de Renal, the wealthy heiress of a religious aunt, married at sixteen to a worthy gentleman, had never in her life felt or seen anything that bore the faintest resemblance to love. Her confessor, the good cure Chelan, was the only person almost who had ever spoken to her of love, with reference to the advances of M. Valenod, and he had drawn so revolting a picture of it that the word conveyed nothing to her but the idea of the most abject immorality. She regarded as an exception, or rather as something quite apart from nature, love such as she had found it in the very small number of novels that chance had brought to her notice. Thanks to this ignorance, Madame de Renal, entirely happy, occupied incessantly with the thought of Julien, was far from reproaching herself in the slightest degree.[33]

The only world that Julien and Madame de Renal are acquainted with is that of the small towns and countryside of the Franche-Comté, a region in eastern France bordering on Switzerland. Since the story takes place in the first quarter of the nineteenth century, cosmopolitan Paris is a world away, at least by the standards of contemporary transportation technology. The author highlights the fact that this relative physical isolation is accompanied by a cultural one as well. Although there exists a print media, its diffusion is quite limited according to modern standards. At the beginning of the nineteenth century, France is still too uneducated, too poor, and too traditional for books and newspapers to make much of an impact outside of the major urban areas. As a result of her narrow and sheltered upbringing, Madame de Renal doesn't even recognize the amorous nature of her feelings toward Julien, and mistakenly attributes her keen interest in him to altruistic impulses. Since she is the respectable wife of the town mayor, her lack of insight into her own emotions and motives is certainly self-interested, but it is also directly related to a specific set of historical circumstances. Given the nearly universal presence of electronic media throughout the developed countries of the modern world, even far-flung rural populations in France are now savvy in a way that was mainly reserved for Parisians in Stendhal's day.

If great authors include details of social context in portraying a character's frame of mind, and thereby achieve heightened realism, shouldn't such factors also be of interest to professional psychologists, insofar as the latter wish to shed light on personality and motivation? From a strictly Freudian standpoint, however, such literary depictions are superficial because they fail to deal with the wholly unconscious inner forces driving the individual. In retrospect, Freud's take on human nature is very much in keeping with eighteenth and nineteenth century romanticism, since his theory reveals our inner nature and dynamic core to be thoroughly impulsive and irrational. Like some of the more radical romantics, he dethrones discursive reason as the mind's monarch by suggesting that it has little sway over or even awareness of the elemental forces that actually determine our most important choices and reactions. In Freud's *Sturm und Drang* conception of mind, reason is often the clueless pawn of intrapsychic power struggles. His theory is a bold one, and his conclusions are startling; by comparison, the psychological insights of a Stendhal appear somewhat banal and commonsensical, the mere products of studious introspection and observation of others.

The reader will recall that Horney's reworked version of the unconscious dispenses with the compartmentalization of mind into id, ego, and superego, and recasts the unconscious primarily in terms of ignorance and subtle denial rather than outright repression:

> Awareness of an attitude comprises not only the knowledge of its existence but also the knowledge of its forcefulness and influence and the knowledge of its consequences and the functions which it serves. If this is missing it means that the attitude was unconscious, even though at times glimpses of knowledge may have reached awareness.[34]

Given this expanded understanding of the unconscious, it is not surprising that she turned to literature for psychological insight, for the pages of the Western literary canon are replete with examples of thinking, feeling, and acting that well illustrate the cited definition. In addition, as Bernard Paris and other literary critics have shown, Horney's ideas can be fruitfully applied to the study of literature. Her version of psychoanalysis has a natural affinity with literature because the two share essentially the same universe of discourse—namely, the human condition as considered in both its private and interpersonal aspects, as experienced firsthand and as an object of thought.

As we have already noted, Freud believed that analytic therapy could and should be pursued independently of any value judgments, a view that dovetails with Kant's identification of ethical behavior with conduct conforming to a universal law or principle. If we assume that the ultimate warrant for morals lays in the existence of such a rational law to which all moral judgments should conform, then considerations of personal motivation and decision making are not directly relevant for determining how the individual ought to act. While it is unclear from his writings where Freud stood in regard to the actual existence of a moral law, his approach tacitly assumes that if morality is anything more than wishful thinking or propaganda, then it must be grounded in some such principle of reason. His description of the unconscious leaves little doubt that our native instincts and emotions are devoid of any genuinely charitable or philanthropic impulses. Although the libido fuels desires that may be deflected into more socially acceptable forms, such as compassion and friendship, even sublimated libidinal desires are essentially sexual and, hence, bent on self-gratification. Given the essentially amoral nature of our native emotional endowment, it would appear that whatever real regard for others exists must spring from reason.

As a psychologist, Freud felt free to leave ethical speculation to philosophy, and to devote himself to the scientific study of the psyche. Due, however, to his implicit acceptance of a Kantian dualism between empirical human nature and rational ethics, he propounded a depth psychology that intentionally ignored the individual's moral qualities, just as some moral philosophers have continued to assume that psychological considerations are irrelevant to morals.

Notwithstanding the influence of the Kantian heritage on ethics and psychoanalysis, writers of fiction have continued to artistically explore interpersonal situations in which the analysis of individual psychology is pregnant with moral meaning. Literature is an inherently moral enterprise, not in the sense that it directly imparts "good" morals, but in the sense that it serves as a particularly effective medium for communicating and reflecting upon the moral dimension of various interpersonal situations. Needless to say, its probings of conscience and character also have a psychological dimension. In addition, because custom in the form of acquired habit and attitude constitutes the inevitable mental background for moral judgment, literary depictions of personality naturally include the relevant features of environing social conditions. Insofar as such literary depictions are realistic, they are often more successful than many social scientific theories in vividly conveying the complex interplay between moral, psychological, and cultural factors in the individual's mental makeup and behavior.

We have argued that the modern novel is the most psychological form of art, and it should now be evident that the psychology in question is that of the modern individual. In fact, the natural readership of the modern novel is the self-aware inhabitant of the society of the advanced type, for whom both identity and morality are no longer purely customary but involve a significant degree of personal choice. This is the same modern individual who experiences a gap that can never be completely closed between the inner dictates of conscience and the public demands of prevailing norms, and between his or her sense of self and the social roles he or she occupies. For such a person, the investigation of the manifold forms of individuality proposed by modern literature can be enticing. The work of fiction creates a bridge between personal subjectivity and communal objectivity, permitting the reader to gain a new awareness of the constellation of features unique to his or her own self by imaginatively donning the situation and character of others.

I have also argued that the personality and identity of the modern self are particularly individuated. As we have seen, this individuation is the result of a process of social evolution that has led to the gradual dissolution of an overarching cultural pattern based on custom. Such a unifying system of culture is a hallmark of traditional societies, and to those reared in its embrace it ascribes both identity and a life narrative, providing for an extensive integration of the individual with the social milieu. In the modern social setting, the rise of individualism has meant that the individual must take an active hand in the creation of his or her identity and life narrative. Custom and tradition, formerly the undisputed guides in human affairs, have ceded their preeminence to personal choice based on private conviction and calculated self-interest.

The new freedoms enjoyed by the individual have tended, in turn, to create a more diverse social landscape. The most important social institution to be impacted in this regard is the family, which is arguably the primary bearer of cultural values in advanced societies. As we have already remarked, if psychoanalysis has identified childhood as the crucial era in the development of personality, it is largely due to the fact that family life has become so diversified. Even within the same geographical location and the same social class, families can differ radically from one another. It is by no means unusual for the modern family to have its own observances and culinary traditions, its own sexual mores, or its own distinctive political or religious orientation. What we have called the micro-culture of family life has become such a significant element in the psychological make up of its members that the contemporary journey of self-discovery usually involves a phase of coming to terms with the distinctive features of one's own upbringing. Once again, many authors of serious fiction have proven themselves to be astute psychological observers, since in all likelihood no social institution has received more attention in modern literature than the family.

The close affinity of Horney's views with literary character studies demonstrates just how seriously her approach takes the uniqueness and complexity of modern selfhood. The fact that her theory accords so nicely with character depictions found in great works of fiction should not be discounted as evidence in support of her views just because such corroboration stems from an unorthodox source. One of the qualities of a good novelist is the capacity to paint convincing psychological portraits, and it stands to reason that great novelists often have a gift for psychological realism. Likewise, it has repeatedly been remarked about Horney's writings that their popular success is at least partially due to the fact that so many of her readers recognize themselves or others in her theories and descriptions.

It may be objected that popular appeal is no measure by which to gauge the accuracy of a scientific theory. After all, perhaps the average person's firsthand experience of the psyche through run-of-the-mill introspection and observation of others has nothing to do with the real nature of human motivation. Such, of course, is Freud's contention. Although it is certainly conceivable that the reality of human psychology is wholly belied by our everyday experience of it, we have argued that the case Freud makes for his version of depth psychology is weak. If we are to reject some of our most basic intuitions regarding mind, then we should at least be provided with persuasive grounds for doing so.

Notes

1. Karen Horney, *Self-Analysis* (New York: W. W. Norton & Company, 1942), 10.
2. Horney, *New Ways in Psychoanalysis*, 34.
3. Ibid., 33.
4. Ibid., 18.
5. Ibid.
6. Bernard J. Paris, *Karen Horney: A Psychoanalyst's Search for Self-Under-standing* (New Haven and London: Yale University Press, 1994), xx–xxi.
7. Ibid., xx and 150–153.
8. Ibid., 215.
9. Ibid., 153–160.
10. Ibid., 157.
11. Horney, *New Ways in Psychoanalysis*, 34.
12. Ibid., 11.
13. A nice example of such a "translation" appears in the title of Irving Solomon's book, *Karen Horney and Character Disorder* (New York: Springer Publishing Company, 1995).
14. Horney, *New Ways in Psychoanalysis*, 7.
15. Ibid., 187.
16. Ibid.
17. In *New Ways*, she quotes from William James' *Principles of Psychology* to illustrate the mechanistic version of evolution [ibid, 42–43.]. The passage she cites is from the book's sixth chapter, entitled "The Mind-Stuff Theory" [see William James, *The Principles of Psychology: Volume One* (New York: Dover Publications, Inc., 1950), 146.]. Unfortunately, Horney seems to read James as a proponent of the mechanistic view, failing to recognize that his description of the mechanistic standpoint actually forms part of a criticism of that very perspective.
18. Horney, *New Ways in Psychoanalysis*, Chapter VIII: The Emphasis on Childhood, sic passim.
19. Dewey, *Human Nature and Conduct*, 93.
20. Horney, *New Ways in Psychoanalysis*, 68.
21. Ibid., 20–21.
22. Dewey, *Human Nature and Conduct*, 31–32.
23. Ibid., 29–30.
24. Ibid., 30.
25. Horney, *Self-Analysis*, 10.
26. Horney, *New Ways in Psychoanalysis*, 296–297.
27. Horney, *Neurosis and Human Growth*, 368.
28. Dewey, *Human Nature and Conduct*, 7.
29. Karen Horney, *Our Inner Conflicts: A Constructive Theory of Neurosis* (New York: W. W. Norton & Company, Inc., 1945), 24–25.
30. Horney, *Self-Analysis*, 10.
31. Ibid., 12.
32. Ibid.
33. Stendhal, *The Red and The Black: A Chronicle of the Nineteenth Century*, trans. C. K. Scott Moncrieff, 1925.
34. Horney, *New Ways in Psychoanalysis*, 20.

6

Psychotherapy as Moral Education

Morals concern nothing less than the whole character, and the whole character is identical with the man in all his concrete make-up and manifestations. To possess virtue does not signify to have cultivated a few namable and exclusive traits; it means to be fully and adequately what one is capable of becoming through association with others in all the offices of life.[1]
—John Dewey

Government, business, art, religion, all social institutions have a meaning, a purpose. That purpose is to set free and to develop the capacities of human individuals without respect to race, sex, class or economic status. And this is all one with saying that the test of their value is the extent to which they educate every individual into the full stature of his possibility. Democracy has many meanings, but if it has a moral meaning, it is found in resolving that the supreme test of all political institutions and industrial arrangements shall be the contribution they make to the all-around growth of every member of society.[2]
—John Dewey

More than a few moral philosophers have held that psychological considerations of intent and motivation are relevant to ethics. In order to accurately assess a moral agent's degree of responsibility for a given act, these thinkers have maintained that we need to know what the agent explicitly hoped to achieve by his or her action, and we need to identify the factors that predisposed him or her to perform it. It might seem as if these considerations exhaust the contribution psychology has to make to ethics. Horney goes a step further by suggesting that psychotherapy can not only help to ascertain moral responsibility but also play an important role in personal development.

In the course of repeated revisions to her theory, the notion of personal development or growth came to figure prominently in Horney's work. In *Self-Analysis* she writes,

> Psychoanalysis is still and will remain a method of therapy for specific neurotic disorders. But the fact that it can be an aid to general character development has come to assume a weight of its own. To an increasing degree people turn to analysis not because they suffer from depressions, phobias, or comparable disorders but because they feel that factors within themselves are holding them back or injuring their relationships with others.[3]

This new view of psychoanalysis as a tool in character development became the unifying theme of her last book, *Neurosis and Human Growth: The Struggle Toward Self-Realization*, as is clearly signaled by the title and subtitle. In the introduction, "A Morality of Evolution," Horney relates the notion of growth to the development of what she terms "the real self." She intends the real self as a contrast to the illusory, idealized self that she identifies as a key component of character disorders. On her view, one of the most insidious effects of such disorders is that they prevent the individual from realizing his or her unique human potential.

Horney contrasts three different conceptions of human nature that respectively inform three different views of conscience. The first standpoint she discusses takes a dim view of the human psyche, holding it to be inherently sinful or impulsive and self-centered. She argues that this attitude leads to a conception of conscience as a system of inner dictates which society must impose upon its members in order to curb their asocial tendencies. A second standpoint adopts a Manichean view of human nature and generally holds that the victory of the positive tendencies over the negative depends upon supernatural aid or upon a strict regimen of reason and willpower. Although this conception of the human condition is more optimistic than the first, Horney stresses that it, too, ultimately has recourse to a system of internalized prohibitions and commandments. She maintains that when the inner empire of ideals and values is erected upon the basis of fear and awe, rather than upon that of understanding and enlightened desire, the individual inevitably loses some of his or her native spontaneity and flexibility.

Horney also criticizes the "original sin" and Manichean models of human nature due to the fact that they both "presuppose a given knowledge of what is good or bad."[4] In other words, they don't allow for a type of moral conscience based upon individual experience and personal judgment. Her own view posits the existence of "evolutionary constructive forces" in the human psyche that naturally prompt the individual to seek self-realization. In a healthy course of development, the individual's values are not simply rationalized versions of custom but rather the results of reflective choice made against the backdrop of his or her own growth and experience. Horney argues that the process of personal moral development offers an attractive alternative to the various strategies subconsciously employed by individuals to deal with their asocial or destructive tendencies. Rather than dissimulating the existence of disruptive elements in the personality through a reaction formation or via projection, the individual is able to outgrow undesirable tendencies by becoming aware of them. Horney describes such work on oneself as at once constituting the prime moral obligation and the prime moral privilege.[5]

The conception of the good life as naturally incorporating personal and moral growth originated in antiquity. In his discussion of the great civilizations of the Axial Age, Hallpike notes that, "The moral life is increasingly seen as a slow struggle to develop one's character by bringing one's desires into harmony with the right, and the image of the path or way becomes a predominant symbol of this dynamic model of the moral life as a series of choices lasting until death."[6] While Western intellectuals readily identify this view with Greek philosophy in general, and with Aristotle's ethics in particular, Hallpike points out that detailed doctrines of virtue were also elaborated by Confucians in China and Buddhists in India. Whether Greek, Chinese, or Indian, the life of virtue was associated with the individual's cultivation of self-understanding and growth in wisdom. For instance, Plato's dialectic of knowledge assumes not only a transformation of understanding but also one of desire: To catch sight of the highest Forms is to undergo a change that is both cognitive and emotional.

A nice illustration of the Platonic dialectic is presented in Diotima's speech in the *Symposium*, in which she outlines the ideal growth of love in beauty. Love is first awakened through the perception of a beautiful body, but the young lover soon realizes that the beauty of all attractive bodies is one and the same, and so will come to view his attachment to just one body as shortsighted and foolish. A particular instance of beauty thus serves as the springboard to an appreciation of beauty per se. The next step involves yet another enlargement of perspective, as the lover shifts his focus from the pulchritude of bodies to that of souls. He realizes that beauty of character is more precious than physical beauty, and so will even desire to dedicate himself to someone who is physically unattractive if that person has a beautiful soul. The focus on spiritual beauty leads to a new understanding and appreciation of laws and customs, since these promote the development of good souls. After love for social institutions and activities has arisen in him, the lover will begin to adore various kinds of knowledge until he ultimately gains access to the form of Beauty itself. Diotima's ideal scheme of development reveals that as the questing individual grows in understanding, his affections undergo a continual process of modification and reorientation.

Although it is couched in his metaphysics of eternity, Plato's key insight in this account is that the individual's values can mature through growth in experience and understanding. While this idea is far from uncommon, it has played a surprisingly minor role in the main currents of modern moral philosophy. Writing of the relationship of science to social progress, Dewey observes that

> progress is sometimes thought of as consisting in getting nearer to ends already sought. But this is a minor form of progress, for it requires only improvement of the means of action or technical advance. More important modes of progress consist in enriching prior purposes and in forming new ones. Desires are not a fixed quantity, nor does progress mean only an increased amount of satisfaction. With increased culture and new mastery of nature, new desires, demands for new qualities of satisfaction, show themselves, for intelligence perceives new possibilities of action. This projection of new possibilities leads to search for new means of execution, and progress takes place; while the discovery of objects not already used leads to suggestion of new ends.[7]

Although Dewey is clearly writing from a social perspective in this passage, his remarks about the development of ends could apply to the individual as well. The human growth that Horney identifies as a therapeutic goal largely consists in the individual's capacity to adopt new and improved ends. During the course of her career, she came to believe that not only can the psychotherapist assist the individual in thinking critically about his or her own values but also, in order to be effective, the therapist must confront the patient's moral difficulties.[8]

As early as 1939, in *New Ways in Psychoanalysis*, she declared that every neurotic has moral problems, and that the challenge for the analyst is to distinguish "pseudo-moral" difficulties from genuine ones.[9]

She notes many patients are actually eager to call the therapist's attention to their personal moral issues, but that these are often red herrings, since such self-professed difficulties are typically just a reflection of the patient's particular neurotic strivings. Horney presents psychoanalysis as an inherently moral enterprise, in the sense that it constitutes a type of reeducation, and she attributes the characterization of psychoanalysis as reeducation to Freud. However, insofar as he held moral issues and value judgments to be irrelevant to analytic work, she argues that he contradicted his own vision. Freud assumed one could educate without making value judgments—an assumption that Horney points out is mistaken, since all education requires goals and standards, and these imply precisely such judgments. The psychotherapist inevitably makes value judgments insofar as he or she offers the patient any guidance whatsoever, including even mere encouragement to explore a particular feeling or attitude in more depth, or to move on to another topic. Horney urges that the analyst be forthright about his or her value judgments, arguing that a candid approach can help the analysand to face up to his or her real problems.

Horney's conception of psychotherapy as a type of moral education is based on the distinction she draws between "pseudo-morals" and genuine moral ideals. She describes the latter as "the standard of feelings or behavior which the individual himself recognizes as valuable and obligatory to him. They are not ego-alien but are an integral part of the self."[10] True moral ideals presuppose that the individual has sifted through his or her cultural inheritance of received mores and has chosen his or her own priorities. On Horney's view, it is by no means a given that even the average non-neurotic person has developed such a reflective morality, since many people find it easier to simply pay lip service to conventional morality and to live with inconsistent attitudes and values. Nevertheless, neurotic persons are at a significant disadvantage when it comes to formulating a personal code of ethics because their inner conflict is essentially unconscious. They are the victims of unrealistic pretensions that they believe to be reasonable and in which they have a considerable emotional investment. In order to protect these inherently fragile beliefs, they have subconsciously adopted strategies that serve to blur or even deform inconvenient facts. The unconscious capacity to make the perceived world square with desire is not limited to external circumstances, but can extend to the self's own feelings. A dictatorial, bullying father can be transformed into a favorite parent, admired for his decisiveness and force of character, and the existence of natural desires for creature comforts can be denied for the sake of a frugality that serves as a badge of virtue. The neurotic interprets his or her human environment in such a way as to compliment the idealized self-image. The various unconscious strategies of dissimulation leave the afflicted individual ill equipped to confront moral issues, since he or she is, in fact, fundamentally divided in commitments and ambivalent in feeling.

Horney begins the first chapter of *Our Inner Conflicts* with the observation that conflicts involving values are par for the course in the modern individual due to the complex and rapidly changing nature of modern civilization. She notes that even in relatively stable, tradition-bound societies, life is not wholly conflict-free for the individual, who may have to negotiate a path between incompatible loyalties or between personal predilection and duty to others. The situation is, of course, even more dramatic in modern civilization, and her description of this state of affairs echoes points we made earlier about the largely independent activity systems of the modern social order, and the progressive loss of a unifying cultural narrative.

In order for the individual to be able to recognize and resolve conflicts involving competing goods or duties, Horney identifies four preconditions: The individual must be aware of his or her wishes and feelings, have developed his or her own set of values, be capable of renouncing at least one of the goods or duties at stake, and be able to assume responsibility for the consequences of his or her decision.[11] The sort of personal evaluation and judgment she has in mind is clearly that popularly associated with conscience. Since a character disorder usually impairs a person's ability to fulfill all four preconditions, one of the goals of Horneyian therapy is to enable the patient to confront moral dilemmas. Her approach to personal morality represents a golden mean between the extremes of value-neutrality and moralistic preaching. She recognizes that since psychotherapy involves the assessment of behavior, the psychotherapist is inevitably guided by a set of general value judgments as regards certain character traits and patterns of conduct. In order to safeguard against misjudgment on the part of the analyst, she recommends that he or she be frank with the patient as concerns the values informing his or her therapeutic approach. Furthermore, Horney stresses that morality is not primarily a matter of mere personal opinion but rather "one of fact coupled with consequences,"[12] and she urges the therapist to ground his or her evaluations of the patient's attitudes and conduct in a realistic consideration of their impact on the patient's growth and relationships.

Individuals afflicted with character disorders are fundamentally compromised in their personal autonomy, due to the compulsive nature of certain underlying attitudes. The key ends toward which they strive are not life goals that have been freely chosen after careful consideration but rather obligations that must be met at all costs. The deontic-like quality of these ends—Horney dubs them "the shoulds"—stems from the individual's desperate attempts to maintain the appearance of superiority or perfection demanded by his or her idealized self-image. Hence, the goal of the therapist is not to constitute a moral authority for the patient but rather to enable the latter to become his or her *own* moral authority.

Psychotherapy qua moral education could be likened to education in appreciation of the arts, wherein learning is not just abstract but involves firsthand experience of the relevant subject matter. For Horney, the crucial element of therapy is transference, by which she understands the patient's "emotional reactions to the psychoanalytical situation."[13] Due to the special nature of the therapeutic relationship, there are two levels of interaction that can provide the therapist with clues to the patient's character structure. The first level is simply that of general human interaction, through which the analyst gains an intuitive feel for the patient by noting such telltale signs as overall bearing, tone of voice, quality of gesture, and so forth. The second level of interaction constitutes the unique feature of the analytic relationship, since it involves the patient's commitment to the principle of free association, that is, the patient's pledge to tell the analyst everything he or she thinks and feels. It is on the basis of this principle that the therapist is capable of making the sort of accurate and detailed observations that are likely to disclose the patient's underlying personality structure. Horney essentially understands psychoanalytic therapy as a special relationship and form of communication in which the analyst develops tailor-made strategies to overcome the patient's resistance to accepting a more realistic self-understanding. The art of the analyst consists in making an accurate diagnosis, and then in presenting it in such a way to the patient that the latter becomes the recipient of a communication that has the potential to transform his or her self-awareness.

Although Horney believes that the psychoanalytic relationship has great potential for increasing our understanding of individual psychology, she readily admits that it is not the only source of help for neurotics. As she points out more than once in her writings, life itself can be a good therapist, as can a caring and insightful family member or friend. Nonetheless, psychoanalysis enjoys the distinct advantage of being an applied science or art that gives us a more reliable method for dealing with neurotic difficulties. As she notes, although life experience can be instructive, it is often either too harsh or too diffuse to do much good, and while an intuitive layperson can sometimes provide considerable assistance, one has to be lucky enough to befriend such an individual. Psychoanalysis offers a body of knowledge and a set of skills that can be taught and mastered, and Horney holds that a sufficiently motivated patient can even employ self-analysis to good effect.

While the main source for her belief in the therapeutic potential of self-analysis was probably her own lifelong quest for self-understanding,[14] Horney's view of self-analysis is consistent with her overall reconstruction of Freud's depth psychology. Although she still employs the term "drive" to describe the emotional forces that endow the personality with its fundamental motives, her view of a drive is much more akin to Dewey's notion of a disposition or attitude as forms of habit than to Freud's instinct-based conception. One effect of this theoretical revision is to reveal the kinship of analysis to critical thinking.

Personal identity is what some philosophers refer to as a "thick concept," that is, an idea that is not only descriptive but also normative. The foundations of identity are laid throughout childhood, long before the individual is capable of critical thinking. So basic a logical distinction as that between fact and value nevertheless constitutes a cultural achievement and must be acquired, at least indirectly. Even among adults, one major source of poor reasoning is the natural propensity to allow comprehension to be led by values rather than facts. This type of error generally involves the failure to give ostensibly unappealing alternatives a fair hearing. The less the individual is aware of his or her own desires and fears, the more likely he or she will be to succumb to their unconscious influence in thought and deed. For instance, several of the so-called fallacies of relevance, such as the various forms of *argumentum ad hominem*, involve the undue influence of sentiment and value on reasoning. Obviously, the evaluation of values or ends should conform to the facts, and not vice-versa. Because the neurotic's leading interests are not chosen, and often appear to him or her in only a vague and fragmentary fashion, it is very hard for the afflicted individual to adopt a critical stance toward them.

Social Factors in Self-Deception

A perennial complaint about Western civilization is that it suffers from poor morals, and the knowledge that such laments have existed since at least the glory days of ancient Greece and Rome tends to put contemporary denunciations of moral decline into proper perspective. Nevertheless, there is at least one sense in which modern society decidedly suffers from poor morals, and that is in terms of our understanding of the individual's personal moral problems. Horney's brand of psychoanalysis has an important contribution to make in helping us to better comprehend and confront these troubles. As she points out in the introduction to *Our Inner Conflicts*, we inhabit a difficult civilization, one that provides fertile soil for the seeds of self-deception. The social basis for self-deception involves several different factors that we have noted in the course of this essay, and that we will now briefly pass in review.

The very individualism that is the hallmark of Western societies has often been identified as a cause or symptom of moral decay. The growth of social and political liberalism has spelled a progressive individualization of preferences and lifestyles, and those who equate morals with fixed custom or universal principles have often seen in such cultural pluralism a slide into thoroughgoing moral relativism. The increasing role of personal judgment in morals has often appeared to such thinkers as more of a threat than a promise. As we have argued, modern moral philosophers have generally failed to appreciate the inspirational and creative potential of conscience as personal judgment. As a result, both our intellectual and popular cultures are inhabited by a vague sense of moral disarray and impending cultural calamity.

Of course, the deeply divided state of contemporary moral theory has not helped matters. Woe to the layperson who, confused by the modern welter of competing principles, rights, duties, virtues, and maxims, turns to philosophy for moral guidance! There he or she will likely learn that morality either hinges entirely upon having the right intentions, or alternatively upon achieving the right results; that moral goodness is almost wholly a matter of reason, or rather of feeling; that good conduct is directly related to the quest for personal happiness, or that it has nothing to do with it, and so forth. One unfortunate consequence of these sharp and chronic differences of opinion among the experts is that they indirectly provide many in the lay public with yet another reason for professing moral relativism. Such self-professed relativists rarely act upon their doctrine in a consistent manner, and it primarily serves them as a handy way of anesthetizing and subsequently ignoring pangs of conscience that should provoke introspection. However, despite the persistence of ideological rifts, there are some indications that a meeting of minds is gradually taking place among contemporary moral philosophers. The new rallying point is naturalism—a naturalism fueled by the discoveries of the human sciences—of which Horney's personality theory represents an important, albeit neglected, instance.

In modern society the abstract nature of most ethical principles and the vagueness of many key moral terms constitute another important source of confusion over morals. As we have seen, guidelines for behavior become more abstract in complex societies because detailed, context-specific rules are unworkable in a highly differentiated social landscape. As the social structure becomes increasingly complex, values tend to become more subjective, in the sense that the mental leap the individual must make in order to relate goods and duties widens. By the same token, terms descriptive of moral character, such as "kindness" or "generosity," tend to be afflicted with vagueness, since such words directly draw their meaning from a shared human context. We have argued that in societies that clearly distinguish between public and private spaces, families develop unique micro-cultures of value, in which roughly the same activities can be performed with very different attitudes. This progressive individualization of family life has created a patchwork backdrop of meaning in reference to which the contemporary vocabulary of virtue and vice is employed. Since different families often have conflicting views as to what constitutes good parenting, or genuine love, or group solidarity, using the vocabulary of everyday moral psychology to communicate with the general public is often a delicate affair. Individuals may have insular or idiosyncratic understandings of certain moral terms without being aware of it, and so be prone to equivocation.

Whereas simple societies are almost entirely organized on the basis of a shared cultural pattern, advanced ones depend on specialized activity systems that operate in relative independence from the cultural framework. Although members of an advanced society are still more often than not united by a common language and shared religious, moral, and social customs, the largely autonomous activity systems of modern life introduce additional ends and motives into individual conduct that sometimes conflict with traditional values. Whereas simple societies often display a high degree of cultural integration and harmonization, the modern social order tends to confront its members with competing ends and duties whose ordering and prioritization is often left up to the individual.

In her first book, *The Neurotic Personality of Our Time*, Horney identified three contradictions inherent in American culture that she believed constituted factors in neurotic self-deception.[15] The first and arguably most important tension she discusses is that between the competitive and meritocratic ideals that originated in the free market economy and the Christian values of brotherly love and humility. The former emphasize individual self-interest, ingenuity, and assertiveness, while the latter involve putting others before oneself and turning the other cheek. If the ethos of competition were limited to the economic sphere, the tension between these two moral frameworks would be less extreme, or at least more readily identifiable. However, Horney observes that the competitive spirit pervades the American way of life, and is present at both work and at home. It permeates virtually all manner of human relationships: both those between the sexes and within the sexes, friendships as well as family ties. The principle of competition not only serves to structure relationships in the private sector and in public service but also is reflected in the organization of our education and recreation.

Indeed, from the perspective of social evolution, it is clear that competition has been the natural companion piece to the growth of modern individualism. Nearly everywhere that status has been replaced by contract, this transformation has ultimately involved the incorporation of competition as the main mechanism for determining how differentials of wealth, power, and prestige are to be distributed. Regardless of whether the individual likes it or not, from the standpoint of the modern social order nearly everyone is both free agent and potential participant in structural competition. While the generous application of the principle of competition to contemporary life has arguably played a key role in the breathtaking economic, technological, and scientific advances of modernity, Horney believes that it has exacted a high toll in terms of the individual's mental well-being.

She identifies a number of different ways in which the competitive ethos tends to undermine the individual's self-esteem and sense of security. The structural or built-in nature of competition throughout modern institutions and groups leaves us feeling isolated and at risk of losing out to others. The knowledge that someone's win usually implies someone else's loss serves to generate what Horney refers to as a diffuse background sense of hostility, a hostility that is all too often exhibited in rivalries between siblings, friends, and even between parents and their offspring. She argues that the individual's vague sense of impending aggression in turn feeds other fears and anxieties. In any system based on competition we may quite reasonably fear failure in our chosen pursuits, and even success is bittersweet, since it engenders the fear that our competitors will be left feeling envious and angry toward us. In addition, she notes that most people automatically gauge their own self-worth based on their successes and failures, and that, given the vagaries of human existence, this constitutes an unreliable basis for self-esteem. The net outcome of competitive fear and loathing is the individual's sense of being ultimately on his or her own in the world, and in many people this creates an exaggerated craving for affection. In Horney's opinion, this reaction is so typical that it has led to a general over-evaluation of love in our culture. Though she affirms that love can be genuine, she holds that many people treat it as a psychological panacea, thereby freighting their close relationships with unrealistic expectations.

The second cultural contradiction she mentions is that which arises due to desires shaped by the virtual world of advertising and media, where pleasure is boundless, consumption carefree, and youth eternal, versus the sober reality of the actual impediments and limits we inevitably encounter in trying to satisfy our desires. In pursuing their business, media and the advertising industry indirectly lend a patina of reasonableness to inflated expectations, and so are instrumental in widening the gulf between the individual's wishes and their fulfillment.

The third contradiction she notes results from the tension between the modern social and political ideology that the individual is free to pursue his or her dreams, and can realize them with sufficient will power, perseverance, and hard work, and the fact that everyone's possibilities are actually constrained by circumstances outside his or her control. For their respective purposes, our economic, political, and legal institutions attribute a freedom of choice to the individual that often conflicts with what the social sciences have taught us about the determination of human thought and action. Caught between an ideology that assumes nearly limitless personal liberty on the one hand, and the very real restrictions of everyday life on the other, many people oscillate between a feeling of great freedom and a sense of deep helplessness.

Horney by no means intended the brief discussion of cultural conditions in *The Neurotic Personality of Our Time* to be exhaustive, and even indicated that the detailed investigation of these conditions was a task better suited to the sociologist than to the psychoanalyst. For our purposes, it will suffice to note that if psychotherapy is to approximate its full potential for moral education, it will have to incorporate social and cultural criticism, and that such inclusion would not simply embrace therapeutic theory, but also therapeutic practice.

Anticipation of Objections

By way of a conclusion, we will consider two objections that can be raised to the notion of psychotherapy involving moral education. Contra Freud, Horney argues that the psychotherapist inherently employs standards of mental health and well-being in order to treat the patient, and that such standards presuppose value judgments. Assuming she is correct, on what grounds does the analyst base his or her value judgments? What is to prevent the therapist from simply imposing his or her values on the patient?

We have already provided a partial answer to these questions by indicating that the therapist's goal is to enable the patient to render his or her own moral judgments in freedom from the constraints associated with personality disorders. Such disorders compromise the individual's ability for moral judgment in several regards. The behavior of people who suffer from a character disorder is always inflexible in some important respects, since such persons strive to achieve ends that are part and parcel of their idealized self-image. Generally speaking, the afflicted individual is neither fully aware of the unrealistic nature of his or her ideals, nor of the existential importance that said ideals have for him or her. Because the idealized self constitutes the foundation upon which the individual erects his or her identity and self-esteem, it must be defended at all costs. In addition, since the idealized self is largely the work of the imagination, crises and conflicts with the world of fact are virtually unavoidable.

Given the individual's lack of insight into his or her predicament, and the high nature of the psychological stakes involved, most afflicted persons are driven to desperately cling to their private illusions. In order to shield the idealized self from potentially dangerous encounters with reality, the afflicted individual usually develops a number of unconscious strategies. Students of psychoanalysis know these strategies under the moniker of "defense mechanisms," and some of the most common are reaction formations and projections. Regardless, however, of the specific nature of the mechanisms employed, the overall effect of these unconscious measures is to undermine the individual's capacity to correctly interpret interpersonal situations, and to weaken his or her relationships to others. Hence, the individual's alienation from himself or herself goes hand in hand with alienation in his or her human relations in general. Consequently, for the person suffering from a character disorder, the range of potential options in any given interpersonal situation is often less than it appears to be.

However, does the very goal of liberating the patient to make his or her own value judgments itself constitute a value judgment? It clearly does and throws us back to the issue of how the therapist is to justify the standards he or she uses to distinguish mental health from its opposite. In *The Neurotic Personality of Our Time*, Horney finds only a partial solution to this problem. As announced in the book's title, her personality theory aims to take account of the cultural factors at work in neurosis. As one of the leading psychoanalytic "culturalists" of the day, and as someone familiar with the work of her contemporaries in cultural anthropology, she readily acknowledges that standards for mental health are culturally relative. Actions and attitudes that we find to be humdrum would be greeted with shock or indignation in some other societies, and vice versa. If this is so, however, how can we define "neurosis" so that it can be meaningfully applied across different cultures?

Her answer is to posit that a significant deviation from normalcy is a necessary—but not sufficient—condition for neurosis, so long as we bear in mind that normalcy itself is a culturally relative conception. In addition to deviation from standard expectations and popular norms, the neurotic typically displays a peculiar rigidity in conduct, and also suffers from a noticeable discrepancy between his or her potential and actual accomplishments.[16] Although Horney appeals to these two traits as a way of shoring up a cross-cultural definition, she overlooks the fact that both characteristics can only clearly emerge in societies that enjoy a considerable degree of structurally sanctioned individualism.

In simpler social orders, where social organization is still primarily a matter of unwritten custom and tradition, the individual has comparatively few opportunities to deviate in either thought or deed from the reigning cultural pattern. The worlds of social atomism or corporate order offer scant resources to those of their members who cannot content themselves with the conventional forms of life. When the individual's identity is primarily a function of ascribed social roles, and the know-how and standards for role performance constitute an integral part of a general cultural pattern, people have relatively little leeway in how they enact their roles. The rigid reactions of the modern neurotic stand out due to their stark contrast with the flexibility of the non-neurotic individual. However, suppleness in social interactions and situations can only become the norm where the average person has the possibility to bend custom to his or her own experience and sound judgment—a circumstance that is more prevalent in modern societies than in traditional ones.

By the same token, our potential for achievement is, to a great extent, a function of the concrete options offered to us by our social setting: Even the natural-born athlete requires a culture that has invented organized sport in order to become an actual athlete. In general, modern society provides it members a larger range of options for self-development, as well as greater equality of opportunity, than social orders of the traditional type. Hence, disparities between an individual's potential and his or her actual achievements that are mainly due to factors of personal psychology are more likely to appear in the former than in the latter.

Given that she has identified deviation from the social norm as a key feature of the neurotic personality, one could reasonably expect that Horney's standards for mental health would be based on the average member of a given population. However, to draw this conclusion would be to ignore her claim that the inner conflicts of the individual are often embedded in the tensions and contradictions of the surrounding culture. In *New Ways in Psychoanalysis*, published just two years after the appearance of *The Neurotic Personality of Our Time*, she argues that the failure to distinguish psychic health from psychic normality can result in an incapacity to recognize the true nature of the patient's problems.[17] For instance, a sufficiently ethnocentric analyst could fail to fully register a patient's inability to make up his or her mind concerning certain issues of directly human import and automatically credit such indecision to typical liberal-minded tolerance. If the analyst fails to see that the much-touted virtues of being nonjudgmental and open-minded often serve in our society as excuses for inaction and being preoccupied with oneself, he or she is liable to miss the potential significance of ongoing indecision on the part of a patient.

If the standard for mental health cannot be equated to a sociological average, how is it to be derived? By the time she authored *Neurosis and Human Growth*, Horney had at least indirectly incorporated a moral dimension to her conception of mental health. In other words, her mature theory implies that the healthy personality has certain basic features in common with what we normally think of as good moral character. By this period she had also adopted a view almost as old as Western moral philosophy—namely, that truly good character is relatively rare and that the character of most people is actually quite mediocre. In her next-to-last book, *Our Inner Conflicts*, published in 1945, she remarks that modern society confronts its members with a series of dilemmas involving competing values whose successful resolution usually requires a clear-cut choice on the part of the individual:

> There is no doubt that choices like these have to be made very often by people living in our civilization, and one would therefore expect conflicts along these lines to be quite common. But the striking fact is that most people are not aware of them, and consequently do not resolve them by any clear decision. More often than not they drift and let themselves be swayed by accident. They do not know where they stand; they make compromises without being aware of doing so; they are involved in contradictions without knowing it. I am referring here to normal persons, meaning neither average nor ideal but merely non-neurotic.[18]

Although Horney's conception of good character is more pluralistic than the monism of virtue generally assumed in Greek moral philosophy, her belief that good character is relatively rare and often difficult to achieve is quite in step with the ethical views of Socrates, Plato, and Aristotle. Compare, for example, Aristotle's remarks about the effort and talent required to be virtuous:

> It is also hard work to be excellent. For in each case it is hard work to find the intermediate; for instance, not everyone, but only one who knows, finds the midpoint in a circle. So also getting angry, or giving and spending money, is easy and everyone can do it; but doing it to the right person, in the right amount, at the right time, for the right end, and in the right way is no longer easy, nor can everyone do it. Hence doing these things well is rare, praiseworthy, and fine.[19]

Aristotle grounds the virtues on the claim that they are the states that arise when the individual fulfills the *telos*, or function native to human beings, in an outstanding manner. This rationale assumes that the universe is ordered according to a master plan that endows nearly all natural entities with species-specific purposes or ends. Hence, Aristotle directly relates human flourishing to the fulfillment of a human being's natural office, which he describes as a life of action informed by reason.

Horney cannot employ a similar argument to support her value claims for at least two reasons. The teleological universe which Aristotle assumes as the backdrop to his rationale did not survive the successive revolutions of thought that resulted in the birth of modern science. Particularly in the wake of Darwin, the assumption that the universe manifests an intelligent design has become suspect among intellectuals, and is at best viewed as highly speculative. In addition, Aristotle's ethics suffer from ethnocentrism, since he tends to think of the various institutions and products of his own time and place as simply the most mature expressions extant of humanity's potential for civilized life. Horney, on the other hand, is keenly aware of the contribution that existing social and cultural arrangements make to individual psychology, and she treats cultural relativism as a fact. But if she acknowledges that values are relative to culture, then what basis can she have for giving some value claims priority over others in the treatment of patients?

Cultural relativism does not necessarily entail moral relativism. One can recognize that, as a matter of historical fact, customs and their associated values have differed from society to society and from era to era, without being forced to conclude—upon pain of logical inconsistency—that it is impossible to provide reasons for preferring some cultural arrangements to others. I have argued that the evaluation of values presupposes the existence of goods within the experience of the individual, and that this experience is inherently social. All judgment of value is situational, if we include a perspective arising out of a certain set of experiences as an inherent part of every human situation. While this formula points to the relativity of value judgments to experience, it involves a limited form of relativism, since experience includes what can be potentially witnessed, reproduced, or inferred by a community of inquirers, and this dimension constitutes the very basis of scientific objectivity. On the other hand, value judgments are relative to the goods we have experienced or to those we can imagine and believe to be attainable. As concerns the appearance of new goods in human behavior, experience is open-ended, a point memorably illustrated by the New Testament metaphor involving the "pearl of great value."[20]

Writing of the need to divest philosophy of its traditional pursuit of fixed ends, Dewey argues that

> the conception which looks for the end of action within the circum-
> stances of the actual situation will not have the same measure of
> judgment for all cases. When one factor of the situation is a person
> of trained mind and large resources, more will be expected than with
> a person of backward mind and uncultured experience. The absurdity
> of applying the same standard of moral judgment to savage peoples
> that is used with civilized will be apparent. No individual or group
> will be judged by whether they come up to or fall short of some fixed
> result, but by the direction in which they are moving.[21]

The values guiding Horney's therapeutic outlook reflect a culture that has discovered the goods of individualism and a democratic way of life. The standards for mental health and well-being she assumes are not set by statistical survey but are rather determined through critical examination of happy, well-adjusted individuals and the goods such people pursue. Of course, no single person or society ever fully realizes the ideals for which the words "individualism" and "democracy" stand. Indeed, the discrepancies between the ideal and the real along these lines are almost too patent to require mention. The trick, as Dewey remarks in regard to education, is to "extract the desirable traits of forms of community life which actually exist, and employ them to criticize undesirable features and suggest improvement."[22] In order to determine the desirable traits, the highest courts of appeal are rational argument and individual judgment, as well as whatever consensus in opinion emerges through their employment. No appeal to a perfect and eternal standard that transcends human experience, to an *a priori* principle of right and wrong, can take the place of the collective experience and intelligence of a community of researchers guided by the experimental method of inquiry. While it would be naive to expect that even such a community will reach a unanimous consensus as regards value claims, it is reasonable to suppose that through prolonged investigation and debate at least such working consensuses of opinion will emerge as presently exist in modern polities and scientifically oriented professions.

Individualism is a value central to Horney's therapeutic approach because the degree to which it exists in a given society bears a direct relationship to the presence of social circumstances favoring personal development, on the condition that individualism is not equated with mere absence of social constraint but includes those active forms of support that can strengthen and enrich personality and character. Democratic government constitutes one such support, since it endows the individual with a political and legal status—that of citizenship—that allows citizens to interact with one another in a way that, under favorable circumstances, can promote a form of critically minded cooperation and a spirit of mutuality. On the one hand, it furnishes the individual with considerable leeway in thought and deed by allotting personal choice a crucial role in affairs both public and private. On the other, it places duties on him or her to respect the right of fellow citizens to the same liberties. By formally ensuring the equality of citizens before the law and guaranteeing universal suffrage, representative government contributes to conditions that favor the growth and vitality of civil society. While the most obvious features of democracy are its institutional aspects, the realm of civil society constitutes its heart and soul, for it is primarily in the latter that public opinion is formed and bonds among citizens are forged. Also, insofar as they are more than mere paperwork, the liberties of expression and association are mainly realized in the civil sphere.

Arguing that democracy constitutes more than simply a type of government, Dewey describes it as "primarily a mode of associated living, of conjoint communicated experience."[23] This conception of democracy finds indirect support in the central thesis of Rose Laub Coser's *In Defense of Modernity*, which is that the structure of the modern social order promotes role complexity and individual autonomy. Coser argues that understanding others, in the sense of imagining oneself in their position, constitutes the crux of social interaction.[24] Obviously such interaction takes place in all societies, but modern ones differ from their pre-modern counterparts in that in the former social conditions require the individual to make a greater differentiation between thought and action. Growth in mental maturity largely consists in an increase in the individual's ability to distinguish and differentiate between the objects and relationships of the social world. Consequently, individuation is primarily a function of the extent to which the individual is required to order and synthesize the different viewpoints, attitudes, and expectations of his or her human environment. Given its complexity and internal tensions, modern society obliges the individual to reflect about the social order as well as about his or her own subjectivity.

Democracy is both an effect and a cause of individualism. It is an effect insofar as increasing individuation represents a consequence of social evolution. The modern, self-aware individual, who can take both society and his or her own states of consciousness as objects of thought, is mainly the result of this process. Such a self is predisposed to question authority and to desire the freedoms necessary to determine the course of his or her own life. While the existence of such selves was a precondition to the emergence of democratic forms of governance, democracy in turn served to strengthen nascent individualism. By investing the individual with formal rights and duties, modern societies create conditions that facilitate the communication of ideas and experiences. Of course, even in the most advanced democracies, social conditions that affect association and communication within the citizenry are rarely, if ever, perfect, and Coser concludes her book with an eye to future improvements:

> What we need is a society where, to use an idea dear to Jürgen Habermas, all citizens have an occasion to participate in a rational discourse between many segments of the population, in a give-and-take imbued with sentiments that are tempered by criss-crossing relationships. Such a pluralistic give-and-take can be made into a foundation of a community of equal participants. I hope that such a society could generate both the multiplicity of perspectives and the mutual support it takes for the enlargement of our aspirations, which are needed for efficacious individualism.[25]

Ideally, democratically structured social and political arrangements not only provide legal protections that enable the individual to act on the basis of personal choice but also make a vital contribution to a social climate of active association and communication in which the individual can realize his or her full potential. As to Horney, she explicitly acknowledged the political import of her therapeutic approach, writing during the Second World War that, "An integral part of the democratic ideals for which we are fighting today is the belief that the individual—and as many individuals as possible—should develop to the full of his potentialities."[26]

In *Reconstruction in Philosophy*, Dewey terms growth, in the sense of betterment and progress, "the only moral 'end.'"[27] He reasons that a thoroughgoing naturalism in value theory implies this view, since it transforms the fixed and absolute ends of the Western intellectual tradition into relative ones:

> The end is no longer a terminus or limit to be reached. It is the active process of transforming the existent situation. Not perfection as a

final goal, but the ever-enduring process of perfecting, maturing, refining is the aim in living. Honesty, industry, temperance, justice, like health, wealth and learning, are not goods to be possessed as they would be if they expressed fixed ends to be attained. They are directions of change in the quality of experience.[28]

In her last book, Horney propounds an ethic of growth that is very much in line with Dewey's vision, albeit with her occupational focus on individual psychology. She calls the ethic "a morality of evolution" and proposes that its main criterion is whether or not a particular disposition or trend promotes or retards the individual's growth.[29]

Learning is the key to personal growth, and education in turn largely depends upon the extent and quality of communication. Horney's reconstructed version of psychoanalysis is, in essence, a special form of communication. In his philosophy of education, Dewey allots a central role to the idea of communication, and gives it the following characterization:

> Not only is social life identical with communication, but all communication (and hence all genuine social life) is educative. To be a recipient of a communication is to have an enlarged and changed experience. One shares in what another has thought and felt and in so far, meagerly or amply, has his own attitude modified.[30]

The expertise of the therapist, in combination with the unique nature of the therapeutic relationship, can sometimes succeed in overcoming the patient's barriers to genuine communication and insight. A key feature of all character disorders is the afflicted individual's inability to benefit from experiences and communications that threaten, directly or indirectly, to expose the unrealistic nature of his or her pretensions. There are a myriad of ways in which the afflicted person can evade ideas that could lead to self-understanding, but they all produce essentially the same result—namely, a particularly dogged form of closed-mindedness that constitutes an impediment to personal growth.

A crucial precondition that Horney identifies for moral development is the individual's ability to accept responsibility for himself or herself. Taking such responsibility is an essential part of being able to acknowledge one's shortcomings and realistically work toward alleviating them. It is also a vital element in good human relations, since accepting responsibility for one's own decisions and actions constitutes a precondition for respecting the rights of others and for fulfilling one's duties toward them. In one fashion or another, all character disorders involve warped interpersonal relationships. The neurotic's central inner conflict corrupts the tissue of mutual respect and obligations that characterize healthy relationships. Under the influence of an impossible search for glory, the neurotic invariably makes unreasonable demands upon himself or herself and others. His or her role partners often sense that they are supposed to follow a sort of unspoken script and, at least insofar as they strive for harmonious relations, must learn to read between the lines of the afflicted individual's words and deeds. They discover that failure to respect the subtext is undertaken at their own risk, though the unpleasant consequences can vary greatly depending upon the specific nature of the character disorder and environing conditions.

Healthy human relations, by contrast, involve what Horney calls a "spirit of mutuality." Such a spirit stands for the quality of interaction in a relationship in which reciprocity is explicitly and unambiguously desired by both partners. It implies that the individual has achieved "an acceptance of responsibility toward others, a readiness to recognize obligations in whose value he believes, whether they relate to his children, parents, friends, employees, colleagues, community, or country."[31] Horney remarks that genuine mutuality coincides with "truly democratic ideals."[32] In addition to respecting the rights and individuality of others, the individual has achieved moral autonomy by establishing his or her own "hierarchy of values," and seeks to live by it.

As the reader may have noticed, Horney's account of the autonomous moral agent bears a striking similarity to the post-conventional level of moral development identified by Kohlberg. To what ultimately became the fifth and final stage in his scheme, he gave the following description:
III. Postconventional, autonomous, or principled level

> At this level, there is a clear effort to define moral values and principles which have validity and application apart from the authority of the groups or persons holding these principles, and apart from the individual's own identification with these groups . . .

> Stage 5: *The social-contract legalistic orientation*, generally with utilitarian overtones. Right action tends to be defined in terms of general individual rights, and standards which have been critically examined and agreed upon by the whole society. There is a clear awareness of the relativism of personal values and opinions and a corresponding emphasis upon procedural rules for reaching consensus. Aside from what is constitutionally and democratically agreed upon, the right is

a matter of personal "values" and "opinion." The result is an emphasis upon the "legal point of view," but with an additional emphasis upon the possibility of changing the law in terms of rational considerations of social utility (rather than freezing it in terms of stage 4 "law and order"). Outside the legal realm, free agreement and contract is the binding element of obligation. This is the "official" morality of the American government and constitution.[33]

As we have already noted, the fifth stage was originally followed by a sixth labeled, "The universal ethical principle orientation." Due to lack of empirical support for the existence of this stage, Kohlberg later removed it from his scheme. According to the criticism of modern moral philosophy we have advanced, the sixth stage was primarily inspired by the legislative attitude that has tended to dominate contemporary thinking about ethics. The legislative standpoint assumes that morality can be encapsulated in an abstract law or principle whose authority is based upon purely rational considerations of logical universality, consistency, and comprehensiveness. In opposition to this approach, we have argued that personal experience, sensibility, and preference play a legitimate and irreducible role in many moral judgments. Horney's implicit understanding of psychotherapy as a type of moral education shares this vision. Her aim was clearly not to impose the therapist's values in place of the patient's, but rather to free patients from their unconscious drives, thereby enabling them to reflectively reach their own judgments of conscience.

Before concluding, a second potential criticism warrants our attention. Notwithstanding her professed commitment to democratic ideals, it may be objected that Horney's acceptance of psychic determinism contradicts her affirmation of individual autonomy and freedom. In *New Ways in Psychoanalysis,* she explicitly adopts Freud's "working hypothesis that psychic processes are as strictly determined as physical processes."[34] Indeed, she holds that it constitutes a sort of sine qua non for analytic work: "Without it we could not hope to understand a single one of the patient's reactions."[35] If, however, human thought, feeling, and action are strictly determined, in what sense can she legitimately talk about moral values? Don't assignments of praise and blame assume that the moral agent could have acted otherwise than he or she actually did? If there is no free will and choice, how can there be any true morality?

The contradiction in Horney's theory is only genuine if we construe her principle of psychic determinism to mean that intelligence does not constitute a bona fide force in human affairs. If, indeed, conscious thought, recollection, and judgment have no real empire over conduct and are merely the visible symptoms of unconscious causes, morality is an illusion. Our analysis and evaluation of moral dilemmas would then simply serve (at best) as rationalizations for behavior that is the product of unconscious energies and external forces. Perhaps the most evident drawback of this view is its inability to account for the obvious fact of technological, scientific, and social progress. If human awareness and intelligence are purely epiphenomenal, it becomes difficult, if not impossible, to satisfactorily explain the genesis and development of humanity's increased understanding and control over nature.

The theory of evolution suggests that human intelligence should be considered as a causal factor in nature. The fossil record indicates that relative hominid brain size has doubled over the course of the last two million years, and in absolute terms has tripled.[36] Assuming that larger brains were the neurological precondition for an increase in both the quantity and quality of motor and cognitive skills, it stands to reason that they were favored by natural selection because they conferred some survival advantages to early hominids. Increased intelligence would have meant not only an improved capacity to solve the problems posed by the world of the Paleolithic era but also an increase in the ability to acquire the known solutions. This interpretation is consistent with the available archeological evidence, which shows gradual improvement in hominid tool making.

In concrete terms, the evolution of human intelligence spelled growth in both the size and effectiveness of the cultural skill set employed for meeting the physical and social challenges of Paleolithic life. More and better skills meant an increase in control and prediction of the environment, and herein consisted the emergence and initial growth of freedom. While history presents little evidence for the existence of a metaphysically autonomous "free will," it does provide ample witness to the creative powers of human intelligence and learning. An absolutely "free will" is required not for morality but only the relative freedom we enjoy through learning and reflection. To be free essentially means to choose among various options on the basis of rational considerations, instead of having one's behavior determined by impulse, whim, or external factors. Insofar as it is justified, moral blame or praise does not depend upon the conjecture that the person in question could have acted otherwise than he or she in fact did, since every action is sufficiently determined. Given an identical set of conditions, including the moral agent's beliefs, cognitive abilities, and affective state, it only stands to reason that precisely the same act would result. Our public expressions of moral disapproval or approval are rational to the extent that they are means by which we influence *future* behavior, whether or own or that of others. Condemnation and commendation, in other words, are useful as means of dissuasion and persuasion. Insofar as her approach provides the individual with a better understanding of the psychological forces shaping his or her behavior, Horney's reconstructed version of psychoanalysis has a contribution to make to expanding the individual's freedom. The freedom to be gained through psychotherapy is that which is had when unconscious, unreasonable expectations and motives are replaced by conscious, reasonable ones. Conduct is no less determined than it was before, but now its determination is desirable instead of undesirable.

Freudianism generally assumes a sharp distinction between facts and values. On Freud's view, the former constitute the realm of science; facts are dealt with by analytic reasoning, a type of cognition that presupposes a purely "disinterested" theoretical stance whose only end is truth for its own sake. Reason is quintessentially a power of consciousness, and its most impressive creations are the pure and applied sciences. It represents a derivation from the so-called "ego drives," which are the ensemble of psychic forces that ensure the self-preservation of the organism. The individual's basic sense of reality is enabled by the operation of these drives, since their function is to deal with the hard facts of life that must be surmounted if the organism is to survive. Abstract reasoning constitutes an extrapolated form of the ego drives, in which the recognition of the sheer necessities for existence is expanded to potentially include all facts per se.

Values, on the other hand, merely represent the conscious and usually incomplete awareness of desires rooted in the unconscious. Hence, intellectual pursuits in which values figure prominently, such as art or philosophy, are particularly subject to unconscious influences. Freud's scheme compliments the divide between facts and values with a division between reason and sentiment. The former is almost wholly an ego process, whereas the conscious aspects of the latter are merely the surface effects of submerged forces. Although Freud's instinct theory underwent several revisions, an invariant feature of his views is that the libido constitutes a main source of desires not directly related to self-preservation. By relying on the psychic mechanisms of sublimation and aim-inhibition, Freud believes that he can demonstrate that an astonishingly wide range of apparently non-sexual feelings and attitudes actually have libidinal origins.

Freud's metapsychology has some obvious affinities with the philosophy of Kant. With the exception of the good will and aesthetic judgment, Kant holds that human values have their source in our animal nature. Indeed, he argues that the values which grow out of such desires enjoy no genuine ethical standing, due to the fact that they are part of the phenomenal world of cause and effect, and hence determined by non-rational forces. Furthermore, Kant treats reason as a faculty essentially independent of feeling and desire. Although Freud reorganizes mind upon an instinctual basis, his mental architectonic largely respects the Kantian dichotomies. While Freud dethrones reason from its pride of place in the psyche, he still tends to treat it as an autonomous faculty. Whereas the philosopher, however, relies on the hypothesis of a metaphysical dualism between noumena and phenomena to justify belief in free will and hence to affirm the authority of reason over feeling, the psychologist tends to reverse the latter relationship. As a materialist, Freud has little use for Kantian noumena, and, although he doesn't deny the possibility of an ethics based on purely rational considerations, his work does little to support such a notion; in fact, it tends to undermine the conception of the individual as a rational agent. Of course, minus its noumenal dimension, the Kantian universe becomes purely phenomenal and, hence, wholly subject to determination by natural laws. It is, perhaps, not too much of an exaggeration to say that Freud stands Kant on his head.

For both thinkers human ends are essentially fixed and static. In Kant, they are either determined by our sensual nature or by reason, and in Freud, they are largely the product of the interplay of unconscious instincts. One of the great innovations introduced by Hegel into the Kantian heritage was the insight that human ends have historical careers, and that their growth is an inherent feature of social development. When Horney criticizes Freud's implicit understanding of evolution as mechanistic, she is making a closely related point: "It implies that present manifestations not only are conditioned by the past, but contain nothing except the past; nothing really new is created in the process of development; what we see today is only the old in changed form."[37] By propounding an emergent model of evolution in lieu of the mechanistic one, she effectively plays Hegel to Freud's Kant.

We conclude by borrowing a terminological distinction from an unlikely source: C. G. Jung. Although he, like Horney, was an analytic rebel, once they departed from Freud their respective paths took very different directions. Despite the fundamental dissimilarity between their views, Jung drew a distinction between the words "individualism" and "individuation" that can serve us as a final illustration of Horney's understanding of personal and moral growth, as long as we bear in mind that by the former term Jung understood the priority of individual interests over those of the group:

> We do not sufficiently distinguish between individualism and individuation. Individualism means deliberately stressing and giving prominence to some supposed peculiarity, rather than to collective considerations and obligations. But individuation means precisely the better and more complete fulfillment of the collective qualities of the human being, since adequate consideration of the peculiarity of the individual is more conducive to better social achievement than when the peculiarity is neglected or suppressed. The idiosyncrasy of an individual is not to be understood as any strangeness in his substance or in his components, but rather as a unique combination, or gradual differentiation, of functions and faculties which in themselves are universal. . . . Individuation, therefore, can only mean a process of psychological development that fulfills the individual qualities given; in other words, it is a process by which a man becomes the definite unique being he in fact is. In so doing he does not become "selfish" in the ordinary sense of the word, but is merely fulfilling the peculiarity of his nature, and this, as we have said, is vastly different from egotism or individualism.[38]

Elsewhere Jung describes individuation as the process of "coming to self-hood" or "self-actualization,"[39] terms that are synonymous with Horney's notion of "self-realization" as the ultimate goal of analytic therapy.

The reader will recall that we began the essay with the vision of a future world in which individualism has largely run amok, leaving many of its denizens alienated and morally confused. In the cited passage Jung identifies individualism with its extreme forms, in which the aims and values of the individual are viewed as both being opposed to collective interests, and as taking precedence over them. Jung's distinction between "individualism" thus conceived and "individuation" is useful, because it suggests that individuality per se is not the source of the difficulties, which are due rather only to certain types of individuality. Horney's writings on character disorders provide us with rich descriptions of the various major directions untoward personal development can take. The personality of the afflicted invariably involves an entrenched egoism, which Horney christens a "dark idolatry of self," a phrase she borrows from Shelley.[40] Her work provides evidence that the answer to character disorders is not less individuality but rather deeper and more robust individuality, implying a personal identity founded on a realistic view of oneself and others. Her psychotherapeutic approach merits further consideration and exploration as a way of assisting those who live in our challenging civilization to free themselves from their self-imposed illusions and engage their fellows in a spirit of reciprocity. By helping the individual to grow *as* an individual, Horney's legacy has an important contribution to make in creating conditions that favor the sort of motivation and moral creativity we moderns associate with genuine conscience and virtue.

Notes

1. Dewey, *Democracy and Education*, 357–358.
2. Dewey, *Reconstruction in Philosophy* (New York: Henry Holt and Company, 1920), 186.
3. Horney, *Self-Analysis*, 10.
4. Horney, *Neurosis and Human Growth*, 15.
5. Ibid.
6. Hallpike, *The Evolution of Moral Understanding*, 299.
7. Dewey, *Democracy and Education*, 223–224.
8. Horney, *Our Inner Conflicts*, 178.
9. Horney, *New Ways in Psychoanalysis*, 10.
10. Ibid., 230.
11. Horney, *Our Inner Conflicts*, 25–26.
12. Ibid., 178.
13. Horney, *New Ways in Psychoanalysis*, 33.
14. Bernard Paris makes the case for this view in *Karen Horney: A Psychoanalyst's Search for Self-Understanding*.
15. Karen Horney, *The Neurotic Personality of Our Time* (New York: W. W. Norton & Company, Inc., 1937), 246–247.
16. Ibid., 20–21.
17. Horney, *New Ways in Psychoanalysis*, 179–182.
18. Horney, *Our Inner Conflicts*, 24–25.
19. Aristotle, *Nicomachean Ethics*, 29.
20. "Again, the kingdom of heaven is like a merchant in search of fine pearls; on finding one pearl of great value, he went and sold all that he had and bought it." Matthew 13:45 (NRSV).
21. John Dewey, *Reconstruction in Philosophy*, 176.
22. Dewey, *Democracy and Education*, 83.
23. Dewey, *Democracy and Education*, 87.
24. Coser, *In Defense of Modernity*, 7.
25. Ibid., 169.
26. Horney, *Self-Analysis*, 12.
27. Dewey, *Reconstruction in Philosophy*, 177.

28. Ibid.
29. Horney, *Neurosis and Human Growth*, 15.
30. Dewey, *Democracy and Education*, 5.
31. Horney, *Our Inner Conflicts*, 241.
32. Ibid.
33. Kohlberg, "From Is to Ought," 72–73.
34. Horney, *New Ways in Psychoanalysis*, 21.
35. Ibid., 22.
36. Carol R. Ember and Melvin Ember, *Anthropology*, 6th ed. (Englewood Cliffs, NJ: Prentice Hall, 1990), 70.
37. Horney, *New Ways in Psychoanalysis*, 42.
38. Violet Staub de Laszlo, ed., *The Basic Writings of C. G. Jung* (New York: The Modern Library, 1959), 144.
39. C. G. Jung, *Collected Works*, vol. 7 (New York: Bollingen Series XX, 1953), paragraph 266.
40. Horney, *Neurosis and Human Growth*, 15.

Index

For Product Safety Concerns and Information please contact our EU
representative GPSR@taylorandfrancis.com Taylor & Francis Verlag GmbH,
Kaufingerstraße 24, 80331 München, Germany

Batch number: 08158437

Printed by Printforce, the Netherlands